tear here

Five Principles for Making Homemade Gifts

1. Match the right gift to the right person by getting to know the likes and dislikes of the people on your gift list.

2. The fact that a person doesn't really need the basics in life makes him or her a perfect candidate for a homemade gift.

3. If you decide to make a homemade gift for a friend, the next step is to choose what you want to celebrate.

4. You should consider the location for gift-giving; a local park would be a perfect spot to present a gourmet lunch basket.

5. A homemade gift says, "I care about you." For many people, a homemade gift is more appreciated than a store-bought gift.

Ten Steps for Getting the Job Done

1. Organize your workspace and supplies by setting up a table and chairs and some storage bins in a special area.

2. Make a list of the people in your life who would appreciate a homemade gift.

3. Shop around for craft supplies, and buy them in bulk whenever you find a good price.

4. If you like a bargain (and who doesn't?), look for discounted seasonal objects after the season has passed.

5. Consider buying a kit that contains all the necessary supplies to make a project if you're a novice at crafting.

6. Browse through a local party store occasionally to find unusual items for decorating and wrapping gifts.

7. Check out sites on the Internet to buy craft supplies and get free craft ideas.

8. Save time and energy by shopping at home for supplies using mail-order catalogs.

9. Check out garage sales for obtaining a variety of inexpensive supplies.

10. Ask your family to put recyclable objects into a box you've set up near the trashcan.

alpha books

Eight Tips for Presenting a Homemade Gift

1. Choose the best finishing touch for a homemade gift, such as wrapping paper, a bag, a box, a basket, bows, and so on.

2. Make up kits of craft ingredients for kids and place them in plastic storage containers.

3. Wrap your gifts and help save the environment at the same time by making reusable material bags for your presents.

4. Personalize a special box for a homemade gift by decorating it with paint and stencils.

5. Try making your own wrapping paper out of craft paper and stamps, comic papers, or remnants of wallpaper.

6. A homemade bow is an attractive addition to a present and is durable enough to be reused by the recipient.

7. Watch people look at the back of homemade cards to find your special signature.

8. Turn your old greeting cards into colorful, personalized gift tags.

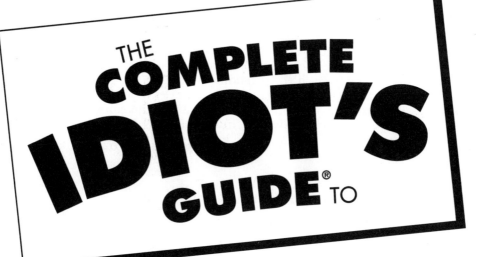

THE **COMPLETE IDIOT'S GUIDE®** TO

Making Great Gifts

by Marilee LeBon

alpha books

201 West 103rd Street
Indianapolis, IN 46290

A Pearson Education Company

International Standard Book Number: 0-02-864001-2
Library of Congress Catalog Card Number: Available upon request.

03   02   01   8   7   6   5   4   3   2   1

Interpretation of the printing code: The rightmost number of the first series of numbers is the year of the book's printing; the rightmost number of the second series of numbers is the number of the book's printing. For example, a printing code of 01-1 shows that the first printing occurred in 2001.

Printed in the United States of America

Note: This publication contains the opinions and ideas of its author. It is intended to provide helpful and informative material on the subject matter covered. It is sold with the understanding that the author and publisher are not engaged in rendering professional services in the book. If the reader requires personal assistance or advice, a competent professional should be consulted.

Publisher
Marie Butler-Knight

Product Manager
Phil Kitchel

Managing Editor
Jennifer Chisholm

Acquisitions Editor
Amy Zavatto

Development Editor
Amy Gordon

Senior Production Editor
Christy Wagner

Copy Editor
Amy Lepore

Cartoonist
Brian Moyer

Illustrator
Melissa LeBon

Photographer
Robert Schroeder

Cover Designers
Mike Freeland
Kevin Spear

Book Designers
Scott Cook and Amy Adams of DesignLab

Indexer
Tonya Heard

Layout/Proofreading
Mary Hunt
Ayanna Lacey
Heather Hiatt Miller
Stacey Richwine-DeRome
Gloria Schurick

Contents at a Glance

Contents

Foreword

The Best Gift of All

Do you think of gift-giving as an obligation or as a celebration? Do you open up that invitation to a birthday party and wonder how you will find the perfect gift? After reading this book, you won't have to ask yourself those questions any more.

The Complete Idiot's Guide to Making Great Gifts gives you everything you need to easily and quickly match the perfect gift with the recipient, regardless of the person, event, or budget. Don't worry—this is not a guide just for the creatively crafty person. Marilee LeBon has seamlessly combined several books into one: a gift-giving lifestyle guide, a resource for traditions, and a step-by-step instructional project book. You can follow the project directions to the letter or integrate your own special flair. And I'm betting you will learn, as I did, the origins of many of the holiday traditions that we still enjoy today.

We each have those "easy-to-shop-for" people in our lives. And we also have those people who "have everything" on our lists. Throughout this book, LeBon gives special pointers on selecting the right gift for the right person. She also gives practical guidelines so you can decide when it is best to buy a gift, make a gift, or combine the two. The true sign of a well-selected, store-bought gift is a need fulfilled. A successful handmade gift gives as much pleasure to the giver as it does to the recipient.

LeBon gives special attention to the beginning of the gift-giving process—the organization of supplies and the mindset of gift-giving. Motivate yourself to complete this step—it isn't expensive or time-consuming. The first and most obvious step is the one that I need to improve upon—mark special days on your calendar—an entire year at a time!

Our lives are filled with so many reasons to celebrate: birthdays, weddings, anniversaries, new babies, new house, new job … the list goes on. Add in the religious and national holidays and suddenly you see the need for streamlining and customizing your gift-giving. And don't forget about giving a gift "just because." Creating a special gift and giving of yourself can be very therapeutic.

As I read this book, I wrote a list of gift ideas for the upcoming year. I've already saved myself hours of "shopping without a plan." When it's time to celebrate my younger daughter's high school graduation and plan a party for my twenty-fifth wedding anniversary, I'll be ready!

So grab this book, get your calendar and a legal pad, and start your list. Create your plan, enjoy your gift-giving, and celebrate the special people and events of your life. The age-old saying is still true: It is better to give than to receive!

Barb Sunderlage
Editor, *Crafts 'n Things*® magazine

Barbara Sunderlage is Editor of *Crafts 'n Things* magazine, as well as the Editorial Director of Clapper Communications Companies, which also publishes *Pack-O-Fun, Painting,* and *The Cross-Stitcher* magazines. She has more than 20 years' experience in the craft industry, including designing, merchandising, account management, and previously owning her own craft business. She lives in the western Chicago suburbs with her very patient and understanding husband of 24 years and has two daughters with whom she shares her love of (addiction to!) crafting.

Introduction

Most of us can name a gift we received that was unforgettable. For me, it was a home-made gift from my parents. One Christmas, they made my sister and me wooden doll cases that contained a doll, hand-sewn clothes, and accessories. Even the little hangers were fashioned from scrap wood and metal hooks.

My parents had just built a new home, and all their money was tied up in the process. I can remember my mother tarring the cement foundation and my dad working on the roof. Little money was available for Christmas presents for my sister and me, still in grade school. Undaunted, my dad took some of the lumber left over from a building project and fashioned it into doll cases that opened into wardrobes. My mom, who was always handy at the sewing machine, made special outfits for the dolls and carefully hung them on the homemade hangers. We were delighted with our gifts and spent many happy hours together dressing our dolls in their matching wardrobes. I received fancy brand-name dolls at other Christmases, but none delighted me as much as my parents' gift from the heart.

I guess it was only natural that I would try to emulate my parents by making home-made gifts for the people in my life. Over the years, I have made clothes and baby carriers for my daughter's dolls and have given gifts of food, home decorations, and sewn creations to the people on my gift list. My father and I worked on a dollhouse together for my daughter, crafting furniture out of spare wood and decorating the rooms with wallpaper and rug remnants. There is nothing more rewarding than seeing your gifts being used and appreciated by friends and relatives over the years.

Of course, in the process, I've also had my share of duds—gifts that I thought would be perfect that just didn't turn out right. I learned from these mistakes and decided to stick to simple-but-elegant handmade gifts for this book. You won't need expensive equipment or an incredible amount of artistic ability to make these gifts. The ingredients can usually be found at a craft or discount store or recycled from household items. The directions are simple and will take you step by step through the creative process.

Many of the gift ideas can also be modified to fit your own personal needs. For example, you could make the get-well dream box in Chapter 16, "On the Mend," for a special birthday gift. Many of the Hanukkah gifts can also be made for Christmas and Kwanzaa, and the summer gifts can be brought inside and used year-round. In some cases, you can change the motif and turn one holiday project into another. For example, you can substitute Easter cookie cutters for the Halloween cookie cutters and pumpkins in the Halloween hanging in Chapter 9, "Fall Fun." You also can change the theme on a carryall or tote bag to match the occasion. Whatever you do, just let your imagination take over, and don't be afraid to try something new!

What's in This Book?

In this book, you'll find guides for getting organized and making handmade gifts for any occasion. This book is broken down into the following four parts:

Part 1, "How to Be a Gifting Genius," explains the process of making homemade gifts—getting organized and deciding the who, what, when, and where of giving a homemade gift. There are tips for buying materials, making special wrappings and gift cards, and presenting your gifts.

Part 2, "The Art of Making the Perfect Holiday Gift," contains ideas for making seasonal gifts for Kwanzaa, Christmas, Hanukkah, Valentine's Day, and the spring and fall holidays. Enough holidays are covered to keep you busy year-round.

Part 3, "Special Gifts for Special People," is just that—gifts tailored to the special occasions in people's lives. There are ideas for birthdays, weddings, new babies, and anniversaries, to name a few.

Part 4, "Showing You Care," delves into the art of making gifts for crafty kids, business associates, hired helpers, retired couples, and soulmates. If you need a gift idea for a special person in your life, you'll find it in this section.

Little Gifts of Information

You'll notice sidebars recurring throughout this book. Valuable information—from tips to warnings to definitions—is contained in these sidebars.

Present Pointers

These tips contain ideas for adding a finishing touch to a gift, changing the theme of a gift, or customizing a gift to the recipient's tastes. You'll also find pointers for using the various mediums involved in the craft project and substituting materials if desired.

Present Tense

These are further explanations of the paraphernalia needed to make some of the gifts. For example, you'll learn that a **spouncer** is a paintbrush used for stenciling or splotching on paint and that **textile medium** can turn ordinary paint into fabric paint.

Gifting Glitches

Here's where experience in crafting gifts pays off. You'll learn what to avoid when making certain projects and how to perfect your technique.

The Gift of Knowledge

These are fun tidbits of information that pertain to the subject being discussed. You'll learn things like the folklore of certain flowers and trees, the origin of the term "honeymoon," and why we celebrate Halloween.

Acknowledgments

Many people were instrumental in the success of this book. I'd like to thank my daughter, Melissa, who expertly illustrated the projects in this book. Her artistic touch to many of the designs helped make them come alive. My husband and soul mate, Joe, was always available to proofread a chapter and to offer advice and emotional support. My son, Ryan, provided technical (computer) and creative support for this endeavor. I'd also like to thank my nephew, Robert Schroeder, whose painstaking attention to detail created the lovely photos of the projects in this book.

I was also fortunate to have the support of family and friends who allowed me to incorporate their suggestions into my projects. I'd particularly like to thank my mother, Mildred, and my sisters Carol and Lisa who provided invaluable advice. My sister-in-law, Anne, helped coordinate the photo shoot, and my friend Hilda listened to me run on about making homemade gifts on our daily walks.

I'd also like to thank my acquisitions editor and development editor for making this project come alive. Amy Zavatto envisioned this book and enriched it with her direction and guidance. Amy Gordon helped shape the chapters into an orderly sequence and added suggestions that improved the content. The senior production editor, Christy Wagner, professionally pulled the book together and ensured technical accuracy. As in any project, good teamwork spells success. Thank you all!

Trademarks

All terms mentioned in this book that are known to be or are suspected of being trademarks or service marks have been appropriately capitalized. Alpha Books and Pearson Education cannot attest to the accuracy of this information. Use of a term in this book should not be regarded as affecting the validity of any trademark or service mark.

Part 1

How to Be a Gifting Genius

There's a lot more to making a homemade gift than meets the eye. You may have the basic talent to create something special for a loved one, but it helps to know how to best put this talent to use. These chapters give you some simple suggestions for making and giving the perfect gift. In this case, a little research goes a long way. You'll learn how to find the right gift for the right person, how to determine when and why to give a gift, and how to make it special.

You'll also learn the ABCs of crafting a homemade gift. There are tips in this section for organizing your workspace, making a gift list, buying and storing ingredients, and recycling household materials. Once you have your supplies and get them organized, the battle is half over.

The final stage of making a homemade gift is presenting it to the lucky recipient. This section will give you ideas for making the present even more distinguished by choosing the best container and wrapping. You'll discover how to make your own bows, gift bags, wrapping paper, gift tags, and greeting cards to grace your gift. So read on to make a beautifully wrapped gift for the perfect person and the perfect occasion.

Getting to Know You

In This Chapter

➤ Who the people on your gift list *really* are

➤ A little research goes a long way

➤ The perfect gift for the perfect person

➤ Why celebrate with a handmade gift?

➤ When not to give a handmade gift

➤ Special occasions and locations for gift giving

How many times has the opportunity to make a perfect gift for a special person passed you by? If you're like me, you like to do something unique to mark the special occasions of your loved ones. If giving a homemade gift is on your to-do list, you know how frustrating it is when the day arrives and you're still wondering what to make. So, instead of giving a homemade gift, you end up running out to a department store for a tie or frantically dialing the florist for a quick fix.

You no longer have to panic at the sight of a circled date on your calendar. If you like to be creative and can hammer a nail and/or paint by number, you can manage to make all, or at least most, of the gifts in this book.

Gifting Glitches

If you do a little research before-hand, you'll be able to match up the right gift with the right person. You don't want to spend time on a stepping stone mosaic for a person who has no interest in gardening or give a gift of potpourri to someone who sneezes at the sight of the smelly stuff.

The Spy Who Loves You

The first step in choosing great homemade gifts is getting to know the likes and dislikes of the people on your gift list. For example, we all know what to give to the college student at Christmastime (hint: it's green and has a president on it), but what do you get for the favorite aunt who's more worried about getting rid of possessions than receiving them? Here's where a little ingenuity will save the day. You might want to consider something as simple as taking an old photo of your aunt—perhaps a baby picture or a wedding picture—and making a *decoupaged* antique frame for it. Or, better yet, you could make a collage of pictures that celebrates a special era in your aunt's life.

Older parents and grandparents usually have special needs that can be discovered with a little thoughtful conversation. For example, you might want to ask your grandparents if they have any daily-living needs that you could provide. If they say yes, a good gift for them may be offering to help them with the lawn or garden, or giving them gift certificates good for chauffeured trips to the grocery store, rides to doctor and dentist appointments, homemade meals shared together, and so on. If you place the gift certificates in a homemade frame, they can put your picture in it when the coupons are gone. You could also include your certificates with a small gift of handmade candles or soaps, stenciled hand towels, or handcrafted sachets for their drawers and closets.

Present Tense

The word **decoupage** is derived from the French word *decouper,* which means "to cut out." It is a creative art that involves pasting and varnishing paper cutouts onto objects. Decoupage has origins that can be traced back to a variety of styles from distant countries. As far back as the twelfth century, Chinese peasants created paper cutouts as decorations. The paper art began to merge with the art of making lacquered furniture in the late seventeenth century and developed into what we know as decoupage today.

If you don't have the time to spend with the senior citizens on your gift list, consider making them practical gifts that won't just collect dust on their shelves. Personalized photo albums to display pictures of their grandkids, homemade candies and cookies in a special tin, or a book lover's basket with homemade bookmarks would be perfect presents for these cherished friends and relatives.

Present Pointers

If you know people who are interested in making crafts, paying for a special art or craft class would be a thoughtful gift. You could give them a coupon good for a class of their choice and then present them with a gift basket of the assembled supplies they'll be using. For example, if they decide upon a knitting class, a gift basket of yarn, needles, and a pattern book would be perfect. Or, if a painting class is chosen, you could give them paints, brushes, and art books. It would also be fun to take the class with them if you have the time.

Of course, you might not always know your gift recipient personally. That makes the gift hunt a little more difficult but not impossible. For example, if the recipient is a fellow employee, you might want to scan the paraphernalia on his or her desk for hobbies or interests that might otherwise elude you.

A few conversational inquiries may also serve the purpose of identifying the perfect gift. Here's how it works: You see a photo of your fellow worker standing in front of a beautiful garden and mention how much work gardening is. She'll either agree with you and tell you that's her favorite spot in the park, or she'll share some of her gardening secrets with you. If the response is the latter, you have the right recipient for a gardening basket, garden stones or mosaics, or painted pots. It's as easy as that!

Maybe your boss is posed with a puppy that is obviously a valued family member. You might want to give a pet gift to acknowledge the new arrival. A few basic pet supplies in a wicker pet bed would be perfect.

And, speaking of new arrivals, you don't want to forget the opportunity to give baby gifts. An individualized scrapbook or photo album would be a perfect choice! Once you get the hang of it, you'll find so many opportunities to surprise people with clever gifts that you'll never be caught in a department store again.

Of course, if someone on your gift list asks for a particular store-bought item, by all means buy it. You could still surprise your loved one with a bouquet of dried flowers or a handmade bow to grace the package.

Present Pointers

Don't be afraid to jazz up a store-bought gift by giving it your personal homemade touch. There are many simple craft ideas in this book that can be included with a present or used to decorate the wrappings. For example, you could make dough ornaments to grace your holiday packages or include a gift of handmade refrigerator magnets with a new teapot. You also might want to check out the homemade bows, gift tags, greeting cards, and handmade bags and wrappings in Chapter 3, "Wrapping It Up," to enhance your presents.

Think about it—doing some basic research not only strengthens the bonds of your relationship, it provides for hours of fun for both the gifter and the giftee. A lot of pleasure can be derived from making personalized gifts, and you'll mark an occasion with a token that says, "I care about you." No matter what your budget, you can find a thoughtful gift that will fit any event.

The Gift of Knowledge

Gift giving was popular in the Victorian era. People were known to make gifts for each other, such as sweets, toys, or crafts, that were highly prized by the recipients. The less-handy Victorians could buy small trinkets at penny bazaars to give as gifts. Queen Victoria encouraged the well-to-do to give presents of food, drink, and money to the poor on Boxing Day, the day after Christmas in Great Britain.

Handmade vs. Store-Bought Gifts

In most cases, you have an idea which people on your list would appreciate a handmade gift. These people probably already have their basic needs met and would be thrilled that you spent the time and energy to customize a gift for them. They could be from all walks of life and in all situations, but what binds them together is the fact that they don't really need the basics. For example, mosaic coasters would probably be lost on a niece who's a struggling actress in New York City. By all means, if you can afford it, send her money. On the other hand, your father, who's gotten a tie from you every Father's Day, would probably love a gift basket of car wash soap, a sponge, car wax, and buffing rags along with a certificate to spend a day together spiffing up his wheels.

In the case of a friend or neighbor with special needs, you might want to explore the possibility of making his or her life easier. For example, if your friend is laid up with a broken leg, you could offer to do some basic house cleaning, run errands, or go to the grocery store for him or her. Or, if your neighbor lost his job, you might want to offer some home-cooked meals or help with the kids until he gets back on his feet. A person who just returned from the hospital following an illness may appreciate a visit from you with a basket of homemade breads and jams and gourmet coffees. You'll find that the gift of your time and energy can make a big difference in a person's life and, in many ways, can enrich your own.

Present Pointers

A perfect gift of pampering for a new mother, grandparent, stay-at-home mom, stressed executive, and so on would be a gift certificate for a day at the spa. Spas offer massages that are relaxing and therapeutic along with a myriad of other services. Be sure to check out the references of the spa and masseuse before signing someone up for a session. If you don't have a spa near you, consider a gift certificate for a makeover or a manicure. You might want to include the certificate in the spa gift basket detailed in Chapter 11, "New Kid on the Block."

Then again, we all know someone whose *basic* needs are met but who could use a little pampering. The new mom comes to mind here. I know from experience how the demands of motherhood can change your life situation. At that point in my life, I would have loved an offer of free baby-sitting and a gift certificate to a restaurant for a dinner out. Along this same line, the retired couple next door, whom you can always count on to let your dog out in a pinch, might appreciate a home-cooked gourmet meal for two. Or maybe you know a busy working mom or dad who would appreciate a sampler tray of Christmas cookies over the holidays. All it takes is a little research to find out what you can do that will be most appreciated by your friends and loved ones.

What Should We Celebrate?

Once you've decided to make a homemade gift for someone, the next step is to decide what you want to celebrate. There are many opportunities throughout the year, besides the obvious ones, that are perfect for gift giving. For example, you might want to celebrate a special birthday or anniversary or start a new tradition of gift giving for Kwanzaa. Then again, you might prefer to celebrate nontraditional occasions such as the addition of a family pet, a neighbor's new pool, new neighbors, a promotion, and so on. Or maybe you just want to show people that you appreciate their friendship (one of the best reasons for a gift, in my book). Once you've decided what to celebrate, be sure to mark the events on your calendar.

The Gift of Knowledge

According to developmental theorist Abraham Maslow's book, *Toward a Psychology of Being*, human needs are divided into the physical and psychosocial needs considered essential to human life. They are physical well-being, physical safety, affection, love and relationships, self-esteem, and self-actualization. You can fill a void in someone's life by being the person who provides one of these needs by giving the gift of yourself.

You'll also want to keep in mind these nontraditional moments in a person's life that could be celebrated with a homemade gift:

➤ Graduation from high school, college, or trade school

➤ New job

➤ Promotion

➤ New house

➤ New baby

➤ Pet adoption

➤ Special anniversary

➤ Special trip

➤ Overcoming adversity in life

➤ Recovery from illness

➤ Retirement

➤ Special accomplishments (such as winning a sporting event or award, succeeding at a dance audition, making an important scientific discovery, and so on)

➤ Success with a life goal

The Right Time and Place

The right time, of course, is anytime! However, if you don't want a first-time recipient of a gift from you to feel awkward, you might want to use a nontraditional occasion for gift giving (as opposed to, say, Christmas or Hanukkah). That way, you can avoid the awkward silence that might occur when they say, "Oh, I feel bad I didn't get you anything …."

Where should you give a gift? Anywhere will do, but for some people, you might want to tie it to an already-scheduled outing or plan an event as part of the gift itself. For example, you could arrange for a special lunch with a newly promoted co-worker and surprise him or her with a congratulatory gift. The lunch itself would be gift enough especially if you include a homemade card extolling his or her virtues. Birthday parties, showers, anniversaries, holidays, and housewarming parties are obvious occasions for giving a homemade gift.

You could invite a special someone to a picnic and provide a gourmet lunch in a basket to celebrate a new job. Or you might want to schedule a trip to the ocean around a kid's birthday and give him or her beach toys in a plastic tote. Consider making a homemade fondue birthday dinner for a special date (see Chapter 7, "My Funny Valentine," for details), or get together with an older friend or relative to help him or her bake Christmas cookies.

Gifting Glitches

Be sure to consider safety and dietary needs when crafting a homemade gift. Many home-made gifts have glued on parts that could become choking hazards for young children. Also, some people have special diets that should be considered if you plan to make them a food gift. For example, a diabetic friend may be checking foods for sugar content or a relative with heart-related disease may have to watch sodium and cholesterol levels. Also, you don't want to tempt a person watching their weight with a box of homemade fudge.

Inspiring Ideas

There are lots of ways to surprise someone with a homemade gift. If you check out the projects in this book, you'll find the perfect gift for any situation. Once you start making homemade gifts, you'll find that ideas for projects are everywhere.

Try checking out the Internet, local craft stores, craft shows, and craft books. The following are a few gift suggestions from this book to whet your appetite:

➤ **Gifts for nature lovers:** Herb gardens, mosaic stepping stones, painted pots, birdhouses, bulb gardens, painted slate welcome signs, bird feeders, perennial gardens

➤ **Gifts for animal lovers:** Catnip toys, a pet bed, a pet gift basket, pet calendars, animal T-shirts

➤ **Gifts for a new baby:** Baby headbands, a Noah's ark hanging, unique picture frames, keepsake boxes

➤ **Gifts for a newlywed couple:** A heart-shaped wreath, etched champagne glasses, homemade candles, decoupaged wedding invitation, kitchen caddy

➤ **Gifts for the aunt or uncle who has everything:** Dried soup mixes with a special mug and crackers, chocolate-dipped spoons with gourmet coffee/cocoa, basket of books and bookmarks, refrigerator magnets, photo albums

➤ **Gifts for the teachers, bosses, or hired help in your life:** A spa in a basket, gourmet wines/foods, tickets to a show, video store gift certificates presented with popcorn and hot chocolate

➤ **Gifts for the kids in your life:** A homemade puppet show, sponge painting, the art of origami, a hand-stamped carryall, beadwork, stenciled aprons, coloring book covers, terrariums

Gifting Glitches

Try to stay away from perishable goods when making up a gift basket, particularly if you are sending it in the mail. If your basket contains gourmet foods that are perishable, be sure to hand deliver it and give instructions for cooking/storing the food.

If you don't want to make all your gifts from scratch, you could always assemble a gift basket that compliments the person's tastes. The following are some examples of the kinds of baskets mentioned in this book that are guaranteed to knock the socks off of the recipient:

➤ **Baby basket:** Rattles, teethers, toys, bottles, cups, spoons, onesies, diapers, and so on

➤ **Wedding basket:** Champagne glasses, champagne, candles, gourmet spreads with crackers, and so on

➤ **Sports-enthusiast basket:** Balls, gloves, sports books, sports videos, training equipment, sports drinks, and so on

➤ **Bird-lover's basket:** Binoculars, birdseed, a feeder, bird books, a hummingbird feeder, a bird house, and so on

➤ **Breakfast-in-bed basket:** A bed tray, pancake mix, exotic fruits, a vase and flowers, a waffle maker, an omelet pan, recipes, and so on

➤ **College basket:** A shower caddy, shower supplies, a laundry bag, a first-aid kit, a tool kit, junk food, and so on

➤ **Picnic-in-the-park basket:** A picnic basket, fruit salad, seafood salad, gourmet cheeses and breads, and so on

➤ **Budding-artist basket:** Craft paint, construction paper, stamps, paintbrushes, stencils, wooden cutouts, how-to books, and so on

The list of possibilities is endless. You only have to think of the person's hobbies and interests and decide on a theme. Gather the ingredients in a basket, add some shrink-wrap and a bow, and voilà —a customized homemade gift!

Present Pointers

If you know someone who could use a monetary gift, you might want to consider putting some money on the bow of a gift box of homemade cookies, candies, or breads. You could fan–fold the money and attach it to the bow as a unique decoration. Just be sure your recipient sees the money in the bow and doesn't toss it out with the wrappings!

Why Give a Homemade Gift?

Why give a homemade gift to a special person? There are so many ways to make a person feel special that go beyond sending a check or a sweater. Of course, I would still recommend money or a practical gift for people who are just getting started in life or could really use material goods. But for many people, a homemade gift says "I care about you" and is often more appreciated than something store bought. You'll be rewarded by the look on their faces when they realize you tailored the gift to their special tastes, interests, and needs. A little research goes a long way in creating the perfect homemade gift.

Here's a personal example of customizing a gift. I wanted to give my mother flowers for Mother's Day, but instead of my usual call to the florist, I decided to visit a garden center, pick out hanging plants and flats of annuals, and make a date to help my mother plant them. We enjoyed spending time outdoors together, catching up on each other's lives. This gift of time made it a wonderful Mother's Day for both of us.

Present Pointers

If you decide to make collages of old family photos and you have a personal computer, you might want to consider getting a scanner. Making multiple copies of photos can get expensive, and the price may even equal the cost of a scanner. With a scanner and some professional photo paper, you can continue to make copies of photos for future projects.

Another present that was an instant success was a collage of old family photos. My husband's family never took many pictures of the kids growing up. I found out that, one year, his sister got a camera for Christmas and took several rolls of pictures of the family. I borrowed the pictures and had copies made for everyone in his immediate family. I then bought frames and made the pictures into collages. I knew my present was a big hit when they all called to thank me for the special gift. It went over so well that I plan to do the same thing for my siblings next Christmas.

It's a great feeling to be able to give something to loved ones that they couldn't go out and buy for themselves (in this case, the gift of their childhood memories). That's the perk of giving a homemade gift—the giver gets as much pleasure from the present as the recipient!

The Least You Need to Know

➤ Knowing the needs and habits of the people on your gift list will help you make the perfect gift for them.

➤ Determine when a handmade gift is appropriate and when it might be sensible to give money or a store-bought gift.

➤ For some people, the gift of your time will mean more to them than anything else.

➤ There are many occasions, in addition to the obvious ones, for celebrating with a homemade gift.

➤ Besides making homemade gifts, you can assemble a unique gift basket for the people on your gift list.

Chapter 2

Gathering the Goods and Setting Up Shop

In This Chapter

➤ Organizing your work space

➤ Stocking up on the supplies you'll need

➤ Shopping in stores for craft supplies and ideas

➤ Buying supplies and learning crafts on the Internet

➤ Searching for garage sale "junk"

➤ Recycling household "trash" into homemade gifts

You finally have the house to yourself and manage to carve out a block of time to work on a special gift for your mother. You get halfway through the project, and your glue gun runs out of glue. You'd run out to the craft store for glue sticks, but it's already closed; your carefully orchestrated plans are ruined. Looks like Mom's going to get another silk scarf this year!

Don't let missing ingredients wreck your creative spirit. You can get your craft supplies organized in no time and learn how to stock up on the tools you'll need for future projects.

Establishing Gift-Making Central

To be efficient, you need an organized place to work and store your supplies. If you can, salvage a corner of an office, rec room, or guestroom to set up a table and chair and some storage bins. If you must work in the garage or basement, be sure to install proper lighting if necessary.

Bare minimum, your office space should contain a work table and chair (which, if desired, could be folded and put away at the end of the day), separate storage bins for different mediums, and a filing system for printed resources, craft catalogs, and gift lists.

A filing cabinet or expandable file box will be invaluable for storing resource materials such as magazine articles, recipes, catalogues, and projects printed from the Internet. You should have several storage bins and group your supplies in these bins according to content. For example, you can place all your painting supplies, such as brushes, paints, sandpaper, and varnishes in one bin and your fabric project ingredients, such as material, fabric glue, yarn, needles, trims, and threads in a second bin. Storage bins with drawers save space and are easy to access. An old filing cabinet or chest of drawers would also do the trick.

Consider keeping storage bins for your recyclables, cleaning supplies, protective coverings, tools, and specialty items like glass etching kits and stepping stone molds. The amount of storage bins you need will depend on how involved you become in making crafts.

The following amenities will make the area more comfortable:

➤ Comfortable chair

➤ Work table

➤ Trashcan

➤ Adequate lighting

➤ CD player, tape player, or radio

➤ Space heater for a garage or basement work area (if necessary)

➤ Personal computer for research, making projects, and filing information

Present Tense

Papier-mâché is a French word that describes a material consisting of paper pulp mixed with glue or paste. It can be molded into various shapes when wet and becomes hard when dry. Many projects can be made from papier-mâché including piñatas, keepsake boxes, ornaments, and jewelry, just to name a few.

To ease clean-up of your work space, you might want to check party-supply stores for clearance sales on plastic tablecloths. You can usually get plastic banquet tablecloths for under a dollar to cover your work area. They may have last month's holiday theme on them, but no one will see them, and they make cleanup a lot easier. You should also save newspapers for messier jobs, but be careful when you use them so you don't transfer newsprint onto your projects. You'll also want to save newspapers to make *papier-mâché*.

Cardboard boxes from cases of canned goods or soda are good to have on hand when spraying your projects with paint or acrylic spray. Place the objects to be sprayed inside the boxes. It's less likely that your projects will stick to the cardboard than newspaper, and they'll be easy to transport outside for drying on a nice day. You can also place a box on its side behind the project to be sprayed to shield the room from paint spray.

Stocking Up on Supplies

Once you have a work area arranged, you're ready to stock up on the supplies you'll need for most of the projects in this book. Having supplies on hand allows you to make gifts as the mood strikes you and insures the successful completion of projects that contain many ingredients.

Following is a list of basic supplies you should keep on hand.

Papers

➤ Construction paper
➤ Tissue paper
➤ Crepe paper
➤ Foam sheets (different colors)
➤ Stationery
➤ Scrapbook papers

Fabrics, Trims, and Sewing Aids

➤ Felt (different colors)
➤ Fabric remnants
➤ Trims (rickrack, laces, ribbons)
➤ Pompoms
➤ Feathers
➤ Yarn
➤ Embroidery thread/needles
➤ Lace
➤ Elastic
➤ Sewing machine or needle and thread
➤ Cord
➤ Ribbons
➤ Polyester fill

Glues

➤ *Glue gun/glue sticks*
➤ *White glue* and/or clear glue
➤ *Tacky glue*
➤ Fabric glue

Present Tense

There are so many kinds of glues and adhesives out there that it's easy to get them confused. A **glue gun** heats **glue sticks** to provide a fast-drying, secure glue job. I recommend this type of glue for most projects that require heavy-duty adhesives, including holding material, light wood, and paper together. **White glue** is an old standby for crafting. You can buy regular school glue, but now it also comes in a clear version that's less messy. **Tacky glue** is especially good for gluing material crafts. It also should be used in place of a glue gun when working with kids to keep them from burning their fingers. I've noticed that there is special glue for gluing foam board, but I have found that a glue gun or tacky glue also works well. Mosaics have their own special adhesive that I would recommend using.

Markers, Paints, and Brushes

➤ Set of magic markers (I'd recommend a set of permanent markers with a broad tip on one end and a fine tip on the other.)

➤ Poster paints

➤ Craft paints

➤ Clear acrylic finish spray

➤ Stencil paints

➤ Varnish

➤ Wood stain

➤ Stamps/stamp pads

➤ Special-effect spray paints (stone finish paint, crackle paint, stained glass paint)

➤ Paintbrushes (different sizes and tips)

➤ Stencil paintbrushes or spouncers

➤ Stencils

Decorative Items

➤ Dried flowers

➤ Silk flowers

➤ Grapevine wreaths and baskets

➤ Foam wreaths and shapes

➤ Shrink wrap

➤ Basket filler

➤ Glitter

➤ Stickers

➤ Decorative rub-on transfers

➤ Beads

Present Pointers

Confused about the variety of paints out there? I use craft paint or acrylic paint for most of the projects in this book; both work well. The paints are waterbase and are easy to clean off of brushes and fingers, but the colors are permanent and vivid. You might also want to try spray paints that create special effects. For example, spray crackle paint gives your project a peeling, antique look (you need a base coat and a topcoat), stone finish paint creates a stone texture, and stained glass spray makes plain glass look like stained glass.

Construction Materials

- ➤ Wooden shapes
- ➤ Wooden candleholders
- ➤ Wooden plaques
- ➤ Wooden frames
- ➤ Wooden boxes
- ➤ Cardboard boxes
- ➤ Peg clothespins
- ➤ Popsicle sticks

- ➤ Clay pots
- ➤ Slate
- ➤ Molding clay
- ➤ Pipe cleaners
- ➤ Beads
- ➤ Bead wire/cord
- ➤ Clay

Cutting and Other Tools

- ➤ Drill with drill bits
- ➤ Automatic sander
- ➤ Wire
- ➤ Wire cutters

- ➤ Scissors
- ➤ Decorative edge scissors
- ➤ Digging tool

Specific Supplies for Specialized Crafts

You'll want to have some specific tools handy if you decide to get into the more specialized crafts in this book, such as mosaics, candle making, or soap making. If you enjoy these projects, watch for the supplies to go on sale and keep them stocked in your work area.

Here's what you'll need for the crafts just mentioned.

Present Pointers

It helps to keep a separate box or bin for each type of ingredient. For example, you can store all your wooden objects in one bin; all your materials such as felt, yarn, ribbon, and so on in another bin; all your paint, brushes, and stencils in another bin; and so on.

The Gift of Knowledge

Several programs that you can buy for your computer will allow you to make calendars, greeting cards, banners, stationery, and so on to accompany your home-made gifts. One of my favorites is Greetings Workshop by Micro-soft. If you get this program, be sure to check out the adorable little dog that directs your commands.

Mosaics

➤ Plastic molds

➤ Grout and spreading tool

➤ Tiles, marbles, decorative glass pieces

➤ Tile cutting tool (if desired)

➤ Mosaic adhesive

➤ Sponge

➤ Mosaic sealant

Candle Making

➤ Sheets of beeswax

➤ Candle wicking

➤ Paraffin

➤ Colored wax pieces or crayons for color

➤ Molds, jars, and glasses to form candles

➤ Liquid candle scent

Soap Making

➤ Block of clear glycerin

➤ Decorative soap chips

➤ Food coloring

➤ Soap molds

➤ Liquid soap scent

Now that you know what to buy, it's time to get out there and shop. If you're serious about trying new mediums, I suggest you photocopy the list provided and head to your local craft or discount store, computer source, or supply catalog. If you just want to feel your way through and see where your talents lie, you could check through the chapters and copy down the ingredients of the projects that interest you the most.

Gifting Glitches

Learn which ingredients can be substituted in projects and which ones can't. The wrong kind of paint *can* ruin a project:

Don't substitute craft paint for stencil paint; it will smear and run under the design.

A thick paste made from flour and water can substitute for glue when gluing *paper* only.

You can usually substitute super glue or tacky glue for hot glue.

Fishing line can replace bead wire, and a shoelace can usually replace cord for larger beads.

Feel free to substitute shredded paper towels, crepe paper, or cardboard for newspaper in papier-mâché. You'll like the different look and texture of these materials.

Buying Smart

Making a homemade gift doesn't always mean you'll spend less money than what you'd pay for a store-bought gift. When you consider the prices of craft materials and factor in your time, you may have a significant investment in the project. That's why it pays to shop around for craft supplies and buy them in bulk whenever you find a good price. I've found five sources for obtaining the goods you need to make homemade gifts: stores, the Internet, catalogs, garage sales, and home recyclables. Depending on the price you want to pay, you could get almost everything you need at a major craft store like *Michaels* or *ACMoore*. However, if you like to shop smart, you might want to take a look at some of the following buying tips.

Present Tense

Michaels and **ACMoore** are two large craft store chains that are devoted to craft making. I've shopped at both of these stores and have found that they carry an extensive collection of craft and hobby supplies at competitive prices. The stores are fun places to shop for materials, get ideas for projects, or take a class on a new art form.

Shop Until You Drop

Let's start with probably the easiest and most accessible source for supplies—stores. You can find supplies at craft stores, department stores, party stores, home-improvement, and discount stores, to name a few. You could purchase all your supplies at a craft store for pretty reasonable prices, or you could shop around for the best deals. For instance, I noticed that the prices in the craft section of a local discount store were slightly better than the craft store prices, but the selection wasn't as good. I found some items I needed but still had to go to the craft store for others. If you watch the papers for sales, you can find weekly discounts on many supplies in your local craft store chain.

One of the benefits of shopping for supplies at a craft store is the wealth of information you can receive for free. If you browse through the aisles, you'll most likely see displays of the current trends in craft projects and free how-tos. The stores are willing to give you ideas whether or not you use their products, but chances are you'll get hooked and end up buying their supplies. Many of the stores offer free craft classes (or charge only the cost of supplies). You may even discover the perfect gift for someone on your list by hanging out in a craft store.

Present Pointers

If you're a novice at crafting, I recommend buying a kit with all the necessary supplies to complete a project. For example, you could buy a kit that teaches you step by step how to make a mosaic stepping stone. Usually a kit contains only enough materials to make one or two projects, but it's a good introduction to the art. It also enables you to try the craft without spending a lot of money. If you like the craft, you can always buy larger containers of the ingredients the second time around.

If you buy a complete kit for making a new craft (such as candle making), you can also avoid the problem of missing an important supply when you begin your project. Kits may cost a few cents more, but the advantage of having complete instructions and all the necessary ingredients is worth the extra money for first-time crafters.

You may find better prices at home-improvement stores on items such as paintbrushes, clear acrylic finish spray, larger unfinished wooden objects, cement for mosaics, clay pots, potting soil, plants, varnish, paint, and so on. If you like to cut wooden objects out yourself, check the scrap boxes at lumber mills. I've found some quality woods in these bins that are perfect for small projects.

Another clue to buying discount materials is to shop for seasonal objects after the season has passed. That way, you can stock up on next year's supply of Christmas,

Kwanzaa, or Hanukkah items when they go on sale in January. You should always check the clearance section in craft and discount stores for discounted materials to use in future projects. When you're buying a lot of supplies, it helps to shop smart.

You probably won't be buying craft supplies at the larger department stores, but I thought I'd mention them because you may find sales on glassware (for glass etching, mosaics, candle making), silk flowers, bows, candles, and so on. You might also find items to use in your gift baskets, such as teapots, gourmet coffees, cooking utensils, candleholders, baby supplies, and so on. If you look for these objects when you shop for home furnishings, you could pick up some nice bargains.

Browse through a local party store occasionally to find unusual items for decorating and wrapping gifts, such as shrink-wrap for gift baskets, candles, stamps, stationery, and so on. You'll be surprised at the variety of decorating supplies that you might not have known existed.

Put That Little Mouse to Work

There are literally thousands of sites on the Internet for buying craft supplies. While I was browsing for mosaic supplies in my local craft store, I learned from a fellow crafter that she bought the supplies cheaper online. That prompted me to check out sites to see what you can buy over the Internet and compare prices.

It appears that you can buy any type of craft item you could possibly need online! The prices are comparable to craft store prices unless you buy in bulk, which may save you some money. You also have to consider shipping and handling when pricing Internet supplies, but many companies will waive these fees if you spend a certain amount of money. If you don't have a craft store chain near you, you may be able to find supplies on the Web that you can't find locally. Check out Appendix A, "Resources and Supplies," for a list of some of my favorite supply sites.

Of course, if you don't want to shop online, you could also shop at home using mail-order catalogs.

The Gift of Knowledge

If you use sewing supplies in your projects, you might want to check out fabric and discount stores for bulk supplies of material, lace, yarn, elastic, and so on. You can buy burlap and felt by the yard for a lot less than you'll find it in craft stores. Occasionally these stores will run half-price sales on special categories of materials (like home décor or seasonal yard goods).

Present Pointers

Party supply stores are a good source for wrapping and decorating presents, putting the finishing touches on a gift, or adding items to a gift basket. You can also decorate a gift with a bouquet of helium balloons to mark a special occasion.

Present Pointers

When shopping at garage sales, check out the "free" boxes. Lots of times people throw objects that they don't feel like pricing into a free box. You might find a loose paintbrush, a can of paint, ornaments, bows, decorations, and many more items that you could use in your projects.

The catalogs are convenient because you can browse through them at your leisure and order supplies quickly and painlessly over the phone. (One word of caution: Once you get on these mailing lists your volume of mail will increase.) You can access Appendix A for a list of available catalogs.

Trash to Treasure

It is said that one man's junk is another man's treasure. Nothing could be closer to the truth when it comes to scrounging up materials for making crafty gifts. Garage sales are the perfect place for obtaining a variety of supplies, craft objects, antique wooden objects, bottles, paints, yarn … you name it. If you look long enough, you'll probably find it at a garage sale. You might even get a hodge-podge of craft supplies for a fraction of the cost you would pay for them new.

I have found glassware, wooden objects, brushes, material, ornaments, decorations, and many more items at my local garage sales. I even purchased (at a reasonable price) some elaborate craft projects that I was able to recycle into my own gifts. If you have the time, it's worth the effort. Think of it as a treasure hunt! You just have to get up early, grab a latte to go along with your garage sale list, and begin your search. It's even more fun if you take the kids or a friend along for company.

Waste Not, Want Not

If you know what to look for, you could gather important ingredients for your projects and help out the environment at the same time! Don't pitch that empty wine or water bottle—recycle it into a lovely vase. Turn empty tin cans into hanging lanterns, and use old spaghetti jars as homemade vigil lights. All you have to do is make a copy of the following list of useful recyclables and tape it to your refrigerator. Ask your family to put these objects into a box you've set up near the trashcan. Sort the items out at the end of the week and store them in your work area. That way, you'll have the perfect can for candle making when you need it.

Here's a list of recyclables:

➤ Newspapers

➤ Tin cans (all sizes)

➤ Foam meat trays (Disinfected with soapy water, these trays make excellent paint palettes.)

➤ Toilet paper rolls

➤ Paper towel rolls

➤ Small cardboard boxes

➤ Oatmeal boxes

- ➤ Cookie tins
- ➤ Plastic soda bottles
- ➤ Clear wine bottles and corks
- ➤ Magazines with colorful pictures
- ➤ Pringles cans
- ➤ Plastic cups
- ➤ Cardboard soda boxes
- ➤ Plastic spoons
- ➤ Straws

- ➤ Sponges
- ➤ Berry baskets
- ➤ Mason jars
- ➤ Jelly jars and jars with unusual shapes
- ➤ Sturdy cardboard gift boxes
- ➤ Gift bags
- ➤ Paper grocery-store bags

Now that your work area is ready to go, it's time to think about the people on your gift list.

Making Your Gift List

It's a good idea to make a list of the people in your life who would appreciate a homemade gift. If you're the organized type, you might want to design a separate list for each recipient that includes his or her hobbies, tastes, likes/dislikes, and so on and copy it for use each year. If you do your lists on the computer, you can update them as you go along and have some fun with them by adding borders, clip art, and so on (which then turns them into "wall art" for your studio).

The nice part about making a list is that you have a record of what you've given everyone from year to year. Keep the lists in a binder or folder and take them along to shop for supplies. Or, if this is too organized for you, just grab an old notebook or tablet to jot down your gift ideas. Here's a sample gift list:

Date: 1/1/2001

Name: Priscilla Jacobs

Relationship: Sister

Interests/Hobbies:

_____

_____

Special Occasions

Birthday: 5/25

Anniversary: 7/8

Christmas

Valentine's Day

Gift Ideas

Wooden peg shelf

Decoupage frame

Ornaments

Wooden hearts with pictures

Supplies

Shelf, paint, brushes, stencils, acrylic finish

Wooden frame

Pictures/varnish

Brush

Glass balls

Clothespins

Material scraps

Wooden cutout hearts, paint, glue, pictures

So far you've read ideas on how to organize your workspace, assemble ingredients, and make your gift list. Whether you decide to follow this method, design your own work system, or pick and choose gifts to make at random, you're ready to move on to the art of making and giving great gifts.

The Least You Need to Know

➤ Organizing your workspace and stocking supplies is half the battle when making homemade gifts.

➤ You can make the most of shopping at craft stores by checking out their craft classes and sample artwork.

➤ You can buy supplies in a variety of stores or check out the Internet and mail-order craft catalogs.

➤ Don't forget to search for cheap craft materials at garage sales.

➤ Save household recyclables for future craft projects.

Chapter 3

Wrapping It Up

In This Chapter

➤ Finishing off your work of art with the perfect wrapping

➤ Choosing the right containers for your gifts

➤ Making homemade boxes and bows

➤ Creating your own gift bags and wrapping paper

➤ Designing personalized greeting cards and gift tags

Now that we've discussed the who, what, when, and where of gift-giving, it's time to give some thought to the "how" of gifting. Although the following chapters take you step by step through making unique gifts for all occasions, we can't forget about the packaging. You wouldn't want to spend all this time and energy making a homemade gift only to mar its appearance with unattractive wrapping, would you? As many renowned chefs would say, "Presentation is everything!"

This chapter is devoted to giving you some ideas for how to finish off your work of art with the perfect wrapping, container, bow, and even handmade bags, paper, greeting cards, and gift tags. You might say there's more to giving the perfect gift than meets the eye!

Choosing the Perfect Container for a Homemade Gift

Before you even get started making your gift, you might want to consider your options for presenting it. There are several choices that depend on the gift you've chosen to make. For example, if you put together a gift basket for someone, the obvious choice for a container is a basket with shrink-wrap and a bow. You can find shrink-wrap in craft stores, discount stores, and party or card stores. It's easy to use and adds a professional touch to a gift basket.

However, you should also consider the type, size, shape, and utility of the container. For example, if you choose to make a gift basket for a college student, you might want to put it in a plastic shower caddy or a laundry basket. The obvious choice for a picnic for two would be a picnic basket, but you might not think to put art supplies for a budding artist in a plastic storage container. If the recipient is a child, the parents will appreciate your thoughtfulness, and the child will be delighted with his or her surprise box. As an added bonus, the gift is easily transportable, and the box could even be used as a "desk" in the car.

Present Pointers

A homemade surprise ball is a unique way to present a number of small gifts. All you have to do is tear or cut newspaper, wrapping paper, or tissue paper into strips and start rolling the gifts into a big ball. Then sit back and watch the excitement on your friend's face as he or she opens the gift.

You might want to package smaller homemade presents, such as Christmas ornaments, in papier-mâché boxes or personalized acrylic boxes. You can also buy cardboard boxes in a craft store that can be painted or stenciled to match the season. For example, a gift of homemade Easter candles could be packed in a cardboard box painted pink with a bunny stenciled on the top. You could also assemble homemade soaps into a small wooden box or a lacey basket that could be displayed in the recipient's bathroom.

Larger items can also be packaged in baskets, tins, homemade boxes, or storage bins. Think about putting several decorated clay pots in a stenciled wooden crate along with other gardening supplies. Or you could make up craft kits for kids (such as kits containing pompoms, fun foam, feathers, scissors, glue, and pipe cleaners) and present them in a plastic shoebox.

The Gift of Knowledge

Although the Chinese probably produced paper from silk fibers earlier, the invention of papermaking is generally attributed to the Chinese court official Ts'ai Lun. He succeeded in making paper from vegetable fibers in about 105 C.E. For some reason, this process was kept a secret for 500 years until 770 C.E. when the Japanese acquired it and began making paper. They produced the first mass publication—1,000,000 copies of Buddhist prayer papers. When the Chinese attacked the Arab city of Samarkand in 751 C.E., some of the Chinese prisoners taken in the attack were skilled in the art of papermaking. They were forced to create and operate a paper mill, making Samarkand the papermaking center of the Arab world. The process quickly spread westward to European countries, and by the sixteenth century, papermaking mills existed in most major cities in Europe.

Bagged Gifts

Don't bag the wrapping, wrap it in a bag! You'll find a huge variety of beautiful, cute, and funny gift bags in all types of gift stores. One of the keys to making your bag work is choosing an appropriate filler. You might want to make your own filler out of shredded crepe paper or several colored sheets of tissue paper. There are tools you can buy that will shred and crumple paper for this purpose. Colored saran wrap is also a good choice for filler. If you're not interested in making the filler, you can buy bags of it in craft or party stores. For example, I bought colored, crimped tissue strands to place in a matching bag. The colors complemented the country-style stenciled vase I was giving to a friend.

If you really want to get creative, you could make your own gift bags by using plain white or brown bags found in a craft store and decorating them with stamps or paint. This would be clever wrapping for a gift of stamps, stamp pads, art paper, and cards with envelopes. See the following directions for making a reusable gift bag from material.

Present Pointers

You can make your own home-made stamps by cutting a raw potato in half and carving a design in the middle. Just make the design on the potato first using a sharp knife and cut away the edges so the design is raised. Use a regular stamp pad or pour some craft paint on a paper plate and begin stamping your creations.

Sponging It On

A gift bag decorated with sponge painting.

(© Robert Schroeder)

A variety of sponge shapes and some craft paint can transform a plain paper bag into a lovely gift bag. After you're finished with the bag, try making homemade wrapping paper using the same technique on brown or white craft paper.

Time frame: One to two hours

Level: Easy

What you need:

> Paper tote bag
>
> Dark-colored spray paint (optional)
>
> Craft paint
>
> Paper plate or foam tray for paints
>
> Sponge shapes
>
> Curling ribbon
>
> Scissors for curling the ribbon
>
> Tissue paper or shredded crepe paper

1. If you're using a recycled commercial shopping bag for this project, you'll have to spray out the printing on the bag with dark-colored spray paint and allow it to dry before stamping. Dark blue or green would work well. Then choose

lighter colors for your sponges. Otherwise, you could purchase a plain, ready-to-decorate bag at a craft shop for under a dollar and save the cost and time of the spray paint step.

2. Place about ¼ cup of paint on your tray in a small pool. Dip one side of the sponge shape into the paint and press the painted side onto the bag. Continue stamping different designs in a pattern on your bag. Start at the front of the bag, allow it to dry, and then proceed to the back of the bag.

3. You could do rows of shapes, circles of shapes, or random shapes; use your imagination. They all look nice!

4. Allow your bag to dry thoroughly and decorate the top with curling ribbon in colors that match the stamped shapes. Use scissors to curl ends of the ribbon. Fill your bag with crumpled tissue paper or shredded crepe paper in a matching color.

Under the Sea

"Under the Sea" gift bag.

(© Robert Schroeder)

Here's a gift bag that's easy to make and can be reused by the kids for hours of fun.

Time frame: Two to three hours

Level: Moderately easy

What you need:

    Gift bag

    Ruler

Gifting Glitches

Be careful when using a glue gun on foam sheets. If you're trying to glue two pieces together to make 3D shapes, it can squeeze under the slippery surface and burn your fingers. Just use a small amount and hold it together for a few minutes with your fingers protected by rubber gloves, or try using the special glue designed for fun foam projects.

Scissors

Blue foam sheet (found in craft stores, trade-marked Flexi-foam or Fun Foam)

Glue gun, tacky glue, or foam sheet glue

Package of foam sea animals (found in major craft stores)

Blue raffia bow

Tissue paper filler

1. Measure the width of the front of your bag. Cut three waves out of the blue foam sheet. Make the waves as long as the width of the bag and about three inches tall.

2. Using a glue gun or tacky glue, glue the three equally spaced waves across the bag, gluing only the bottom edge and side edges of the waves. The top should be open to allow insertion of sea animals. If you have a larger bag, you could include more waves of animals.

3. Insert the foam sea animals into the waves. Make a bow out of the blue raffia and attach it to the handle. Fill the bag with tissue paper.

Simple Stitchery

Environmentally friendly gift bag.

(© Robert Schroeder)

You can wrap your gifts and save the environment at the same time by making re-usable material bags for the presents you'll exchange. Just follow these simple directions:

Time frame: Two to four hours

Level: Moderately difficult

What you need:

> Material (can use assorted fabrics, burlap, or felt)
>
> Thread
>
> Sewing machine
>
> Iron and ironing board
>
> Rope or heavy cord
>
> Pins
>
> Large safety pin
>
> Trims, buttons

1. Cut the material into different-size rectangles. I'd recommend making two sizes of bags to accommodate large and small packages. I used material that's 22×36 inches and 16×32 inches. You'll need one rectangle for each bag you make.
2. Fold the material in half with the right sides of the material together. Use the folded edge as the bottom of the bag and stitch up the two side edges using a ½-inch seam.
3. Using an iron, press a ¼-inch seam around the top of the bag toward the wrong side of the bag. Fold this pressed edge down again to the wrong side of the bag, forming a one-inch casing along the top. Press the casing down and pin it in place to prepare for sewing. The pressed casing should be seen on the wrong side of the material (which at this point is on the outside since it hasn't been turned right side out yet).
4. Stitch the casing, using a ¼-inch seam around the bottom of the casing. Leave a two-inch opening on one side of the side seams to insert the cord. Reinforce the stitching at the opening by reversing over the original stitching.
5. Cut a piece of cord for the drawstring that is double the width of the bag plus eight inches (for the larger bag, approximately 48 inches; for the smaller bag, approximately 40 inches).

Present Pointers

Craft stores sell all types of decorative buttons that are perfect for craft projects. The buttons come in bagged assortments that represent different interests (for example, sports, flowers, gardening supplies, shapes, seasonal objects, and so on). These buttons would be perfect to sew or glue onto your homemade bags.

6. Secure a pin on the end of the cord and thread the cord through the opening, around the casing to the other side. Tie a secure knot in the two ends of the cord. Do not resew the opening because the cord will be pulled through the hole.

7. Turn the bag right side out. Sew rickrack or a lacey trim along the top of the bag under the casing, being careful not to sew the top opening shut. Sew some buttons on the bag for decoration or draw a simple design on the front using fabric paint.

Box It Up

Another option for wrapping a gift is to make a special box for the item. You can buy boxes made of wood or cardboard at a craft store or use sturdier boxes that department stores give out for free. A little paint with stencils or stamps will give them a finished touch, or you could check out the following directions for making your own small gift boxes out of old greeting cards.

Recycled Boxes

Gift box from recycled greeting cards.

(© Robert Schroeder)

These decorative little boxes made from old greeting cards are perfect for little gifts like jewelry or rare coins or gems.

Time frame: Half hour

Level: Moderately easy

What you need:

> One greeting card per box
>
> Scissors
>
> Ruler and pencil

1. Cut the card in two along the folded edge.
2. Cut the front of the card into a perfect square using a ruler.
3. Cut the back of the card into the same shape but trim approximately ⅛ inch off two sides.
4. Draw an "X" on the nonpicture side. Fold ends to the center.

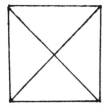 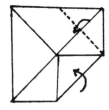 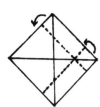

How to fold greeting cards into a gift box.

(© Melissa LeBon)

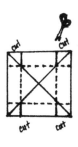 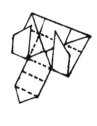 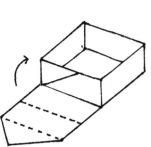

Present Pointers

If you enjoyed the art of box making, you might want to try doing it on a larger scale by using pictures from magazines glued onto cardboard. Be sure to glue the pictures securely onto the cardboard by spreading the glue evenly over the entire surface of the cardboard before applying the pictures. Allow the glue to dry for several hours before folding so that it won't buckle.

5. After all ends are folded to center, fold each side horizontal to the center line and then unfold to crease top of box.

6. Cut along the vertical creases on two opposing sides to the point until it would start to cut another side.

7. Unfold except for two corners. Unfold long arms and fold up to meet and form the box shape.

8. Fold the uncut portion to cover and then meet the tips in the middle.

9. Repeat steps 4 through 8 for the back of the card. You should now have a colorful top and plain bottom to make a small gift box.

Make Their Day with Papier-Mâché

Papier-mâché boxes make lovely keepsake boxes that can be used for presenting a special gift. The box itself becomes part of the gift!

A finished papier-mâché keepsake box.

(© Robert Schroeder)

Time frame: Two to three hours, plus two nights to dry

Level: Moderately difficult

What you need:

Newspaper (for covering work surface and pasting)

Flour

Water

Shallow bowl

Cardboard box

White and green craft paints

Paintbrushes

Sponge

Magazine picture or picture from a greeting card

White glue

Varnish

1. Cover your work area with newspapers. In a shallow bowl, make a paste from ¾ cup of flour and a little less than ½ cup of water. The paste should be thick enough to thoroughly coat a piece of paper dipped into it, without it dripping off the paper. If the paste is too runny, add more flour; if it's too dry, add more water.

2. Tear or cut a section of newspaper into one-inch-wide strips.

3. Dip the strips into the paste and run your fingers down them to remove excess paste. Paste the strip of paper onto the box. Continue pasting strips on the box until the sides, bottom, and inside of the box are covered. Do the same to the lid. You may want to rub extra paste along the strips as you go to smooth out any wrinkles or puckers. Allow this to dry overnight.

4. Paint the box with white craft paint and allow it to dry. Dab green paint onto the box with the sponge to create a marbled effect.

Present Pointers

You can change the look of your papier-mâché keepsake boxes by pasting on a layer of comic paper or tissue paper before varnishing the box (instead of using paint and a picture) or by painting the box and stenciling a design around the sides and top. Be sure to add a layer of varnish at the end to protect the finish.

5. Glue the picture onto the top of the box. (I used a picture of a bunny from a greeting card.) Coat the box with a layer of varnish and allow it to dry overnight.

Wrapping Paper

Let's not forget the old standard in the gift business—wrapping paper. One nice effect can be accomplished by buying brown craft paper and decorating it yourself with stamps. Or you could use the Sunday comics for a different look. I also like tissue paper with some decorative confetti glued to the top. I know some people who shop for cheap remnants of wallpaper to use as wrapping paper, and come to think of it, remnants of material would also work well.

Paper Pizzazz

Time frame: Four to five hours, including drying time

Level: Easy

What you need:

Newspapers or plastic tablecloth (to cover work area)

Two contrasting colors of craft paint (I used blue and white.)

Foam tray or dish for paint

One to three textured sponge stamps (Craft stores sell sponge stamps that create textured designs on the object being painted. You can reuse one sponge or use three different designs for this project.)

Brown craft paper large enough to fit the gift (You can use the paper sold for wrapping postal packages.)

Matching bow

1. Cover your work area with newspaper or a plastic tablecloth. Pour approximately ⅓ cup of blue craft paint onto the paint tray. Dip the textured sponge stamp into the paint and stamp the design onto the top left of the paper. Continue this process until there is a blue design covering the paper. Add more paint to the tray as need. Allow to dry.

2. Add a small amount of white paint to the blue paint on the tray and mix well. Dip the second sponge (or cleaned first sponge) into the paint and stamp intermittently onto the paper. Allow to dry.

3. Wash the paint off the paint tray and pour about ⅓ cup of white paint onto the tray. Dip the third sponge (or cleaned first sponge) into the paint and stamp

white designs onto the paper intermittently. You should have a piece of wrapping paper with blue, powder blue, and white textures covering the brown paper. Allow to dry thoroughly.

4. Wrap your gift in the paper and add a matching bow.

The Gift of Knowledge

Although wood is the main ingredient in paper, only about half of the fiber used in the papermaking process comes from trees cut for this purpose. The remainder of the fibers used comes from recycled newspapers, wood chips from sawmills, and a small quantity of nonwood fibers such as sugarcane bagasse, flax straws, reeds, and cotton and linen rags. The finest handmade papers are made from pure linen or cotton rag pulp. The fibers are washed, boiled, and beaten to break down their structure. They are then molded into paper on a screen supported by a frame. A deckle is another frame that is placed on top of the bottom frame to keep the fibers from being washed away by the process.

Bodacious Bows

A handcrafted bow.

(© Robert Schroeder)

A handmade bow is an attractive addition to a present and is durable enough to be reused by the recipient. Make your own bows from wired ribbon by following these simple directions.

Time frame: 10 to 20 minutes

Level: Easy

What you need:

    Five yards of stiff ribbon or ribbon with wired edges

    Wire

    Scissors

1. Start at one end of the ribbon and leave a tail about eight inches long. Make a bow at this point with each loop about eight inches long. Hold the middle of the bow in one hand and twist each loop around one time to keep it firmly in place.

2. Add another loop on each side and twist in place.

3. Add a third loop on each side and twist in place. Then add a final five-inch loop in the center of the bow and twist in place. End with an eight-inch tail on the other side and cut the ribbon.

4. Use a piece of wire to catch all the loops, starting through the middle loop, around the back of the bow, and back through each side. Fluff up your bow and notch the ends of the ribbon as shown.

You might want to add a sprig of dried flowers or silk flowers to your bow for a finishing touch. You could also put glue on the edges of the bow and sprinkle them with glitter for a special effect.

The steps to creating a beautiful handmade bow.

(© Melissa LeBon)

The Gift of Knowledge

The tradition of giving Christmas cards began in London in 1843. Sir Henry Cole asked artist John Calcott Horsley to design a card for him to send to his friends and business acquaintances at Christmastime. It was tradition to write to family and friends over the holidays, but Cole didn't have the time to write personal greetings. The card portrayed a typical English family celebrating the holidays and performing charitable acts. The message was "A Merry Christmas and a Happy New Year to You." A thousand copies of the card were printed and sold for one shilling apiece. Twelve of the original cards still exist today. Hallmark issued its first Christmas card in 1915.

Hallmark, Here You Come!

Greeting cards created by Lourie Russell.

(© Robert Schroeder)

Trust me, people will look at the back of the card to find your special signature when you give them a homemade greeting card. When you think about it, what could be better than giving a card that captures your own special feelings for the recipient?

Lourie Russell of Alexandria, Virginia, does a beautiful job with greeting cards and stamps. She purchases blank paper and envelopes at a craft store and decorates them with a variety of stamps and ink. She also uses different textured and colored papers that she cuts to fit the card for special effects. A touch of glitter for the right card and a handwritten message is the finishing touch. You always know when a Lourie card is coming—her trademark of a tiny engine is always stamped on the back.

Present Pointers

Making greeting cards is a fun project for anyone, including kids. You might want to give someone on your gift list a pack of blank cards, stamps, stamp pads, magic markers, textured paper, scissors, and glue and package them in a keepsake box.

You don't have to be an artist to create a homemade card—a blank note card and envelope, a rubber stamp and stamp pad, and some markers would fit the bill. Simply stamp the front with the stamp and write your message inside. You can stamp a matching stamp on the back or side of the envelope. It's the thought that counts, and your written thoughts will be appreciated long after the gift is gone. Or try this simple design to relay your greetings.

Card Creations

Time frame: Half to one hour

Level: Easy

What you need:

> Rub-on transfers and Popsicle stick, or packs of paper cutouts and white glue (found in craft stores)

Blank note card and envelope (You can buy these in packs at craft or stationery stores.)

Hole punch

Matching thin satin ribbon

Fine tipped marker

1. Use a rub-on transfer to create a design on the card by placing the design centered on the front with the tacky side down. Rub the transfer with a Popsicle stick until it is completely transferred to the paper. Gently lift a corner of the transfer off the paper. If there are areas that aren't transferred completely, rub again with the Popsicle stick until transferred.

2. If using cutouts, glue a random pattern of paper cutouts on the front of the card. I've used Christmas cutouts for Christmas greetings, hearts for Valentine's Day, and everyday shapes such as leaves, musical notes, flowers, and so on for everyday greeting cards.

3. Using the hole punch, make two holes in the front center top of the card. Thread the ribbon through the holes from the back to the front and tie a bow in the ends, so the bow is on the front, top of your greeting card.

4. Write your message inside the card and place in the envelope. If desired, decorate the envelope with matching transfers or cutouts on the back flap or front left side.

Recycled Gift Tags

Turn your old greeting cards into colorful gift tags. You can personalize the tags with a special message to the gift recipient.

Time frame: One hour

Level: Easy

What you need:

Old greeting cards

Pinking shears or *decorative-edge scissors*

Hole punch

White or clear glue

Glitter

Yarn

Present Tense

Pinking shears have been around for years, and most people are aware that they make a notched edge around paper, fabric, cardboard, and other assorted materials. A newer variation on pinking shears is **decorative-edge scissors** that cut various designs into materials in the same manner. These special scissors are great for making greeting cards and gift tags.

1. Cut the front of the card into shapes of your choice using pinking shears or decorative-edge scissors. You could cut out rectangles, circles, triangles, hearts, and so on. Punch a hole in the top of the tag.

2. Squeeze glue around the edges of the shapes and sprinkle glitter on top. Shake the excess glitter off the gift tag onto a piece of paper. Either fold the paper in half and pour the excess glitter back into the container or discard.

3. Thread a six-inch piece of yarn through the hole and knot the ends.

If desired, you could use the front and back of the greeting card when cutting out your shapes and tie the two pieces together with the yarn forming a gift tag that opens up to include a message.

Present Pointers

Another fun gift tag to make for a present is a stenciled wooden shape. Simply paint a flat wooden shape, such as a heart, star, Christmas tree, dreidel, and so on, with craft paint and allow it to dry. Stencil the front with a seasonal stencil and write "To" and "From" messages on the back with a fine tipped marker. Drill a hole in the wood and string it with yarn or cord to tie to the bow.

The Least You Need to Know

➤ In addition to the traditional wrappings for presents, there are many creative ideas for packaging gifts.

➤ You can easily make your own special boxes and bows to present your presents in a unique manner.

➤ Gift bags are a great substitute for wrapping paper and can also be handmade.

➤ Don't pay out big bucks to the greeting-card industry. Make your own cards and gift tags for a fraction of the cost.

Part 2

The Art of Making the Perfect Holiday Gift

Holidays have a way of creeping up on us. This year, don't let these special days pass you by without making that homemade gift you've been putting off for years. Take a look at the following chapters to discover the perfect gift ideas for all your holiday needs. You'll find suggestions for making homemade presents for Kwanzaa, Christmas, Hanukkah, Valentine's Day, Easter, Passover, Halloween, and Thanksgiving.

Chapter 4

Kwanzaa Kumba (Creativity)

In This Chapter

➤ Understanding the meaning of Kwanzaa

➤ Learning how to celebrate Kwanzaa

➤ Making symbolic Kwanzaa gifts

➤ Finding the perfect homemade Kwanzaa gift (zawadi)

Whether you plan to celebrate *Kwanzaa* with your family this year or you've only recently heard enough about the holiday to pique your interest, you should check out this chapter. Every year from December 26 to January 1, many African-Americans celebrate their past, present, and future during a season called Kwanzaa. Individual families determine the significance of Kwanzaa by starting their own family traditions. In most cases, these traditions reflect the historical and present-day background of the African-American heritage. An important aspect of this holiday is planning for the year ahead and attempting to enrich community life.

If you decide to celebrate Kwanzaa, don't let the holiday be one more chore on your already-busy agenda. Celebrate this great event in your own style and enjoy this season of positive values and unity. Enhance the holiday by trying some of the easy gift ideas in this chapter.

The Meaning of Kwanzaa

You may already know that the Kwanzaa rituals include lighting candles, celebrating with friends, and exchanging daily homemade gifts. But are you aware of the special meaning behind the candles in the kinara (traditional Kwanzaa candleholder) that are lit at dinnertime?

Each candle represents one of these seven principles or rules of learning how to live each day:

1. **Umoja** (*oo-MOE-jah*): Unity. Sticking together as a family. Symbolized by lighting the black candle in the center of the kinara (candleholder).

2. **Kujichagulia** (*koo-jee-cha-goo-LEE-ah*): Self-determination. Being proud of who you are and what you do in life. Symbolized by lighting the first red candle.

3. **Ujima** (*oo-JEE-mah*): Collective work and responsibility. Working together as a team to support the goals of the family and/or community. Symbolized by lighting the first green candle.

4. **Ujamaa** (*oo-JAH-mah*): Cooperative economics. Taking pride in the cultural expressions of African-Americans, such as music, art forms, dance, clothing styles, and so on. Symbolized by lighting the second red candle.

5. **Nia** (*nee-AH*): Purpose. Trying to be the best you can be and being responsible for your own actions. Symbolized by lighting the second green candle.

6. **Kumba** (*koo-OOM-bah*): Creativity. Being able to express yourself in a creative fashion through music, art, dance, and so on. Symbolized by lighting the last red candle.

7. **Imani** (*ee-MAH-nee*): Faith. Having faith in the creator, parents, family, community, and the goodness of the struggle for excellence. Symbolized by lighting the last green candle.

Seasonal Symbols

The Kwanzaa celebration is rich in symbols. You might want to try creating some of these family heirlooms for your friends and families to display at their Kwanzaa dinners.

Present Tense

Kwanzaa (Swahili for "first") is an African-American celebration designed to promote unity. It was developed in 1966 by Dr. Maulana Karenga, a noted black ideologist. Dr. Karenga wanted to instill in the African-American community a sense of pride in its culture. The elements of the Kwanzaa celebration include certain standard principles, symbols, and rituals. The principles are unity, self-determination, collective work, economic cooperation, purpose, creativity, and faith. There are also seven basic symbols: a unity cup, a candleholder, crops, seven candles, a woven mat, ears of corn, and gifts. The colors that represent this season are red, green, and black.

Woven Mats

One of the seven basic symbols of Kwanzaa— Mkeka.

(© Robert Schroeder)

Spend special time with your family making these unique holiday mats (mkeka) that represent traditions and family origins. Be sure to set your Kwanzaa table with these colorful woven designs.

Time frame: Two to three hours

Level: Easy

What you need:

Two pieces of burlap cut into 18 × 12-inch rectangles

Scissors

Crochet hook or large yarn needle

20-inch long strands of red, green, and black thin satin ribbons

Glue gun or tacky glue

1. Fray the edges of the first burlap rectangle to about ½ inch. With a crochet hook or yarn needle, pull out three strands from the sides of the burlap, every inch or however far apart you'd like your design to occur.

2. Thread the yarn needle with the ribbon and weave the ribbon through the pulled out burlap, leaving about five strands of burlap material in between the weavings (see illustration). Alternate the colors—I chose to use black, red, black, green, black, red, and so on—or pick a pattern that appeals to you. You may want to use three red ribbons, one black ribbon, and three green ribbons to represent the kinara. Be sure the ribbon is flat when you pull it through the burlap.

3. After all the openings are filled with ribbon, lay the mat on top of the other piece of burlap and glue the two pieces together around the perimeter. Be sure to catch the ends of the top mat onto the glue.

4. Take two pieces of trim ribbon and glue them onto the right and left sides.

Present Pointers

You can make a woven mat using red, green, and black raffia in place of the ribbon, or you might want to make a banner out of the leftover burlap. Remove some of the strands to make open spaces of various widths. Reweave the open part using twigs, flowers, weeds, leaves, and so on. Fringe the ends if desired. Fold the top over about 1½ inches and glue with a glue gun to make a sleeve for a dowel. Tie a piece of cord to each end of the dowel for hanging purposes.

Light Up Their Lives

A traditional, handmade kinara.

(© Robert Schroeder)

Make a special *kinara* (candleholder) for the people on your Kwanzaa gift list using these trendy clay pots.

Time frame: Three to five hours, including drying time

Level: Moderately easy

What you need:

> One piece of wood, approximately 18 × 3½ inches
>
> Red, black, and green craft paints
>
> Paintbrush
>
> Clear acrylic finish spray
>
> Seven 2-inch clay pots
>
> One 1½-inch clay pot
>
> Seven wooden candle cups with a ⅞-inch hole (These can be found in a craft store.)
>
> Glue gun
>
> One black, three red, and three green candle tapers

1. Paint the piece of wood black and allow it to dry. Spray it with clear acrylic finish spray and allow it to dry.

2. Paint the outside of the two-inch pots—three green, three red, and one black. Paint the outside of the 1½-inch pot black. Paint the seven wooden candleholders—three green, three red, and one black. Allow the pots and candleholders to dry and spray with clear acrylic finish spray. Allow them to dry approximately three hours.

Present Tense

A ceremonial **kinara** is a candle-stick holder that holds seven candles—three red, three green, and one black. The black candle represents the face of the African people. The three red candles signify the blood of the African people. The three green candles represent the hope of new life.

3. Glue the two-inch pots upside down across the piece of wood in the following order: the three red pots on the left, the one black pot in the middle, and the three green pots on the right. Then glue the black 1½-inch pot upside down onto the bottom of the black 2-inch pot as shown.

4. Glue the painted wooden candleholders onto the bottoms of the matching pots.

5. Place the black candle in the middle, the three red candles on the left side, and the three green candles on the right side.

6. Be sure to include directions for lighting the kinara. The black candle should be lit first, followed by the red and green candles, which should be lit alternately from left to right.

Candle Magic

Homemade Kwanzaa candles.

(© Robert Schroeder)

Make your kinara (candleholder) for Kwanzaa even more special by burning home-made candles. Candles are relatively easy to make, but it's important that adults supervise due to the nature of the materials. Wax reacts much like oil when heated and is very flammable. Be sure to have some sand available in the event the wax catches on fire. You shouldn't have any trouble if you follow these simple steps.

Time frame: Three to four hours plus overnight to harden

Level: Moderately difficult

What you need:

> Newspapers
>
> Candle wicking
>
> Masking tape
>
> Spoon
>
> Seven 8-ounce plastic drinking cups
>
> Three 16-ounce boxes of paraffin wax
>
> Plastic bag
>
> Hammer
>
> Three 12-ounce coffee cans
>
> Red, green, and black crayons (paper peeled off) or red, green, and black wax pieces (one bag of each color)
>
> Large frying pan
>
> Pot holders
>
> Toothpick

1. Cover your work area with newspapers.
2. Prepare the candle molds: Cut a four-inch piece of candle wicking and tape it onto the middle of the handle of a spoon. Lay the spoon over the plastic cup so the wick hangs down into the cup. Tape the other end of the wick to the bottom of the plastic cup. (You can also buy individual stiff candle wicks with a metal disk on the bottom that will stand up in the cups without using the spoon. Be sure to hold the top of these wicks when pouring the wax to keep them in the center of the cup.) Repeat this step with the other six cups.
3. Place the paraffin wax in a plastic bag. Hit the bag several times with a hammer to break the wax into small pieces.

Gifting Glitches

Keep in mind these four don'ts of candle use:

➤ Don't light candles and leave them unattended.

➤ Don't let kids put candles in their bedrooms.

➤ Don't light candles in a drafty area where they'll burn unevenly.

➤ When making candles, don't throw the unused hot wax down your drain.

4. Place the wax pieces into the tin cans until two cans are approximately two-thirds full of wax and one can is one-third full.

5. If using crayons, break them into small pieces keeping each color separate.

6. Fill the frying pan half full of water (about one-inch deep). Keep the water at this level by adding more as it evaporates.

7. Place the cans of wax in the boiling water.

8. Once the wax melts, add the black crayons or wax pieces to the can with the smaller amount of wax and the red and green crayons or wax pieces to the other cans. Add a few pieces at a time, until you have the desired shade of color. Stir well with a stick or spoon until the wax is melted.

9. Using a pot holder, carefully pour the melted wax into the prepared plastic cups to within one inch of the top. If any bubbles form around the wick after pouring the wax, pop them with a toothpick and add more wax. Repeat these steps until you have three red candles, three green candles, and one black candle. (Do not discard any leftover wax down a drain.)

10. Allow the wax candles to harden in the refrigerator overnight before removing them from the cups.

11. When the candle is hard, tap the bottom of the cup until the candle falls out or cut away the plastic from the candle with a pair of scissors. Cut the wick from the spoon, leaving a ½-inch length of protruding wick to light. Be sure to place a plate or tray under your candles to catch any wax that drips when you light them.

Give the Gift of a Kwanzaa Celebration

Treat the novices on your list to a special Kwanzaa celebration prepared for them at your home or their home.

Time frame: Six to eight hours

Level: Moderately easy

What you need:

Straw mats (Mkeka), representing reverence for tradition

Unity cup (Kikombe cha umoja), a communal libation

Corn (Vibunzi), one ear for each child

Fruits and vegetables (Mazao), representing the product of unified effort

A candleholder (kinara), holding seven candles (Mishumaa saba) representing the seven principles

Gifts (Zawadi), related to African-American heritage

Family dinner

Music

Present Tense

A **unity cup** is a communal cup filled with a drink. Usually, water is used to symbolize the essence of life. The celebrants should pour the water in the communal cup in the direction of the four winds: north, south, east, and west. The cup should be passed to family members, allowing each person to take a sip from the cup or make a sipping gesture. You might want to use the following libation statement from a model developed by Dr. Karenga:

For the Motherland cradle of civilization.
For the ancestors and their indomitable spirit.
For the elders from whom we can learn much.
For our youth who represent the promise for tomorrow.
For our people the original people.
For our struggle and in remembrance of those who have struggled on our behalf.
For Umoja, the principle of unity, which should guide us in all that we do.
For the creator who provides all things great and small.

1. Set a table with straw mats. Place a unity cup, ears of corn, fruits and vegetables, and the kinara (candleholder) in the center of the table. Greet each guest with the traditional Kwanzaa greeting: Habari Gani, which means "What's the news?"

2. Make the family the center of the celebration, and give each member a turn to light the kinara. The kinara should have three red candles to the left, three green candles to the right, and one black candle in the center. Light a candle each night of Kwanzaa, starting with the black candle and alternately lighting the red and green candles from the left to right. Re-light the candles that were lit on previous nights until all the candles are lit on the seventh night. For example: on the first night, light the black candle. On the second night, light the black candle and the first red candle. On the third night, light the black candle, the red candle, and the first green candle. And on the fourth night, light the black candle, the red candle, the green candle, and the second red candle (going from left to right) and so on until all candles are lit on the seventh night. When a candle is lit, recite and discuss one of the seven principles of Kwanzaa. Conclude the lighting ceremony by calling out "Harambee!" seven times. (Swahili for "Let's all pull together!")

3. Pour libation from the unity cup during the celebration.

4. Following the ceremony, serve refreshments or dinner and exchange gifts (zawadi) if desired. If possible, gifts should be handmade or homegrown and should reflect the black heritage. Gifts can be given each night or can be saved for the Kwanzaa feast (Karamu) on December 31.

5. If you'd like, you could encourage expressions of song and dance during the celebration.

Traditional Kwanzaa symbols: fruits of the harvest.

(© Melissa LeBon)

United We Stand

Symbolic unity cup.

(© Robert Schroeder)

Express your desire for unity by making this lovely stained glass unity cup. All you need to make stained glass that looks like the real thing is special stained glass paint and simulated liquid lead.

Time frame: Two to three hours plus overnight to dry

Level: Moderately easy

What you need:

> Paintbrush
>
> Stemmed glass drinking cup
>
> Red and green stained glass paints
>
> Simulated liquid leading (A squeeze bottle of simulated lead can be found in a craft store.)

1. Paint the top of the glass red and allow it to dry. Paint the stem and bottom half of the glass green. Allow it to dry.

2. Using the liquid leading, draw a design in black on the front of the glass. You could make your own design (such as an ear of corn, a kinara, and so on) or use the design shown.

3. Write the word "Unity" on the top or base of the glass. Allow it to dry overnight before using.

Kwanzaa Gifts with Kumba

Running out of homemade gift ideas for the seven nights of Kwanzaa? You might want to check out this next section for meaningful and useful Kwanzaa gifts.

Corn Jewelry

One of the symbols of Kwanzaa is an ear of corn. Save your dried corn from Halloween to make these unique necklaces and bracelets.

Time frame: One to three hours plus overnight to soak the corn

Level: Easy

What you need:

Dried ears of corn (Halloween corn)

Bowl of water

Food coloring (optional)

Heavy thread

Large embroidery needle

Present Pointers

If you enjoyed this activity, you might want to visit a local bead store or craft store and buy different sizes and varieties of beads. Spend an afternoon making necklaces and bracelets to give at Kwanzaa. I'd recommend making gemstone necklaces and bracelets on elastic thread. You could customize a gift for Kwanzaa by using the recipient's birthstone in the jewelry.

1. Remove the dried corn from the cob.

2. Soak the corn overnight in a bowl of water to make it soft.

3. If desired, you can make different colored beads. Add several drops of different colors of food coloring to individual bowls of water, and place the corn in the bowls to soak overnight.

4. Measure a piece of heavy thread that, when shaped into a necklace, will fit over your head (or the head of the recipient) and then add five inches to the length.

5. Thread a large embroidery needle with the thread and string a kernel of corn on it. (You could also use bead wire for this step and earring wire to make earrings.)

6. String on the rest of the kernels and tie the ends together in a knot.

7. Allow the corn to dry before wearing it.

A Tisket a Tasket, a Lovely Kwanzaa Basket

Homemade basket to hold the fruits of a Kwanzaa dinner.

(© Robert Schroeder)

You'll be surprised how easy it is to make these simple baskets to hold the fruits and vegetables for a Kwanzaa celebration. They also make a special Kwanzaa present for friends or relatives.

Time frame: Two to four hours

Level: Easy

What you need:

> Yarn needle
>
> Red, green, and black yarn, raffia, or ribbon
>
> Plastic basket with cutout grids on the sides (see photo)
>
> Piece of red or green felt
>
> Scissors
>
> Tacky glue
>
> Assorted fruits and vegetables

1. Thread the needle with one color of the yarn. Start at one corner at the bottom of the basket and weave the strands of yarn in and out of the grids until you reach the starting point. Cut the yarn, leaving an extra eight inches of length. Pull the yarn ends through the corner hole and tie the ends of the yarn into a bow.

2. Re-thread the needle with a different color of yarn and repeat step one, moving up the grids until all the levels of holes are filled with yarn. You should have layers of bows tied in one corner of the basket.

3. Cut the felt to the size of the bottom of the basket, and glue it onto the inside of basket with tacky glue.

4. Fill the basket with fruits and vegetables.

Kwanzaa Lights

A stone textured vigil light for Kwanzaa.

(© Melissa LeBon)

All it takes is a little kumba to make this stone fleck votive light for one of the nights of Kwanzaa gift giving.

Time frame: One to two hours plus overnight to dry

Level: Easy

What you need:

> Mason jar
>
> Can of spray stone/fleck paint
>
> Red, green, and black ribbons or yarn
>
> Glass votive holder and candle

1. Spray the first jar with a light layer of stone fleck spray in your color of choice. Allow it to dry. Spray a second layer on the jar and allow it to dry overnight.

2. Wrap the ribbon or yarn around the neck of the jar and tie a bow.

3. Place the votive light in the opening of the Mason jar.

Whenever you work with special-effect paint sprays, be sure your surface is clean and free of any dust or oils. Always spray the object with a light coat first and add coats as needed. Keep the sprayer from getting clogged by turning the can upside down and spraying a small amount of paint to clear the cap. (Make sure it doesn't get in your eyes!)

A trivet fashioned in the traditional Kwanzaa colors.

(© Robert Schroeder)

Design your own trivet to give as a gift on one of the nights of Kwanzaa. This gift is a functional work of art!

Time frame: Two to three hours plus two days to dry

Level: Moderately difficult

What you need:

> One pound bag or box of white grout (can be found in craft stores)
>
> Disposable plastic bowl or cup
>
> Water
>
> Mosaic trivet mold
>
> Popsicle stick or old spatula
>
> Bag of red, green, and black tiles
>
> Sponge

Soft cloth

Can of mosaic sealer isolant

Paintbrush

Present Pointers

If you choose square mosaic pieces for a project, you might want to break them for effect. Place several of the same color pieces in a zipper bag. Lay the bag on a flat, hard surface such as cement. Sort the tiles out in a single layer in the bag. Hit each piece with a hammer, using a quick light blow. The tiles should split into two to four pieces. Repeat the process until all the tiles are broken.

1. Place about ½ cup of grout in the bowl or cup. Mix with water according to the directions on the package of grout (usually about three parts grout to one part water). Stir the mixture well until it is a thick, smooth consistency.

2. Fill the mold with grout almost to the top of the mold. Use a Popsicle stick or spatula to smooth over the top.

3. Lay the tiles on top of the grout in the pattern you desire or use the pattern shown. Apply a small amount of grout on top of the design and push it into the crevices.

4. Once the grout has set, approximately 10 to 15 minutes, wipe off the excess grout with a damp sponge. Continue this process until all grout is removed from the top of the tiles. Allow this to dry overnight.

5. Carefully apply pressure to the back of the mold to remove the trivet. Polish the tiles with a soft cloth, and apply a coat of mosaic sealer isolant. Allow this to dry overnight.

Homemade Spice of Life

A homegrown Kwanzaa gift.

(© Robert Schroeder)

Add a touch of spice to your Kwanzaa celebration by giving this lovely gift of potted herbs.

Time frame: Three to five hours including drying time

Level: Moderately easy

What you need:

Eight-inch clay pot and saucer

White craft paint

Paintbrush

Sunflower stencil (I used a border stencil)

Stencil paintbrush or spouncer

Brown, yellow, and green stencil paints

Clear acrylic finish spray

Potting soil

Herbs (basil, oregano, cilantro, and so on)

Thick ribbon for bow

1. Paint the clay pot white on the outside below the rim. Allow it to dry.

2. Place the stencil over the painted area of the pot, and hold it in place with tape or the pressure of your hands.

3. Using the stencil brushes, apply stencil paint to the appropriate areas. Remove the stencil, being careful not to smudge the design. Allow it to dry.

4. Spray the pot with clear acrylic finish spray and allow it to dry.

5. Add potting soil to your pot and plant a variety of herbs in the soil. Place the pot of herbs on the saucer, and tie the ribbon into a bow around the top.

Potent Potions

Herb and fruit flavored oils and vinegars.

(© Robert Schroeder)

Strive for Ujima (pronounced *oo-jee-mah,* meaning "collective work") by making these cooking helpers with your friends or family.

Time frame: One to two hours plus one week to seep

Level: Easy

What you need:

Gallon-size jug of white vinegar

Six Mason jars with lids

One cup each of fresh raspberries, blueberries, and strawberries

Gallon-size jug of olive oil

½ cup each of assorted fresh herbs (basil, rosemary, thyme)

Strainer

Six cups or bowls

Funnel

Six decorative bottles with corks, or six wine bottles with corks (You can buy new corks for wine bottles in craft stores.)

Fine-tipped marker or calligraphy pen

Labels

Tacky glue

Small basket

Raffia filler

Bow

Present Pointers

You might want to try adding other ingredients to your vinegars and oils such as garlic, scallions, red chile peppers, oregano, cranberries, and so on. Use your imagination and come up with some great combinations.

1. Divide the vinegar into three Mason jars. Add a cup of different berries to each jar and seal with the lids. Divide the oil into the remaining three Mason jars. Add ½ cup of different fresh herbs to each jar and seal with the lids. Allow the filled jars to steep in a dark area for about a week.

2. Strain the vinegars into separate cups or bowls. Using a funnel, pour each flavor into a recycled wine bottle or decorative bottle. Add a few whole berries to the jars before sealing with corks.

3. Strain the oils into separate cups or bowls. Using a funnel pour each flavored oil into a wine bottle or decorative bottle. Add a sprig of the herb to the oil for decoration before sealing. If desired, you could re-use the Mason jars for this project in place of the decorative or wine bottles.

4. Hand print the ingredients in each bottle onto the labels. Glue the labels onto the bottles. Place the bottles in a small basket filled with raffia, and catch some sprigs of dried herbs in the bow for decoration.

Family Calendar

This personalized family calendar is perfect for keeping in touch with faraway relatives. They'll delight in seeing your faces month after month.

Time frame: Three to four hours

Level: Moderately easy

What you need:

> 12 family photos
>
> Photo lab services
>
> Blank yearly calendar (found at office-supply or craft stores)
>
> White glue

1. Choose 12 family or individual poses that correspond to each month (for example, a pose by the pool for July or sleigh riding for December).
2. Take the photos to a photo lab and have them blown up to fit the calendar size.
3. Paste the finished photos onto the calendar.

You might want to circle important family dates such as anniversaries and birthdays on the calendar.

Be a Poet!

There's nothing like a special poem written in your honor. You can make these simple gifts that express your feelings for your loved ones in no time. Be sure to share the poems with your friends and relatives on one of the nights of Kwanzaa.

Time frame: One to two hours plus overnight to dry

Level: Easy

What you need:

> Parchment paper
>
> Wooden plaque
>
> Original poem
>
> Calligraphy pen or fine-tipped marker (or use a fancy computer font)
>
> White glue
>
> Rub-on transfers
>
> Popsicle stick
>
> Can of varnish
>
> Paintbrush
>
> Paint remover (to clean brush)

1. Cut your parchment paper to fit the plaque you'll be using. Leave about ½ inch around the edges of the plaque. Write your poem and copy it onto the parchment paper. If you're using the computer, type your poem in the font of your choice (the *Brush Script* font looks nice) and print your project onto good-quality paper. Be sure to leave space on the paper for your decals.

2. Glue the paper to the wooden plaque. Cut out the rub-on transfer of your choice and position it (or them) tacky side down on your paper. Apply the transfer by rubbing the entire surface with a Popsicle stick.

3. Apply varnish over the plaque with a paintbrush. Allow to dry and then add another coat. Allow it to dry overnight. Remove varnish from brush with paint remover.

You can drill a hole in the top of the plaque and add a leather shoe string for hanging, or you can buy frame-hanging hardware at your local home-improvement store and attach it to the back of the plaque.

Gifts for the Kids on Your List

Don't forget the kids when planning your Kwanzaa gift list. Enjoy the look of wonder in a child's eye when you present him or her with these special gifts.

Box of Fun

Give the kids on your Kwanzaa list this present that will allow them to express their kumba (creativity).

Time frame: Two to four hours

Level: Easy

What you need:

> Book of African tales
>
> Tape or CD of African music
>
> Wooden beads
>
> Bead cord
>
> Plastic storage box
>
> Acrylic paint (optional)
>
> Paintbrush (optional)

Place the book, tape or CD, beads, and bead cord in a plastic storage bin. You might want to personalize the bin by painting the word "Kwanzaa" and the year on the lid with acrylic paints.

Here are some suggestions for finding the supplies listed:

➤ Check out the selections of African folktales and music at Amazon.com and barnesandnoble.com. Use the keywords "African folktales/music" for available books, CDs, and reviews.

A visit to a local bookstore will also produce many selections.

➤ Wooden beads and cord can be found at a craft store.

Sponge Painting

A box of art supplies for the kids on your list.

(© Robert Schroeder)

Many different types of sponges and foam stamps are available in craft stores. Give a lucky kid on your list a variety of these sponges and stamps, some paints, and paper to help them create their own works of art.

Time frame: One to two hours

Level: Easy

What you need:

Sponges in various shapes and sizes

Kid foam stamps

Poster paint in different colors

Art paper

Storage bin

Apron (optional)

1. Assemble the sponges, stamps, paint, and paper in the storage bin.

2. You might want to include an apron to protect the child's clothing. (See directions for a stamped apron in Chapter 10, "Birthday Bash.")

If you can, spend time with the child to help him or her get set up and share some techniques with the sponges and stamps.

The Least You Need to Know

➤ Kwanzaa is an African-American celebration designed to promote unity.

➤ There are guidelines for celebrating Kwanzaa, but you can decide how to make this event meaningful to your family.

➤ Gifts can be given on each night of Kwanzaa or saved for the last day of celebration (January 1).

➤ Kwanzaa gifts should be homemade or reflect the African-American heritage.

Chapter 5

Making a List and Checking It Twice

In This Chapter

➤ Using homemade Christmas ornaments as decorations and presents

➤ Painting and stenciling wooden gifts

➤ Concocting homemade soaps and containers

➤ Creating a Christmas decoration for a front door

➤ Making gifts for the kids on your list

➤ Crafting gifts for the young at heart

Christmas is one of the best holidays for showing off your gift-making expertise. For most of us, Christmas is a time spent in a frenzy of buying and wrapping gifts, decorating the house and tree, and baking cookies and other treats. What we don't realize is that, with a little planing and foresight, we can change this frantic pace to a slower, more enjoyable time. Why let the ghosts of Christmas past haunt you? This year, vow to spend some time relaxing with family and friends and making great gifts to celebrate this joyous occasion.

You can make this Christmas a stress-free, exciting holiday by taking the time to check out the fun gift ideas in this chapter. Be sure to get started ahead of time so you can make creative gifts for all the people on your list.

Christmas Tree Treasures

You might want to spend some of your rainy weekends or Christmas vacation time making decorative Christmas tree ornaments. I guarantee they'll become family favorites that everyone will cherish for years. A box of Christmas ornaments is the perfect gift for anyone but would be especially appreciated by a young couple starting out in life or a single person who has moved into a first apartment.

Baked to Perfection

*Puffy salt dough
Christmas ornaments.*

(© Robert Schroeder)

You don't need a lot of "dough" to decorate your tree with these ornaments. Let your imagination run wild to create these unique decorations.

Time frame: Four to six hours including drying time

Level: Easy

What you need:

> Newspapers
>
> 2 cups flour
>
> 1 cup salt
>
> 1 cup water
>
> Mixing bowl
>
> Rolling pin
>
> Cookie cutters
>
> Cookie sheet

Paintbrush

Paperclips (optional)

Acrylic paints

Clear acrylic finish spray

1. Cover your work area with newspapers and preheat the oven to 350°F.

2. Place the flour, salt, and water in a large bowl. Mix the ingredients well with your hands, working out any lumps that may occur, until it forms a ball. (You may want to wear gloves for this step.) If the mixture is too dry, add a few drops of water; if the mixture is too wet (slimy), add a small amount of flour.

3. Now you're ready to form your ornaments. You could roll out the ball of dough to about ¼ inch using a rolling pin and make ornaments with cookie cutters, or you could make your ornaments free-form or follow the patterns illustrated. Place the ornaments on a cookie sheet sprayed with cooking spray.

4. Be sure to put a hole in the ornament with the pointed end of a paintbrush to accommodate an ornament hanger. For heavier dough ornaments, you might want to press a paperclip onto the back of the ornament with the end sticking up about ¼ inch from the top to form a hanging loop. You can either cover the clip with existing dough or add some extra dough to the back.

5. Bake the ornaments in a preheated oven for 8 to 15 minutes, depending on the dough's thickness. The ornaments will be done when a slight golden-brown edge appears and they are firm to the touch. Check the ornaments occasionally so they don't get too brown. The ornaments will puff up while cooking. Allow them to cool on a cooling rack.

6. Paint your creations with acrylic paints. Spray clear acrylic finish on your ornaments to protect them and to give them a glossy appearance.

Present Pointers

When making your own dough Christmas ornaments, use a garlic press to make dough into angel hair, roll small balls for eyes and noses, or roll "snakes" and braid them into a wreath. You can also add food coloring to portions of the dough to make colored accents. Use your imagination and see what works best.

Present Pointers

You might want to try this with your dough ornaments: Buy a wooden wreath form at a local craft store. Paint the form green by dabbing a sponge coated with green craft paint onto the wood until it's completely covered. Use a glue gun to glue your dough ornaments onto the form. Finish it off with a matching bow.

Steps to creating a teddy bear ornament.

(© Melissa LeBon)

Steps to creating a Santa Claus ornament.

(© Melissa LeBon)

Holiday Messages

Want to send a special holiday message to a loved one? These pretty glass ornaments are perfect for the job.

Time frame: One to two hours

Level: Easy

What you need:

> White paper
>
> Calligraphy marker or fine-tipped marker
>
> Red curling ribbon or thin red satin ribbon
>
> Green tinsel

Clear glass Christmas balls

White or clear glue

Plastic holly sprig (optional)

Red or green craft paint (optional)

Message in an ornament.

(© Robert Schroeder)

1. Cut the white paper to approximately three × two inches.
2. Write a special message for your loved one on the paper with a calligraphy pen or a fine-tipped marker.
3. Roll up the paper and tie it in the middle with the red ribbon.
4. Place the tinsel in the ornament along with the message.
5. Decorate the ornament by gluing a red ribbon around the top. If you like, add a plastic sprig of holly to the top.
6. Also, if desired, paint the name of the recipient on the outside of the glass with red or green paint or a permanent marker.

Etched Glass Ornaments

Be a trendsetter by personalizing glass ornaments for your loved ones. Your friends will love the way these ornaments catch the light on their Christmas trees.

Time frame: Two to four hours

Level: Moderately difficult

Etched glass Christmas ornaments.

(© Robert Schroeder)

Present Pointers

You can purchase a small plastic box at your local craft shop to store and protect your glass creations. They would also fit nicely in a computer disk storage box. Paint the words "Merry Christmas" and the date on the box with red or green craft paint or a permanent magic marker. Be sure to put a layer of tissue paper between each ornament.

What you need:

Precut glass forms from a craft store (I found glass Christmas ornaments with a hole in the top for stringing.)

Glass etching stencils

Masking tape

Popsicle stick

Gloves, eye protection, and protective clothing

Armour Etch solution

Paintbrush

Window cleaner

1. Clean the glass ornament with water and a paper towel.

2. Select a stencil design and position the stencil on the cleaned glass. Secure the stencil to the glass temporarily with pieces of masking tape (as shown).

3. Rub the stencil with a Popsicle stick to transfer it onto the glass. Rub up and down and left and right, being careful not to gouge the stencil. The stencil will change in appearance when rubbed.

4. Remove the top sheet of the transferred stencil by carefully peeling it back. If the stencil is not completely transferred, put the sheet back down and rerub the stencil.

5. Apply a border of masking tape around the entire stencil, overlapping the tape on the blue stencil by ⅛ inch to prevent the etching cream from running over the stencil and etching unwanted areas.

6. Shake the Armour Etch cream thoroughly. Be sure to wear protective clothing, gloves, and eyewear for this step! Using a paintbrush, apply a thick layer of the cream on top of the stencil. Keep the cream out of the reach of children.

7. Allow the cream to remain on the glass for one minute only. Then immediately wash off all the etching cream under warm water.

Gifting Glitches

Be sure to wear a protective apron, rubber or plastic gloves, and protective eyewear when working with etching cream. The cream is an acid and should not touch your skin. Be sure to work in a well-ventilated area and have all your supplies assembled ahead of time. Also work near a source of running water.

After all the traces of etching cream are washed away, remove all remaining tape and stencil pieces and clean the glass with window cleaner. Your etching is now complete.

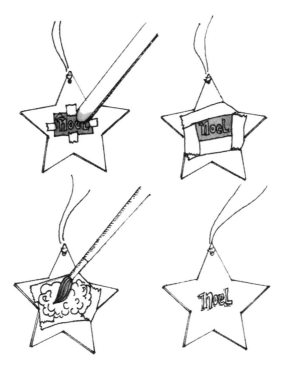

Steps to etching glass ornaments.

(© Melissa LeBon)

The Gift of Knowledge

You might want to buy a special pickle ornament at a Christmas store to include with your handmade ornaments. The pickle is a German symbol of good luck. Traditionally, German parents decorated their Christmas tree on Christmas Eve, hiding the pickle ornament last. The first child to find the pickle on Christmas day received an extra gift from Saint Nicholas. You could also make your own pickle ornament out of dough.

Popsicle Stick Nostalgia

If you can remember white Christmases, you probably have fond memories of riding your sled down neighborhood hills. Bring back happy memories with these easy-to-make wooden sleds.

Time frame: One to two hours

Level: Easy

Christmas sled ornament made out of Popsicle sticks.

(© Robert Schroeder)

What you need:

> Paint or stain
>
> Nine wooden Popsicle sticks
>
> Tin shears or an Exacto knife
>
> Sandpaper
>
> White glue or glue gun
>
> Clear acrylic finish spray
>
> Six-inch piece of yarn or twine
>
> Decorative Christmas sprig
>
> Glue gun

1. Paint or stain Popsicle sticks and allow them to dry.
2. Using tin shears or an Exacto knife, cut two Popsicle sticks three inches long, making a curved edge on the cut end. Sand the curved edge with sandpaper to make it symmetrical with the other end.
3. Lay five of the sticks vertically in the pattern shown.
4. Glue the two three-inch sticks horizontally on the top and bottom of the five sticks as shown.
5. Turn two sticks on their sides and glue them to the two three-inch sticks to form runners. Spray the sled with clear acrylic finish spray and allow it to dry.
6. Tie the cord or yarn to the top of the sled and using a glue gun, attach a decorative sprig of holly and berries.

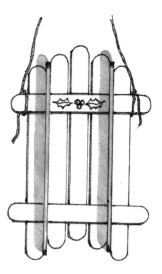

Assembling a Popsicle stick sled.

(© Melissa LeBon)

The Gift of Knowledge

Each year, approximately 40 million live trees are bought and decorated in the United States alone. According to Pastor Richard P. Bucher, one of the first records of a Christmas tree being decorated (without lights) dates back to 1521 in the Alsace region of Germany. Some of the items that decorated the first trees were apples, paper roses, gold, communion wafers, sweet treats, and dolls. Christmas trees began to appear in the United States around 1700, when German people immigrated to Western Pennsylvania. Dating back to the Roman era, people of many cultures brought evergreens into the home to symbolize life in the midst of death.

Pinned on Pine

Transform simple wooden clothespins into whimsical wooden ornaments to add to your gift boxes. Following you'll find supplies and instructions for both Santa Claus and Reindeer ornaments.

Time frame: Two to three hours

Level: Easy

Christmas ornaments handmade from clothespins.

(© Robert Schroeder)

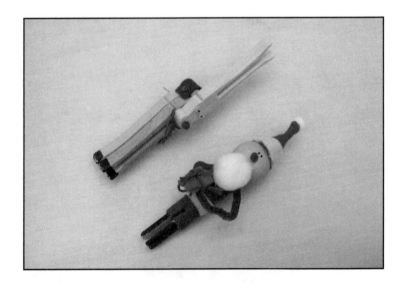

What you need:

Red, white, and green felt

Glue or glue gun

Small wooden heads (In craft stores you can buy bags of round wooden heads with or without painted facial features that fit over the end of a clothespin.)

Peg clothespins with round heads and squared off heads (see illustration)

Small and large white pompoms

Red nose pompoms

Black marker

Red pipe cleaner

Popsicle stick

Red string

Two plastic eyes

Glitter (optional)

For the Santa Claus clothespin:

1. Cut a two × one-inch strip of red felt. Next cut a 2 × ¼-inch strip of white felt. Glue the white felt to the bottom of the red felt to form coat trim.

2. Glue the wooden head onto the knob of the clothespin. Glue the large white pompom onto the chin for a beard and one red pompom onto the head as a nose. If the type of head you bought doesn't have facial features, mark two dots for eyes with a black fine-tipped marker.

3. Glue the felt to the top of the clothespin as shown.

4. Cut a red pipe cleaner to be seven inches long. Wrap the pipe cleaner around the head of the pin to form arms.

5. Make a Santa hat out of red felt. Cut a 4 × 1½-inch red triangle with a 4 × ¼-inch white felt trim glued to the bottom of the hat. Glue the sides of the triangle together to form a hat. Glue the small white pompom on the end of the hat as shown. Attach the hat to the head with glue.

6. Cut a two × one-inch rectangle out of red felt, and glue it onto the clothespin as shown to form pants. Push the felt into the clothespin with a Popsicle stick to form legs (see illustration).

7. Color the bottom of the clothespin with a black marker to make boots.

8. Cut a piece of green felt and tie it with a piece of red string to form a present. Glue the present onto the Santa's hands as shown.

For the reindeer ornament:

1. Glue two of the flat (not rounded) peg clothespins together side by side to form the body. Glue a third clothespin upside down on one end of the body to form the head and antlers (see illustration).

2. Glue plastic eyes and a red pompom nose onto the head.

3. Decorate the reindeer with a red and green felt saddle or felt holly leaves and berries. Add glitter if desired.

Making a Santa and a reindeer out of clothespins.

(© Melissa LeBon)

Crafty Christmas Gifts

The following Christmas gifts are made from unfinished wood objects found at a craft store. With a little paint and ingenuity, you can transform these rough designs into works of art.

Ornament Keepsake Box

You worked hard making perfect ornaments for your loved ones; now make this decorative box to store and protect your delicate creations.

Time frame: Two to four hours

Level: Moderately easy

A painted and stenciled keepsake box.

(© Robert Schroeder)

What you need:

Unfinished wooden or cardboard box

Sandpaper

Cream-colored craft paint

Paintbrush

Stencils

Stencil paint

Stencil brushes or *spouncers*

Clear acrylic finish spray

Raffia filler

Red silk bow

Present Tense

You have to buy special **stencil paints** and brushes to make clear and clean stencils. Stencil paint is dryer and doesn't smear the designs. You may have to peel a thin protective layer from the top of new stencil paints with your fingernail or tweezers.

1. Sand any rough edges on the box with sandpaper. Paint the box with cream-colored paint and allow it to dry.
2. Place a Christmas stencil on the box and hold or tape it in place.
3. Use the stencil brush or spouncer to apply stencil paint to the stencil area.

81

Present Tense

A **spouncer** is a tool used for painting stencils. It looks like a round sponge attached to a wooden handle and comes in different sizes. You can use this tool for pouncing, stippling, or swirling on paint. The spouncer uses less paint than paintbrushes and does a good job covering the stencil area without smearing it.

4. Remove the stencil, being careful not to smear the design. Allow the paint to dry.

5. Spray the box with clear acrylic finish spray and allow it to dry for at least five hours.

6. Add raffia filler and ornaments and tie the box together with a big red ribbon.

A Touch of Country

Use your new stencils to decorate this handy Shaker peg shelf. You might want to check out your friend's décor and try to match the colors for this project. Or, you could use holiday stencils and colors to create a Christmas shelf to hang extra ornaments or stockings.

Time frame: Six to eight hours including drying time

Level: Moderately difficult

Stenciled Shaker peg shelf.

(© Robert Schroeder)

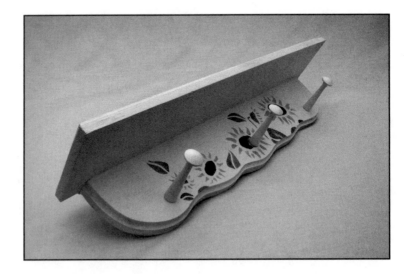

What you need:

Unfinished wooden Shaker peg shelf

Sandpaper

White paint

Paintbrush

Sunflower border stencil

Stencil paint

Stencil paintbrushes

Clear acrylic finish spray

1. Sand any rough edges on the shelf.
2. Paint the shelf white and allow it to dry for several hours.
3. Hold or tape the stencil in place and paint the stenciled areas with designated colors.
4. Remove the stencil, being careful not to smudge the colors.
5. Allow the stencil paint to dry. Spray the shelf with clear acrylic finish and allow it to dry overnight.

Present Pointers

When presenting your Shaker peg shelf, you might want to include candles and homemade wooden hearts on a string to compliment the gift. Two candles connected by the wick look great hanging from the pegs.

Tugging at Their Heartstrings

Decorative country hearts.

(© Robert Schroeder)

Keep stringing them along with these decorative country hearts. These trinkets are a perfect accent to give with a Shaker peg shelf.

Time frame: Four to six hours including drying time

Level: Easy

Present Pointers

You could also make string hangings out of other shapes. You might want to try pine trees, Christmas ornaments, or wreaths for Christmas; tulips or eggs for Easter; shamrocks for St. Patrick's Day; and so on.

What you need:

Unfinished wooden hearts (three different sizes)

Sandpaper

Red and green craft paints

Paintbrush

Clear acrylic finish spray

Drill with ¼-inch bit

Cord or yarn

1. Sand any rough edges on the hearts. Paint the top and sides of each heart red or green and allow them to dry.

2. Turn the hearts over and paint the other side.

3. Spray clear acrylic finish on one side of each heart and allow it to dry. Turn the hearts over and spray the finish on the other side. Allow this to dry approximately four hours.

4. If your hearts are at least ½-inch thick, drill a hole in the center of each heart, through the top of the heart to the bottom, to create a hole through which the cord or yarn can be thread. Thread three hearts of different sizes onto a 12-inch piece of yarn and tie a knot in the yarn above the top and bottom of each heart.

   If you have thinner hearts, drill a hole in the top center and bottom center of each heart and thread the yarn through the top hole around the back of the heart and then through the bottom hole. Repeat this process until you have three hearts on a 12-inch piece of string.

Bathtime Baubles

You don't have to spend your day boiling lye over an open flame to make these decorative soaps. Soap making is a simple process if you use the glycerin blocks, soap chips, and molds available in your local craft store. A cute wooden box in which to store the soap is the perfect accompaniment to this gift.

Time frame: Five to six hours including drying time

Level: Moderately easy

The Gift of Knowledge

One of the earliest literary references to soap was found on clay tablets dating from the third millennium B.C.E. in Mesopotamia. These tablets contained a recipe calling for a mixture of potash and oil to be used in the manufacture of cloth, as well as a recipe for a medicated soap. The first authentic reference to soap as a cleansing agent appears in the writings of Galen, the second century C.E. Greek physician who noted that soap helped cure skin diseases. The ancient Romans spread this knowledge, and centers for soap making began to spring up in different countries.

Handmade soaps in a decorative box.

(© Robert Schroeder)

What you need:

Unfinished wooden box, preferably with a sea or nautical design.

Oak wood stain

Clear acrylic finish spray

Decorative excelsior moss

Block of glycerin

Knife

Plastic microwavable cups

Food coloring

Small bottle of liquid soap fragrance

Soap molds

Bag of soap chips (optional)

Plastic wrap

Thin ribbon

Present Tense

Decorative excelsior moss is a form of filler that resembles Spanish moss, but it comes in different colors. You might want to use this filler in flower arrangements, gift bags, or anywhere you might use Spanish moss.

1. Stain the wooden box with wood stain and allow it to dry. Spray the box with clear acrylic finish. Allow this to dry for three to four hours. Fill the box with decorative excelsior moss.

2. Meanwhile, cut two one-inch squares out of the glycerin block and place them in a microwavable cup. Cook in the microwave on high for 40 seconds until melted or according to manufacturer's directions. Stir two drops of food coloring and one or two drops of liquid fragrance into melted glycerin.

3. Pour the mixture into soap molds. You might want to add the soap chips to your mixture for texture.

4. Repeat step 2 using different food coloring until all molds are filled.

5. Allow the soaps to dry overnight. Remove them from the mold by applying pressure to the back of the mold.

6. Wrap the soaps in plastic wrap and arrange them in the prepared wooden box. Place a homemade bow on top of the box.

Present Pointers

It may seem like the kids in your life will believe in Santa Claus forever, but before you know it they'll be grown up, and the whimsical nature of the season may diminish. It's never too late to give them the gift of yourself by spending time with them and making special gifts for the people in your lives. Hopefully, the love that binds you together as a family will last longer than the latest trading card craze.

You might want to make holiday soaps by using Christmas soap molds and a box with a Christmas design. Add red and green food coloring to the melted glycerin and use evergreen or cinnamon liquid scent.

Treats for the Tots

When you're making your list and checking it twice, don't forget to check out these cool gifts for kids.

All Dolled Up ...

Handmade button doll.

(© Melissa LeBon)

Give the older kids and country buffs on your list these cute country button-and-spool dolls. Don't stop there, though; make a gift out of the supplies and teach them how to make their own country dolls. Don't forget to present your gift in a small wooden crate or plastic storage box.

Time frame: Two to four hours

Level: Moderately easy

What you need:

> Yarn or cord
>
> Masking tape or nail polish
>
> Doll head bead (This is a round wooden bead with facial features that can be found in craft stores.)
>
> Buttons, plastic or wooden

Gifting Glitches

Button-and-spool dolls are not recommended for children under six because the pieces could present a choking hazard. This project also takes some patience and manual dexterity and would be more appreciated by kids over eight years old. Consider making button dolls for adults who like to decorate with a country theme.

Wooden spools of different sizes

Large wooden button for skirt

1. Cut 20 6-inch-long strands of yarn for the hair. Then cut one strand of thin cord 30 inches long for the body and another piece 12 inches long for the arms. Roll a piece of masking tape on the ends of the cord or harden the ends with nail polish to make it easier to thread the buttons and spools.

2. Place the middle of the strands of yarn on top of the wooden bead head. Thread the cord through the top of the head, catching the yarn in the knot in the middle. You should have a head with hair and two long strands of cord approximately 15 inches long. Thread several small buttons onto both strands of cord to form the neck. Tie a knot and thread a larger button onto the neck buttons for shoulders. Bring the cord through a larger wooden spool and large wooden button to form the body and skirt. Tie a slack knot under the skirt.

3. Separate the cord into two legs. Tie a knot in each leg about one inch away from the skirt. Leave this area as string only so the doll can sit down on the skirt. Thread buttons and spools onto the legs, ending with a spool for each foot. Tie a knot at the end of each leg.

4. Tie the 12-inch piece of cord under the shoulder button, making two 6-inch arms. Thread buttons and spools onto the arms as desired, ending with a spool for each hand. Tie a knot at the end of each spool.

Budding Artist

Here's what to give that creative kid on your list who seems to have everything—a storage box full of art supplies. All it takes is a little time to assemble the ingredients and paint the child's name on the box.

Time frame: One to two hours

Level: Easy

What you need:

For the box:

> Plastic storage box (The see-through plastic ones are nice to paint on.)
>
> Acrylic paints
>
> Paintbrush
>
> Stencils (optional)

To put inside the box:

> Sketch pad
>
> Watercolors
>
> Paintbrushes
>
> How-to-draw books (for example, how to draw animals or how to draw faces)
>
> Crayons
>
> Markers
>
> Coloring books for younger children
>
> Construction paper
>
> Blunt scissors
>
> Stencils

Present Pointers

A college student would appreciate a "movie time" basket—the latest video releases wrapped up with a box of microwave popcorn, hot chocolate, and soup mixes.

1. Use acrylic paints to write the child's name on the box. If you like, you could include some simple flower designs, or you could use your stencils to create a special effect.

2. Assemble all the supplies and place them in the plastic storage box.

It's Showtime!

Get the creative juices flowing by giving the kids on your list this puppet show in a box. Make these easy finger puppets from craft store foam and include the ingredients to make their own puppets to add to the fun.

Time frame: Two to four hours

Level: Moderately easy

*Puppet show fashioned
from foam sheets.*

(© Robert Schroeder)

Present Pointers

If you enjoyed making puppets
out of foam sheets, you might
want to try making a Nativity
scene. Use blue foam for Mary's
gown and brown for Joseph's gar-
ments. Include a manger and baby
Jesus, three wise men, an angel,
and barn animals. Fashion a stable
out of the shoe box and add a
large white foam star on top.

What you need:

Several different-colored foam sheets, including
six sheets with sticky backing for the stage

Scissors

Foam sheet glue or glue gun

Shoebox for stage

Extra foam sheets, glue, feathers, pompoms,
blunt scissors

1. Make the body of your puppet by cutting a 3½
   × 2-inch rectangle of foam. Glue the two ends
   together to form a body that can slip over your
   finger.

2. Make a head and decorate the puppet following
   the samples or use your imagination to create
   your own designs. (You can also buy precut
   foam animals and shapes and glue them onto
   the puppet body.)

3. For the stage: Cover a shoebox with the sticky back foam inside and out. Cut a
   hole in the bottom of the box, large enough for your fist to go through.
   Decorate the opening with foam stars. Cut out lights and microphone shapes
   and glue them inside the box.

4. Assemble several foam sheets of different colors, glue, feathers, pompoms, and
   blunt scissors so the kids can create their own puppets to add to the cast.

Steps to making a puppet show out of foam sheets.

(© Melissa LeBon)

Gifts for the Young at Heart

Don't forget to make special gifts for the adults on your Christmas list. Impress them with these useful presents that they won't have to stand in line to return after Christmas.

Trivet Treasures

Mosaics are a newly recycled trend in the craft business. These colorful coasters are easy-to-make, useful gifts for any occasion.

Time frame: Two to three hours to assemble plus overnight to dry

Level: Moderately easy

What you need:

Gloves

Popsicle stick to mix grout

One pound bag or box of grout (can be found in a craft store)

Water

Disposable mixing bowl (A plastic tub from margarine or foam or paper bowls work well.)

Mosaic coaster mold

One bag each of red, green, and white tiles

Clear acrylic finish spray

The Gift of Knowledge

Did you know Bunraku is the name commonly used for the art of puppetry and storytelling? A long line of storytellers and puppeteers have operated throughout history, but it is believed that Bunraku began in 1684 when Takemoto Gidayu set up his own theater in Osaka.

Trendy mosaic coasters.

(© Robert Schroeder)

1. Put on disposable gloves. Using the Popsicle stick, mix the grout with water in a bowl according to the manufacturer's directions. The consistency should be slightly thicker than cake mix.

2. Pour the grout into the coaster mold and smooth it with the Popsicle stick.

3. Lightly press different-colored tiles in the grout in your pattern of choice (see the photo for an example).

4. After 15 minutes, lightly wipe the top of the tiles with a soft, moist towel or sponge.

5. Allow this to dry overnight. Wipe the surface of the coaster with a damp towel to remove excess grout. Carefully remove the coaster from the mold. Spray your finished work with clear acrylic finish.

Gifting Glitches

Always wear protective clothing when mixing grout. Be sure to throw away the mixing bowl, and don't dispose of leftover grout down your drain.

Wine Lover's Delight

Give the wine lovers on your list a gift to help toast to the holiday season. They'll appreciate these tasty treats.

Time frame: Two to three hours

Level: Easy

What you need:

> Basket with filler (shredded paper or decorative Spanish moss)
>
> Red or white wine (Mulled wines and ciders would be perfect for the holiday season.)
>
> Set of wine glasses
>
> Gourmet cheeses and crackers (Buy ones that don't need to be refrigerated.)
>
> Basket shrink wrap (found in a party supply stores)
>
> Bow

Present Pointers

You could replace the wine in the wine lover's basket with nonalcoholic wine or sparkling cider if desired. If your gift recipient has a sweet tooth, you might want to give him or her a dessert wine and fancy Christmas cookies.

1. Place filler in a wicker basket.
2. Assemble the goodies and arrange them in the prepared basket.
3. Follow the directions on the shrink-wrap to cover the basket. Place a bow on top.

Let It Snow!

Decorative snowman candy dish.

(© Robert Schroeder)

Even if it doesn't snow for Christmas, you can make this fun snowman to celebrate the winter season. Anne Schroeder of Philadelphia, Pennsylvania, taught me how to make this delightful gift.

Time frame: Four to six hours including drying time

Level: Moderately easy

Present Pointers

Buy a can of Krylon Crystal Clear Acrylic Coating to protect finished, painted projects. Once the paint is dry, place the project on newspapers outside or in your garage and lightly spray the acrylic coating. When dry, turn the project over and spray the other side. I recommend two light coats instead of one heavy one to keep the project from dripping.

What you need:

Three round cardboard boxes with lids (one big, one medium, and one small box)

White snow paint (You can find a jar of snow paint in craft stores.)

Paintbrushes

White glue or glue gun

One yard of one-inch-wide red satin ribbon

Black paint

Small wooden Christmas tree painted orange for nose

Sprig of holly leaves

Wrapped Christmas candies

1. Paint the largest box and lid white for the bottom of the snowman and allow them to dry. Don't paint inside the box or lid or you won't be able to get it off later. Glue ribbon around the edge of the lid.

2. Paint the second box white and the lid black and allow them to dry. (The lid is the brim of the hat.)

3. Glue the nose onto the front of the second box and paint black round eyes and a smile on the face.

4. Paint the third box and lid black and allow it to dry. (This box is the hat.) Place a sprig of holly leaves on the front of the box.

5. Stack the boxes on top of each other with the largest box on the bottom and the smallest box on top to form a snowman. The boxes should all open up.

6. Fill the boxes with Christmas candy.

Knocking on Heaven's Door

Surprise your friends and family with this lovely angel to greet their guests at the front door.

Graceful angel door decoration.

(© Robert Schroeder)

Time frame: Three to five hours

Level: Moderately difficult

What you need:

Foam ball for head

Beige or light pink paper ribbon

White glue

Spanish moss for hair

Black paint for eyes

Small paintbrush

Small cardboard tube

White paper ribbon

Glue gun

Decorative straw broom

Trim for angel robe

Bow

White foam sheets

Wire

Tinfoil

1. Cover the foam ball with the beige or pink paper ribbon using white glue to hold it in place. Glue Spanish moss to the top of the ball for hair. Paint eyes, a nose, and a mouth on the angel using black paint and a small paintbrush.

2. Cover the cardboard tube with white paper ribbon. Using a glue gun, glue the head onto the covered cardboard tube. Then glue the head and covered paper tube onto the decorative broom's handle.

3. Cut four strips of white paper ribbon 18 inches long. Glue these strips at the neck to form a gown.

4. Cut a 24-inch-long strip of white paper ribbon for the arms. Glue the strip in the middle to the top of the cardboard tube.

5. Glue lace trim or satin ribbon to the bottom of the angel gown and the ends of the sleeves as shown.

6. Glue a bow on the angel's neck.

7. Make wings for the angel out of large white foam sheets. With a glue gun, glue each arm to the bottom of the wings and fluff out the arms.

8. Make a circle of wire and wrap it in tinfoil to form a halo. Wire the halo to the angel's head.

Steps to making a heavenly angel.

(© Melissa LeBon)

wing

The Least You Need to Know

➤ If you give a craft for a present, you might also want to include the ingredients as part of the gift so the recipient can try his or her hand at the art.

➤ Give the gift of yourself over the holidays by spending some time with your loved ones.

➤ Allow yourself lots of time to make your homemade gifts before the hustle and bustle of the holidays catches up to you. You might want to try making Christmas in July!

Chapter 6

Hanukkah Happenings

In This Chapter

➤ Understanding how and why we celebrate Hanukkah

➤ Making traditional Hanukkah symbols

➤ Creating a handmade menorah and beeswax candles

➤ Crafting homemade gifts for your loved ones

There's much more to Hanukkah than lighting a menorah and spinning a dreidel. This important Jewish holiday celebrates the rededication of the temple of Jerusalem under the Macabees in 164 B.C.E. The eight days of this holy season represent the eight days that the lamp of eternal light miraculously stayed lit in the temple of Jerusalem with only one day's worth of oil.

On each night of Hanukkah, the candles in the menorah are lit. Gifts are exchanged and games are played. One popular game is *dreidel*. The dreidel is a four-sided top with a Hebrew letter on each side. The letters nun, gimel, hey, and shin stand for "nes gadol hayah sham," or "A great miracle happened there." Kids delight in spinning the top to collect a pot of goodies. Each player places a treat (traditionally gelt, which can be regular or chocolate coins) in a kitty and takes a turn spinning the dreidel. If the player spins nun, he gets nothing and loses nothing. For hey he gets half, gimel he takes all, and shin he loses and must put one in the kitty.

The dreidel's origins are thought to come from the Syrian decree that studying the Torah was a crime. The children studied it anyway and would pretend to play dreidel when they spotted Syrian troops.

You can print a pattern to make a cardboard dreidel from several sites on the Internet. Just enter the keyword "Hanukkah" for a variety of options.

Eight days is a long time to celebrate a holiday, and you might find yourself having trouble gathering enough ideas to make each night special. Worry no more! With this chapter, you'll never run out of Hanukkah gift ideas that are sure to make this season memorable for you and your family.

Seasonal Symbols

Set the stage for a special Hanukkah season by making these simple decorations that are suitable for Hanukkah gift giving.

Star Light, Star Bright

Glittering Stars of David.

(© Robert Schroeder)

Brighten your Hanukkah celebration with these decorative Stars of David. Hang them around the house or use them to decorate your holiday packages.

Time frame: One to two hours

Level: Easy

What you need:

> Popsicle sticks
>
> White glue
>
> Gold glitter

1. Glue three Popsicle sticks into a triangle.
2. Glue three more Popsicle sticks into a second triangle.
3. Glue the first triangle onto the second triangle upside down to form a six-pointed star (see illustration).
4. Squeeze glue around the edges of the star and sprinkle with gold glitter.
5. Allow this to dry.

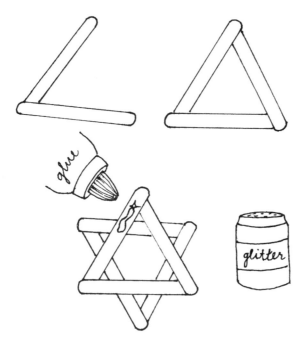

Assembling the Star of David.

(© Melissa LeBon)

Present Pointers

You might want to research the story of King David and the origin of this symbol as well as its current use on the national flag of Israel. Write down the story and include a copy of it with a box of stars. If you do this on your computer, you could choose an appropriate border for your story, or you might want to add glue to the edges of plain paper and sprinkle with the gold glitter.

Festival of Lights

A handmade golden menorah.

(© Robert Schroeder)

Light up someone's Hanukkah table by making this golden-accented menorah.

Time frame: Two to four hours including drying time

Level: Moderately easy

What you need:

A piece of wood, approximately 17 × 4 inches

Sandpaper

Can of gold spray paint

10 wooden candle cups with a ⅞-inch hole (can be found in a craft store)

Gold glitter

Ten 1½-inch wooden wheels (can be found in a craft store)

Blue paint

Paintbrush

Glue gun or super glue

Nine taper candles (blue or gold would look nice)

1. Sand any rough edges off the board. Spray paint the board and candle cups gold. If desired, sprinkle gold glitter onto the board and cups before the paint dries. Allow the paint to dry.

2. Paint the wheels blue and allow them to dry.

3. Glue a wheel onto the bottom of each of the candle cups.

4. Equally space nine candle cups (with wheels on the bottom) on the board and glue them to the board with a glue gun or super glue. Glue the remaining cup (with a wheel on the bottom) onto the top of the middle cup to form a candleholder in the middle that is higher than the other candleholders (see illustration).

5. Place tapers in the candleholders.

candle cup

wheel

Steps to making a hand-made menorah.

(© Melissa LeBon)

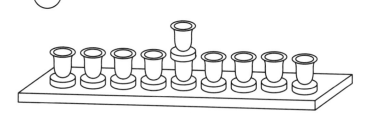
Menorah

The Gift of Knowledge

You may already know how to light a menorah, but here are the directions for first-timers: The candles should be lit at sundown. Each night, a candle should be placed in the menorah from right to left. The number of candles inserted represents the number of nights of the holiday—one candle on the first night, two on the second night, and so on. The shamash (the raised helper candle in the middle) should be lit first and be used to light the other candles. You light the candles, using the shamash, from left to right. In other words, the candles are *arranged* from right to left, but the candles should be *lit* from left to right. A benediction should be read over the Hanukkah lights. The menorah should be placed in front of a window so that everyone can enjoy this festival of lights. You can find a history of Hanukkah lights on the Internet at www.his.com.

Candle Creations

Hanukkah candles made from sheets of beeswax.

(© Robert Schroeder)

These homemade beeswax candles are easy to create and make a lovely Hanukkah gift when placed in an acrylic box.

Time frame: One to two hours

Level: Moderately easy

What you need:

Sheets of beeswax (Three packs of beeswax, 16 × 8 inches, will make a dozen candles.)

Cutting board or cardboard

Ruler

Exacto knife or scissors

Waxed wicking

Hair dryer (optional)

Rectangular acrylic box (I used a doll showcase box.)

Blue acrylic paint

Paintbrush

1. Place one beeswax sheet onto the cutting board.

2. Using a ruler and an Exacto knife, cut the wax in half to form squares that are 8 × 8 inches. Cut wicks into 8½-inch lengths.

3. Use a hair dryer if necessary to warm the wax for molding purposes. (Usually rolling them at room temperature is sufficient.)

4. Place the wick about ½ inch from the edge of the wax. Role the wax firmly together with the wicking inside and seal along the edges. The tighter you roll the candles, the better they will burn.

5. Paint Hanukkah and the year on the top of the box with the blue paint. Let paint dry. Place the candles in the box.

The Gift of Knowledge

You'll need a total of 44 candles to get you through the eight days of Hanukkah. Each night you add a candle and always use a helper candle, or shamash, to light the other candles.

Eight Days of Hanukkah Gifts

Traditionally, gifts are given on the eight days of Hanukkah. Giving a homemade gift is a meaningful way to celebrate this season.

Stack 'Em Up and Spell It Out

Happy Hanukkah greeting.

(© Robert Schroeder)

Say "Happy Hanukkah" with these beautiful, handcrafted, wooden blocks that can be used as a decoration year after year.

Time frame: Two to four hours

Level: Moderately easy

What you need:

> 13 unfinished square wooden blocks (found at craft stores)
>
> Light blue spray paint
>
> Masking tape
>
> Letter stencils
>
> Dark-colored or black stencil paint
>
> Stencil brushes
>
> Clear acrylic finish spray
>
> Plastic shoe-size box
>
> Blue craft paint
>
> Paintbrush

1. Spray paint the 13 blocks light blue and allow them to dry.
2. Tape a letter stencil on a block and, using a dark stencil paint and a stencil brush, apply the color to the stencil area. You'll need three "H" blocks, three "A" blocks, two "P" blocks, one "Y" block, one "N" block, one "U" block, and two "K" blocks. Allow the blocks to dry.
3. Spray the blocks with clear acrylic finish. Allow them to dry.
4. Paint "Happy Hanukkah" and the date on the lid of the plastic box with blue craft paint. Let it dry. Place the blocks inside the box.

Natural Hearth Warmers

Basket of pinecone fire starters.

(© Robert Schroeder)

Your friends who own fireplaces will love to receive this basket of pinecone fire starters. Although Hanukkah falls on different days from year to year, you can almost count on the weather being cold. It's the perfect time to build a fire and create a warm, cozy, holiday atmosphere. These pinecones are perfect for getting logs started and look lovely sitting in a basket of potpourri next to the hearth.

Time frame: Three to four hours

Level: Moderately easy

What you need:

> Newspaper
>
> Box of paraffin wax
>
> Large saucepan
>
> 12-ounce coffee can
>
> Metal tongs
>
> 24 pinecones
>
> Gold glitter
>
> Basket
>
> Potpourri or pine branches
>
> Bow

1. Prepare your work area by spreading sheets of newspaper on the table. Fill the saucepan with about two inches of water and bring to a boil on the stove. Break the paraffin into small pieces and place in the coffee can. Insert the coffee can in the pot of boiling water to melt the wax. Make sure to watch the wax closely, and turn off the burner when it is melted. Wax reacts like oil when heated and can catch on fire if it is not carefully watched.

2. Hold the pinecone from the bottom with a pair of metal tongs and dip it into the wax to coat it. Place it on the prepared newspapers and sprinkle the pinecone with gold glitter. Repeat until all the pinecones are dipped. Allow them to dry.

3. Place some potpourri or pine branches in a basket for filler and lay the pinecones on top. Decorate the basket with a large bow.

Present Pointers

As long as you're already working with pinecones, you might want to make a gift for your feathered friends. All you have to do is smear some peanut butter in the crevices of the pinecones and dip them in birdseed. Place a cord around the top and hang them from a tree that's close to the window. You can enjoy watching the birds dive for this delightful treat, and they might even reward you with a song.

Sensational Scents

A potpourri-filled dreidel.

(© Robert Schroeder)

These potpourri pot coasters will fill your friends' kitchens with a lovely lemon scent each time they brew a pot of tea.

Time frame: One to two hours

Level: Moderately easy

What you need:

> Paper for template
>
> Ruler

Masking tape

Two sheets of felt (I used light and dark brown, but blue and white would also be nice.)

Black permanent marker

Glue gun or sewing machine

Rickrack or trim

Small bag of lemon sachet

1. Make a dreidel pattern from paper. Using a ruler, draw a six × eight-inch rectangle on the paper. Fold the rectangle in half and cut off the bottom two corners to form the point of the dreidel. Cut out a two × one-inch tab for the top of the dreidel, and tape it onto the top of the rectangle. Now you're ready to trace your pattern onto the felt.

2. Place the pattern over the two pieces of felt and trace it with a marker. Cut the dreidel out of the felt. You should have two different-colored pieces of felt in the shape of a dreidel.

3. Using a glue gun or sewing machine, glue or sew all the ends together leaving a two-inch opening to add the sachet. Allow the glue to dry.

4. Decorate your dreidel by gluing or sewing rickrack or trim onto the outline as shown. Draw a Hebrew letter on the front with a permanent magic marker, using the illustration as a guide.

5. Pour the lemon sachet into the open end of the dreidel. (Make a paper cone or use a funnel for easy pouring.) Glue or sew the opening shut. Allow the glue to dry.

The heat from a hot pot or kettle will make the lemon aroma fill the kitchen.

The Gift of Knowledge

If you're wondering why there are different spellings and pronunciations of the word "Hanukkah" (which, by the way, means the festival of lights), it's because there's no exact way to change Hebrew words into English. You may also have seen it spelled "Chanukah." Either spelling is correct because it represents the way the *sound* of a Hebrew letter is interpreted into English.

The Hebrew letters nun,
gimel, hey, and shin.

(© Melissa LeBon)

A Perfect Frame of Mind

Inspirational frame for
Hanukkah pictures.

(© Robert Schroeder)

Make a special picture even more memorable by placing it in this lovely holiday picture frame.

Time frame: Two to three hours plus overnight to dry

Level: Moderately easy

What you need:

> White craft paint
>
> Blue craft paint
>
> Foam or paper plates
>
> Unfinished wooden picture frame (with at least a two-inch wooden surface around the picture area)
>
> Sponge
>
> Gold or silver puffy paint in a squeezable bottle (3D fabric paint works well.)
>
> Eight wooden stars (I've used five-pointed stars, but you can use the six-pointed Star of David if you prefer.)
>
> Yellow paint
>
> Paintbrush
>
> Glue gun
>
> Silver or gold marker
>
> Clear acrylic finish spray

Present Pointers

You could make these felt dreidels into beanbags by filling them with small beans instead of sachet. You should machine-stitch or hand-stitch the outside to reinforce the edges if they will be used in play. You could also cut holes in a box and let the children see if they can throw the beanbags into the holes for points.

1. Mix a small amount (about ¼ teaspoon) of white paint into the blue paint (about ¼ cup) on a foam plate. Paint the picture frame this color. Allow it to dry.

2. Mix about ½ teaspoon more of the white paint into the blue paint. Take the sponge and dab the lighter blue paint onto one side of the frame, creating a cloud-like effect. Allow it to dry.

3. Pour a small amount of the blue paint onto another paper plate. Using the sponge, dab the darker blue paint onto the other side of the frame. You should have three different shades of blue on your frame. Allow it to dry.

4. Using the squeezable silver or gold puffy paint, draw swirls or dots onto the frame.

5. Paint the stars yellow and allow them to dry. Glue the stars onto the picture frame with the glue gun.

6. Use a gold pen or marker to write the words "inspiration," "imagination," and "dreams" on the frame or choose your own selection or words. Allow to dry.

7. Spray your frame with clear acrylic finish and allow it to dry overnight.

Table Accents

Quilted place mats to grace your Hanukkah table.

(© Robert Schroeder)

If you can sew a straight line, you can transform a couple yards of quilted material and some fancy trims into this useful and attractive household accent. Warm up a friend's table by making him or her these beautiful Hanukkah place mats.

Time frame: Five to six hours

Level: Moderately difficult

What you need (makes six place mats):

2½ yards of 44-inch-wide blue quilted material

Pins

Thread

Sewing machine

Wide-width white lace trim

Fabric glue (optional)

Gold fabric paint (optional)

Pack of six complementing napkins

1. Double the quilted material by folding it in half horizontally. Cut six rectangles that are 20 × 15 inches long. You should have 12 rectangles of material.

2. Place two rectangles right side together on a flat surface. Pin the rectangles together to prepare for sewing. Sew along the edges using a ½-inch seam. Leave a three-inch area open on one side to turn the place mat right side out.

3. Turn the place mat right side out and stitch the opening together.

4. Sew the lace trim along the edges or glue the trim to the place mat with fabric glue.

5. Repeat steps 2 through 4 for the remaining five place mats.

6. If desired, draw a small Star of David or dreidel in the corner of each place mat with gold fabric paint.

Present Pointers

You can make lovely napkin holders to include with your gift of place mats and napkins. Purchase unfinished wooden napkin holders at a craft store and paint them blue or white. Allow them to dry. Glue a small wooden dreidel to each holder. Spray the napkin holders with clear acrylic finish and allow them to dry overnight.

7. Buy a pack of six complementary napkins to accompany your gift or make your own napkins by cutting 12-inch squares out of matching fabric and hemming them along the edges with a sewing machine.

Mocha Java

Nothing goes better with Hanukkah cookies than a cup of coffee or cocoa. Perk up a friend's coffee or cocoa with these homemade chocolate-covered teaspoons. One dip into the cup and your friends will think they're in coffee lover's heaven.

Time frame: Two to three hours

Level: Moderately easy

What you need:

Double boiler

Melting chocolate (white, brown, and assorted colors)

12 spoons, either good-quality plastic spoons or metal spoons

Cookie sheet

Plastic wrap

Curling ribbon

Mug

Coffee and/or cocoa mix

1. Place ½ inch of water in the bottom of a double boiler (or use two pans that fit into each other). Slowly melt the brown chocolate in the top pan. Be sure you don't have the heat too high; otherwise, the chocolate might scorch. If you do scorch the chocolate, throw it out and start over or it'll taste burnt.

2. Once the chocolate is completely melted, dip the base of the spoon (not the handle) into the melted chocolate. Allow it to dry a few minutes and dip again until it has a thick coating.

3. Place the spoon over the edge of a cookie sheet and allow it to dry completely.

4. You can stop at this point or melt another color of chocolate to make different-colored spoons. You also could drizzle an accent on the brown chocolate. Use as many colors as you like to make your spoons fancy.

5. Once the spoons are dry, wrap them individually in plastic wrap, and tie a piece of curling ribbon onto each spoon. Place the spoons in a mug and include cocoa or coffee with each gift.

Making chocolate-dipped teaspoons.

(© Melissa LeBon)

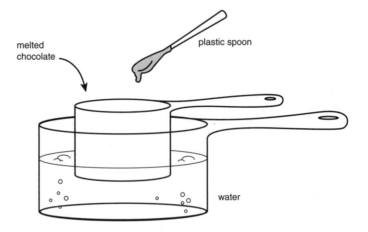

Spa in a Basket

Help the adults on your gift list relieve the stress of the season by giving them this mini spa in a basket. You might want to include a soothing CD with your present.

Time frame: Two to three hours

Level: Easy

112

What you need:

> Bath blanket and washcloth
>
> Body salts
>
> Scented candles
>
> Scented soaps
>
> Body lotion
>
> Facial mask
>
> Body spritzer
>
> Wicker basket
>
> Shrink-wrap
>
> Bow

Present Pointers

You might want to make your own bath salts for this spa in a basket. All you need are Epsom salts, sea salt, scented oil, and food coloring. Experiment with the ingredients or follow one of the many recipes you can find online or at the library. Place your salts in a plastic container, Mason jar, or decorative bottle and decorate with lace or ribbon trim.

Place spa supplies in the wicker basket and seal with shrink-wrap. Tie a bow to the handle of the basket.

You might want to make your own candles and soaps for this gift following the recipes in this book. (See Chapter 4, "Kwanzaa Kumba [Creativity]," this chapter for homemade candles, and Chapter 5, "Making a List and Checking It Twice," for homemade soaps.)

Living Gifts

From plant clippings to full-grown plants.

(© Robert Schroeder)

Since Hanukkah is a winter holiday, it's nice to offer a touch of green growth when the trees outside are bare. Even if you don't have a green thumb, you can grow these hardy plants from scratch to present as Hanukkah gifts. Just follow these easy steps for beautiful foliage in no time.

Time frame: Two to four hours to assemble plus one month to start and begin to grow

Level: Moderately easy

Present Pointers

You might want to start several plants in one pot for variety. If you stick to one type of plant, be sure to plant several rooted slips to give the plant a good start. Add a note with the plant's name and care requirements to your gift.

What you need:

Plant clippings from hardy plants: philodendron, spider plant, ivy, cast-iron plant, and aspidistra are all easy-care choices

Small container of water

Clay or ceramic pots with saucers

Crackle paint base coat

Crackle paint second coat

Potting soil

Fertilizer

Star of David (see project earlier in chapter)

Wooden dowel

Glue gun

1. Either buy several of the plants listed above or ask friends or relatives for clippings from their plants.

2. Cut a slip of the plant at least six inches long. Remove any leaves from the bottom two inches that will be placed in water. If using a spider plant, remove one of the babies (offshoots) from the plant.

3. Place the slips of plants in a container of water. Watch for root growth in about a week. When the roots are about ½ inch long, it's time to plant.

4. Prepare the pots. Spray the outside with a base coat of crackle paint. Allow it to dry. Spray again with a different color (step 2) of crackle paint. You should get a peeling effect when dry.

5. Add soil to the pot. Carefully dig a small hole in the soil and place the roots of the plant into the hole (approximately two to three inches of the stem should be covered). Cover the hole with the displaced dirt and press firmly around the stem. Water thoroughly and add fertilizer as directed on the box.

6. Make the Star of David listed earlier in this chapter and glue it onto a wooden dowel with the glue gun. Place the Star of David in the plant.

Creative Gifts for Kids

Don't forget the kids on your gift list this Hanukkah. Surprise them with these easy-to-assemble gift packages that will keep them busy over the school vacation.

The Ancient Art of Origami

Origami has gained popularity as an art form over the years. You can finds lots of kits in craft stores that explain the mechanics of this art step by step. Combine these kits with some extra supplies for a fun holiday treat.

Time frame: One to two hours

Level: Easy to moderately difficult

What you need:

> Origami kit
>
> Special origami colored papers
>
> Scissors
>
> Book on the art of origami
>
> Plastic shoe-size box

The Gift of Knowledge

The art of folding paper began in China approximately 2,000 years ago. When this art form reached Japan several hundred years later, they called it origami—*ori* means "fold" and *kami* means "paper." The art of origami spread to other countries and developed into the whimsical art form practiced today.

1. Assemble the supplies and place them in the plastic box.
2. Be sure to spend some time with your gift recipient to get him or her started on this art of folding paper.

Check out the free origami video located at www.learn-origami.com to learn how to make a hopping bunny out of an index card.

Clay Play

Provide the youngsters on your list with the ingredients to make these nifty clay beads and watch their creativity soar! If beads aren't their thing, help them make cute miniatures from the clay to display in a shadowbox.

Time frame: Three to four hours

Level: Moderately easy

Necklaces made out of handmade clay beads.

(© Robert Schroeder)

What you need:

Fimo or Sculpy clay (You can buy a kit of clay with all the colors you'll need or buy the clay individually.)

Ruler (optional)

Plastic knife for sculpting

Toothpick

Cookie sheet

Pot holders

Cord for stringing beads

Shadow box for miniatures

Glue gun

To make bead necklaces:

1. Put several colors of clay together, and roll them out with your hands to make a snake that is evenly rounded throughout. If you want to make square beads, use a ruler and your hands to flatten each edge until you have a rectangular shape.

2. With a knife, cut the rolled shapes into individual beads. Put a hole in the middle of each bead with a toothpick.

3. Place the beads on a cookie sheet and bake as directed by the clay's manufacturer (approximately 275°F for 15 to 20 minutes). Remove the beads from the oven using the potholders and allow them to cool.

4. String the beads with bead cord or wire and knot the ends together.

To make a shadow box:

1. Think of things that reflect the child's tastes and interests—certain music, foods, fashion trends, hobbies, sports, and so on. Use the clay to make images that represent these tastes. For example, if the child likes to play an instrument, make a musical note out of clay. If he or she plays baseball, make a ball and bat. If the child is fond of pizza, make a pizza out of clay and so on. Do this until enough favorite things are sculpted out of clay to fill the shadowbox.

2. Bake the clay objects following step 3 for the beaded necklace. Allow the clay objects to cool.

3. Glue the clay objects into the shadow box.

Thanks for the Memories

Hanukkah is the perfect time to get a child started on the art of making scrapbooks. If you throw in a disposable camera with the gift, your loved one will be on his or her way to immortalizing this special time of year.

Time frame: Two to four hours

Level: Moderately easy

What you need:

Blank scrapbook or binder with colored papers

Scrapbook pack of decals

Decorative-edge scissors

Extra paper

White glue

Disposable camera

Glitter pens

Fine-tipped markers

Paper gift bag and bow

Crepe paper filler

Confetti

117

1. If you check the aisles at your local craft store, you'll find all the ingredients you need for this fun gift. I suggest you collect the materials listed above and add things that catch your eye in the store.

2. Place the ingredients for your gift in a paper gift bag and include a couple bags of confetti that can be used on the scrapbook. Tie with a bow made of curling ribbon.

The Least You Need to Know

➤ Besides making the perfect menorah and dreidel for Hanukkah, you can fashion unique, symbolic gifts for your family and friends.

➤ The eight days of Hanukkah are filled with opportunities for presenting a homemade gift to a loved one.

➤ Don't forget the kids on your Hanukkah list. Make them a special gift basket that utilizes their time and talents.

Chapter 7

My Funny Valentine

In This Chapter

➤ Designing special greeting cards for your valentine

➤ Making Valentine's Day gifts for friends and family

➤ Choosing a gift for your favorite valentine

➤ Creating a romantic atmosphere for Valentine's Day

➤ Giving gifts of food to the ones you love

She loves me … she love me not …. This Valentine's Day show your friends and family how much you love them by giving them gifts from the heart. Valentine's Day is a hassle-free holiday devoted to expressing your feelings for others. So relax … you don't have to shop until you drop, set up a cot in the kitchen, or race against time to get your decorations up before the next holiday begins. Just kick back, have a romantic dinner out, and spend your renewed energy making these special gifts for your loved ones.

Valentine's Day Greetings

I love you because …. Let your loved ones know why you love them by making them these unique collage valentines.

Time frame: Half hour

Level: Easy

What you need:

> White card stock
>
> Red foil paper

Present Pointers

Instead of using magazine pictures for your valentine card, you could use photographs of the valentine's recipient and write the reasons why you love him or her beside the pictures. Consider making collage valentines a family activity. Assign each person a collage to create for a family member and exchange them at a special Valentine's Day dinner.

Scissors

Glue

White parchment paper

Fine-tipped magic marker

Magazines

Hole punch

Pink or white yarn or ribbon

1. Fold the white card stock in half to form a card.
2. Cut a heart shape out of the red foil paper and glue it onto the front of the card. Cut a smaller heart out of the white parchment paper and glue it onto the foil heart.
3. Use a fine-tipped marker or calligraphy pen to print the words "I love you because ..." on the white heart.
4. Search through magazines and cut out pictures that represent your feelings for the valentine's recipient. The pictures may reflect the person's personality traits, hobbies, qualities, and so on.
5. Use the marker or calligraphy pen to print the words "You're you!" inside the card.
6. Glue the pictures around the inside message.
7. Punch two holes about an inch apart in the top of the front of the heart. Thread the ribbon or yarn through the holes and tie the ends in a bow.

Creative Gifts for Family and Friends

Bring out the artistic talent lurking inside you by spending an afternoon working on these simple Valentine's Day projects.

Picture Pot

Let your love grow by sharing this unique heart plant with a favorite relative. Or you could keep the plant yourself for a special Valentine's Day centerpiece.

Growing gift of love.

(© Robert Schroeder)

Time frame: One to two hours

Level: Easy

What you need:

    Newspaper

    Six wooden hearts

    Red and green craft paints

    Paintbrushes

    Six Popsicle sticks

    Glue gun or carpenter's glue

    12 small family pictures

    White glue

    Small, green, leafy potted plant (ivy or philodendron is a good choice)

    Approximately two yards of red or white ribbon

1. Cover your work area with newspapers.
2. Paint the wooden hearts red and the Popsicle sticks green. Allow them to dry.
3. Glue the hearts onto the sticks with a glue gun or carpenter's glue.
4. Place the wooden heart over the part of the photo you'd like to use and trace around the heart onto the photograph. Cut the photo into the heart shape.

Repeat this step until you have 12 heart-shaped photos. Using white glue, glue a picture onto each side of the six hearts. Be sure to put the glue only around the perimeter of the picture so it doesn't buckle when it dries.

5. Glue a piece of ribbon around the rim of the pot. Make a bow out of the same ribbon and glue it onto the rim. Insert the hearts into the potted plant.

Present Tense

Most experts agree that **Valentine's Day** can be linked to the Roman festival of Lupercalia, a fertility celebration that was held on February 15 in ancient times. Men participating in this festival would strike people with animal hides to ensure their fertility. Pope Gelasius outlawed this pagan holiday in 496 C.E. and decided to replace it with a Christian event that he felt would be more respectable. He chose to honor the martyred bishop, Valentine, who demonstrated his love by helping persecuted Christians. Valentine was jailed for his actions and eventually was put to death. While in prison, he fell in love with the jailer's daughter. His farewell letter to her was signed, "From your Valentine."

Warm Welcome!

A perfect wreath for your valentine.

(© Robert Schroeder)

Flowers are a perfect symbol of love. Proclaim your love this Valentine's Day by making these simple wreaths for your family and friends.

Time frame: One to two hours

Level: Moderately easy

What you need:

Three wooden hearts

Red, white, and mint-green craft paints

Paintbrushes

Clear acrylic finish spray

Drill

Three 12-inch pieces of cord or yarn

Heart-shaped grapevine wreath

Baby's breath

Dried roses

Wire

Wire cutters

Red or green homemade bow (see Chapter 3, "Wrapping It Up," for bow directions)

Present Pointers

You might want to use "picture hearts" on your grapevine wreath. Just follow the directions for preparing the hearts in the previous craft project, "Picture Pot," but place a picture on only one side of the heart and omit the Popsicle sticks. Then continue with steps 2 through 4 of the wreath project.

1. Paint the three hearts—one white, one red, and one mint green—and allow them to dry. Spray them with clear acrylic finish spray and allow them to dry.

2. Drill a hole in the upper-right and -left sides of each heart. Thread the cord or yarn through the holes and tie the hearts onto the grapevine wreath as shown. Make a bow with the ends of the cord or yarn.

3. Place clumps of dried baby's breath and roses in between the hearts. Wire the flowers onto the wreath.

4. Attach the bow to the top of the wreath with wire. Form a loop out of wire at the top of the wreath for hanging purposes.

You've Been Framed!

Use this simple dough recipe to make a heart picture frame for your loved ones on Valentine's Day.

Adding a country look to a Valentine's Day frame.

(© Robert Schroeder)

Time frame: One to two hours plus overnight to dry

Level: Moderately easy

What you need:

> 1 cup flour
>
> ½ cup salt
>
> ½ cup water
>
> Mixing bowl
>
> Cutting board
>
> Rolling pin
>
> Small, heart-shaped cookie cutters
>
> Nonstick cookie sheet
>
> Cooling rack
>
> Oak stain
>
> Varnish
>
> Paintbrush
>
> Glue gun

Thin calico ribbon (approximately one yard or enough to go around the perimeter of the frame)

Cardboard picture frame

Two cinnamon sticks

1. Preheat the oven to 350°F. Place the flour, salt, and water in a large mixing bowl. Mix the ingredients with your hands, working out any lumps. If the mixture is too dry, add a few drops of water; if the mixture is too wet (slimy), add a small amount of flour. The mixture will stop sticking to your hands when it's ready.

2. Place the dough on a cutting board that has been dusted with flour. Roll the dough out with the rolling pin to about ¼-inch thickness. Use small heart cookie cutters to make six hearts for the frame. If you have extra cookie dough, make more hearts to use in future projects.

3. Place the hearts on a nonstick cookie sheet, and bake them for 15 to 20 minutes until they are firm when touched and have a slight golden edge. Check your hearts frequently so they don't get too brown. The hearts will puff slightly; this is normal.

4. Remove the pan from the oven and allow the hearts to cool for five minutes before transferring them to a cooling rack.

5. Once the hearts are cool, stain them with the oak stain and allow them to dry. Using a paintbrush, apply a coat of varnish to the hearts and allow them to dry thoroughly.

6. Using a glue gun, glue the ribbon around the perimeter of the cardboard picture frame. Glue three hearts on the left side and three hearts on the right side of the picture frame.

7. Break the cinnamon sticks into four pieces. Glue two cinnamon sticks on the top middle and two cinnamon sticks on the bottom middle of the frame. Make two small bows out of the ribbon, and glue one on top of each stack of cinnamon sticks.

8. Place a photo in the frame.

Gifting Glitches

Making items out of dough is much like baking cookies or bread. The cooking time may vary with individual ovens, so you'll want to check the dough frequently to be sure it doesn't get too brown. The finished product should be puffed out a bit with golden brown edges. Allow the dough to cool for about five minutes before removing it from the pan. If you don't use nonstick pans, be sure to spray your cookie sheet first with nonstick cooking spray.

Scent-Sational Sachets

A sweet-smelling Valentine's Day gift.

(© Robert Schroeder)

Even if you're just a novice seamstress, you can make these simple sachets for your valentine. Use several country prints and sachet scents for variety.

Time frame: One to two hours

Level: Moderately difficult

What you need:

    Paper for template

    Scissors

Country print material (remnants or quilting squares work well)

Straight pins

Matching thread

Sewing machine

Iron and ironing board

Packs of scented sachet

Polyester filler

Matching ribbon

Buttons

1. Make a heart pattern by cutting a piece of paper into a seven-inch square. Fold the paper in half and draw half a heart on the paper, starting at the fold. Cut out the half heart and unfold the paper to form your pattern.

2. Double the material and pin the pattern onto both layers. Cut around the pattern to form two material hearts.

3. With both right sides touching, pin the material together with straight pins. Carefully sew around the heart shape using a ½-inch seam. Leave a two-inch opening on one side of the heart so you can easily turn the heart right side out and insert filling. Cut slits in the outside bias of the seam as shown to keep the stitches from puckering.

4. Turn the heart right side out. Push all the rounded areas out to form the heart and press the heart with an iron.

5. Fill the heart with scented sachet and enough polyester filler to give it a nice shape. Sew the open seam on the side.

6. Make a small bow out of the ribbon and sew it onto the top of the sachet. Sew on some buttons for decoration if desired.

Present Pointers

When sewing a project, you should always reverse over the beginning of the seam and the end of the seam to reinforce the stitching. Trim the seams and cut slits into the bias (material outside the seam), without cutting through the seam, to keep the stitches from breaking. Use pins to hold your material together when sewing it or, if sewing a hem, use an iron to press the hem into the material prior to sewing it.

Love Beads

Classy beads that don't cost an arm and a leg.

(© Melissa LeBon)

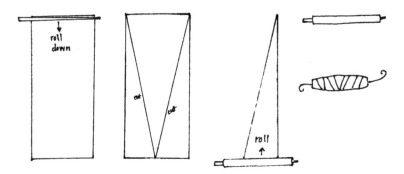

Nothing says love like a piece of jewelry, but that doesn't mean you have to spring for pearls or gold. Try making a necklace or bracelet out of these paper beads for the kids on your gift list. Since half the fun of this gift is making the beads, the kids will love it if you include the supplies and these instructions along with your necklace so they can design their own jewelry.

Time frame: One to two hours

Level: Moderately easy

What you need:

>   Different-colored papers
>
>   Scissors
>
>   White glue
>
>   Water
>
>   Round toothpicks
>
>   Varnish or clear nail polish
>
>   Paintbrush
>
>   Embroidery needle
>
>   Bead elastic

1. Cut the colored papers into strips approximately ½ to 1 inch wide and 5 inches long. Cut ⅓ of the strips into three angled strips as shown. You'll need a whole strip and an angled strip of contrasting colors for each bead.

2. Mix about ¼ cup of white glue with 2 teaspoons of water in a small bowl. Using your fingers or a paintbrush, spread the glue on the wrong side of a whole strip

of paper. Roll the paper onto the toothpick until you reach the end, keeping the ends even.

3. Spread glue on the wrong side of the angled strip of paper. Starting with the wider end, roll the second strip onto the first strip, forming a two-toned bead. Allow the bead to dry. Repeat these steps with the remaining strips.

4. Varnish the beads with varnish and a paintbrush or clear nail polish, and place them over the edge of a shoebox lid or wooden block to allow them to dry. You could also stick one end of the toothpick into Styrofoam or clay until the bead is dry.

5. Remove the beads from the toothpicks. Thread an embroidery needle with bead elastic and string the beads into a necklace or bracelet. Remove the needle and tie the ends of the elastic into a knot.

Present Pointers

Origami paper is perfect for making homemade paper beads. You can find all types of designs and colors of origami paper in your local craft store, or you can order special papers over the Internet. Just use the keyword "origami" in your search.

Gifts for the Someone Special in Your Life

Catch the love of your life with cupid's arrow this year, and reward him or her with a homemade gift from your heart.

Love Story

Is your significant other an avid reader? Consider making him or her a special bookmark and placing it inside a book of poetry or a love story.

Time frame: Half to one hour

Level: Moderately easy

What you need:

Poster board

Small red heart stickers

Small silver heart stickers

Red fine-tipped marker or calligraphy pen

Clear contact paper

Hole punch

Red yarn or thin ribbon

Book of poetry or a love story

1. Cut the poster board into a two × eight-inch strip.
2. Position the red and silver foil hearts in a pattern on the poster board strip.
3. Using a red marker, write the words "Love," "Peace," and "Happiness" (or any words you desire) on the strip in between the hearts.
4. Trace the strip onto the contact paper. Cut out two strips of clear contact paper. Peel the backing off one piece of contact paper and place it on the front of the bookmark. Do the same for the back of the bookmark. Trim any overflow edges.
5. Punch a hole in the top of the bookmark and thread the yarn or ribbon through the hole and knot the ends. You also could make a tassel for the bookmark by gathering several stands of yarn and tying them together with a separate piece of yarn as shown in the illustration.
6. Place the bookmark in the book of poems or a love story. If desired, write a message to the recipient on the inside cover of the book.

Making a tassel for a bookmark.

(© Melissa LeBon)

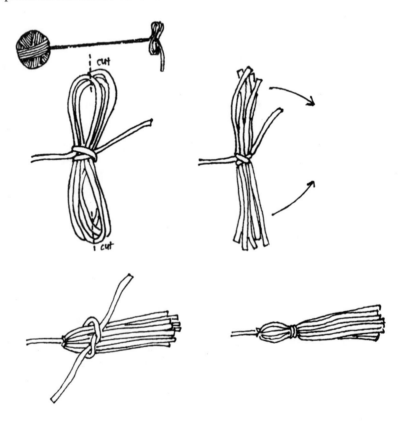

For the Birds

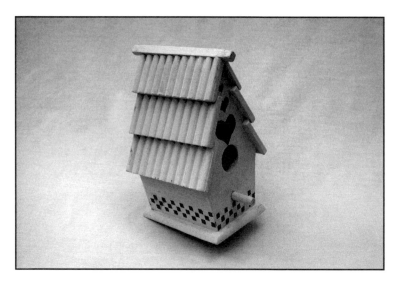

Stenciled house for love-birds.

(© Robert Schroeder)

Attract some lovebirds to your garden by creating this country-style stenciled birdhouse.

Time frame: One to two hours

Level: Moderately easy

What you need:

> Unfinished wooden birdhouse
>
> Sandpaper
>
> Country white craft paint
>
> Paintbrush
>
> Heart stencils
>
> Red stencil paint
>
> Stencil paintbrush or spouncer
>
> Border stencils
>
> Clear acrylic finish spray

The Gift of Knowledge

Lovebirds have been a Valentine's Day symbol since the Middle Ages, when it was thought that they mated each year on February 14. These birds also couple for life, making them a symbol of never-ending love.

1. Sand any rough edges off the birdhouse.
2. Paint the birdhouse with country white craft paint and allow it to dry.

131

3. Place the heart stencil over the front of the birdhouse, and add red stencil paint using the stencil brush or spouncer. Carefully remove the stencil and allow the heart to dry. Repeat this process on the sides and back of the birdhouse if desired.

4. Using the same process in step 3, stencil a border along the bottom of the birdhouse and allow it to dry.

5. Spray the birdhouse with clear acrylic spray and allow it to dry overnight.

The Gift of Knowledge

Remember plucking daisies as a kid to find out if someone special loves you? Valentine's Day customs around the world were based on this same quest for love. In England and Italy, it was thought that an unmarried woman who rose before dawn could look out the window to find her mate. They believed that the first man she saw or someone who looked like him would marry her within a year. Some Danish men send a *gaekkebrev*, or joking letter, to a woman. This letter contains a verse and is signed with dots—one dot to represent each letter in the sender's name. If the woman guesses the sender, she is rewarded with an Easter egg on Easter. Another old Valentine's Day custom was to write women's names on slips of paper and place them in a jar. The men would pick a name out of the jar and become the valentine of the woman whose name they picked.

She Loves Me!

Coloring daisies for a perfect Valentine's Day bouquet.

(© Robert Schroeder)

A bouquet of daisies in a painted vase makes a perfect Valentine's Day gift for the special someone on your gift list.

Time frame: One to two hours plus overnight for coloring daisies

Level: Easy

What you need:

> Three jars or vases
>
> Water
>
> Red, blue, and green food coloring
>
> Bouquet of daisies
>
> Clear wine-bottle or decorative bottle
>
> Red stained-glass spray paint
>
> White ribbon

1. Fill three vases or jars with water. Make three different colors of water by adding six drops of food coloring to each jar.
2. Cut ¼ inch off the ends of the stems off the daisies. Divide the flowers into three bunches and place each bunch in a different color of water. Allow the flowers to soak up the colored water. You'll see them start to change colors overnight.
3. Spray a clean wine bottle or decorative bottle with the red stained glass paint and allow it to dry.
4. Tie white ribbon into a bow around the rim of the bottle for a finishing touch. Place some water and your colored daisies in the painted bottle.

Heart and Soul Food

Check out the following ideas to treat your valentine to a sweet homemade concoction or special picnic lunch.

Sweet and Salty

Feed your honey's sweet tooth with these colorful and tasty chocolate-covered pretzels. A handmade decorated cookie tin makes a perfect storage container for your gift.

Time frame: One to two hours

Level: Easy

What you need:

> Bag of mini pretzels
>
> Cookie sheet
>
> Bag of Hershey Kisses
>
> Cooling rack
>
> Bag of red, pink, and white M&Ms (These can be found in stores around Valentine's Day.)
>
> Plain cookie tin
>
> Picture of Cupid or heart rub-on transfer
>
> Popsicle stick
>
> Plastic wrap

1. Preheat the oven to 325°F. Place the pretzels in a single layer on a cookie sheet.
2. Unwrap Hershey's Kisses and put one on top of each pretzel. Put the cookie sheet into the preheated oven.
3. Bake until the Hershey Kiss is melted, approximately five minutes. Remove the cookie sheet from the oven and press an M&M onto the middle of the melted chocolate kiss. Remove to a cooling rack and allow them to cool.
4. Place the rub-on transfer, tacky side down, of Cupid or a heart onto the lid of a tin canister, and rub it gently with a Popsicle stick until it is completely transferred to the lid.
5. Place a sheet of pink plastic wrap in the bottom of the can and layer the pretzels into it, putting plastic wrap in between each layer.

Chocolate Fundue

Help the endorphins kick in by sharing this yummy chocolate concoction with your special someone. Take the time to enjoy this dessert together and sweeten your relationship.

Time frame: One hour

Level: Easy

A great gift for your chocolate-loving friends.

(© Robert Schroeder)

What you need:

 One pint of fresh strawberries

 Two kiwis

 Two bananas

 Pound cake

 Serving plate or tray

 One 12-ounce bag chocolate chips

 ⅔ cup half-and-half

 Two tablespoons orange liqueur or brandy

 Fondue pot

 Fondue forks

 Sterno

1. Wash and core the strawberries. Peel the kiwis and cut them into wedges. Peel the bananas and cut them into slices. Cut the pound cake into cubes.

2. Arrange the ingredients on a serving plate or tray.

3. Heat the chocolate and half-and-half in a heavy saucepan over low heat, stirring constantly, until the chocolate is melted. Stir in the liqueur.

4. Pour the chocolate mixture into a fondue pot and light the Sterno underneath. Keep the flame low so the chocolate doesn't scorch.

5. Place the cut up fruit and pound cake on fondue forks and dip away!

Present Pointers

You could pair a fondue set with the ingredients for cheese fondue or chocolate fondue (or both) to make a great gift basket for a special friend. For a cheese fondue, you could include a fondue pot with forks, assorted cheeses (usually Gruyere), French bread, fresh vegetables, and a fondue cookbook. A bottle of wine, for both drinking and making the fondue, would complement your gift. For a dessert fondue, include the ingredients listed in the "Chocolate Fundue" project along with a bottle of dessert wine. Place the ingredients in a basket filled with crepe paper filler, and add some shrink-wrap and a bow for a finishing touch.

Picnic in the Park

Surprise your favorite valentine with a gourmet picnic for two. You can make the food yourself or pick up some specialty foods at your local grocery store. Be sure to include a bottle of wine or sparkling cider. If you don't live in a warm climate, you might want to spread your lunch out in front of a fireplace or drive to a romantic, scenic area and eat in the car.

Time frame: One to two hours

Level: Easy

What you need:

    Plastic or paper plates, flatware, and cups

    Tablecloth and napkins (red or pink are always a nice touch)

    Hearts of palm or artichoke heart salad

    Chicken, ham, or seafood salad made into heart-shaped sandwiches (Use a heart-shaped cookie cutter.)

    Imported cheeses and crackers

    Heart shaped cookies

    Chocolate dipped strawberries

    Bottle of wine, champagne, or sparkling cider

Wine opener

Candle and/or flowers (You can use a jar as either a votive or vase.)

Picnic basket (Check your craft store or discount store.)

1. Gather all the ingredients and place them in a wicker picnic basket.
2. Plan a special location to enjoy your picnic.

You may want to send a handmade invitation to your guest beforehand, perhaps keeping the location and picnic a mystery.

The Least You Need to Know

➤ A homemade Valentine's Day card says "I love you" in a unique way.

➤ Valentine's Day is the perfect day to celebrate your love by giving your family and friends a homemade gift.

➤ Include the gift of yourself for Valentine's Day by spending time with the ones you love.

➤ Make Valentine's Day gifts that express your feelings of love.

➤ You can make your significant other feel special by pampering him or her with a gourmet food gift.

Chapter 8

Spring Has Sprung

In This Chapter

➤ Creating a theme to celebrate the Easter season

➤ Peter Cottontail's picks for kids

➤ Designing homemade sweet treats for special Easter baskets

➤ Celebrating Passover with symbolic gifts

➤ Making gifts that symbolize the rebirth of spring

The arrival of spring means that Easter and Passover are right around the corner. Finally, the doldrums of winter are coming to an end, and an exciting rebirth is occurring in nature. This is the perfect time to renew your commitment to friends and family and let the kid in you be reborn. Get a jump on the holiday season by checking out the simple Easter and Passover gifts in this chapter.

Symbolic Easter Gifts

If you think your friends could use a bit of Easter decoration inspiration, these meaningful holiday gifts will add beauty and charm to any home. Give these gifts to someone special and perhaps make extra to decorate your own house.

Eggceptional Tree

Easter wouldn't be Easter without dyed Easter eggs. After you've dyed your usual hard-boiled eggs, dye about 15 uncooked eggs different colors for the following project.

Time frame: One to two hours

Level: Moderately easy

What you need:

Newspaper or plastic tablecloth

Easter egg dye

15 uncooked eggs

Straight pin

Thick nail or knitting needle

Yarn or heavy cord

Toothpicks

Tree branch with several protruding branches

White or gold spray paint

Pot with soil

Spanish moss

Present Pointers

Light up your Easter egg tree with a small set of battery-operated miniature lights. You can buy pastel-colored lights at Easter time that are perfect for this project. Be sure to put the lights on the tree before you hang the eggs.

1. Spread newspaper or a plastic tablecloth on your work area. Prepare the Easter egg dye as directed by the manufacturer. Wash the uncooked eggs and dye them different colors. Allow the eggs to dry.

2. Hold the egg over the sink and make a small hole on each end of it with a straight pin. Then make the hole on the pointed end bigger by carefully inserting a thick nail or knitting needle into the hole and slightly rotating it. This hole should be about ½ inch wide.

3. Keep the egg over the sink and shake out the egg mixture. Wash the inside of the egg with water and shake that out until the egg is clean inside and out. Repeat steps 2 and 3 for each egg.

4. Tie a 6-inch piece of yarn or cord onto a ¾-inch piece of toothpick. Insert the toothpick sideways into the top hole of the egg. Tug on the cord until the toothpick is wedged firmly against the top of the egg. Repeat this step for each egg.

5. Spread some newspapers outside or in a garage. Place the branch on the newspapers and spray it white or gold with the spray paint. Allow the branch to dry.

6. Stick the branch in the pot of dirt and cover the dirt with Spanish moss.

7. Hang your Easter eggs from the branches.

Blooming Art

Paper flowers with pizzazz.

(© Robert Schroeder)

Let your Easter spirit bloom. Make these colorful and majestic flowers to herald the arrival of spring. These flowers, placed in a stained glass bottle, make a colorful Easter centerpiece and are the perfect gift to bring a harried hostess.

Time frame: Two to three hours plus overnight to dry

Level: Moderately easy

What you need:

> Pastel-colored tissue paper (several different colors)
>
> Wire stems
>
> Green florist tape
>
> Glass water or wine bottle
>
> White glue
>
> Paintbrushes
>
> Varnish
>
> Bow
>
> Gift tag

1. Place one piece of tissue paper on top of a second piece. You can use the same color or two different colors for a layered effect.

2. Cut the tissue paper into 3 × 20-inch strips. Fold the strips in half so that each strip is 3 × 10 inches with four layers of paper.

3. Start at the fold and wind the paper strip loosely around your finger.

4. Pinch the ends together at the bottom and fluff up the tissue layers. You should have a flower that resembles a rose.

5. Use one tissue paper flower as a rosebud, or put three or four flowers together to form a carnation.

6. Place a wire stem in the center of the bottom of the flower. Wrap the pinched ends of the flower and the wire stem with florist tape. Repeat these steps until you have the desired number of flowers.

7. To make the matching vase: Soak the label off an empty wine or water bottle. Make a mixture of ¼ cup of white glue and two tablespoons of water.

8. Paint the glue mixture onto the bottle one small area at a time. Cut or tear strips of tissue paper and press them onto the glue, creating a stained glass effect. Repeat until all the areas of the bottle are covered with glue and tissue paper. Allow the bottle to dry.

9. Paint the bottle with a layer of varnish and allow it to dry overnight.

10. Place your flowers in the vase and attach a homemade gift tag and bow.

The steps to making tissue paper flowers.

(© Melissa LeBon)

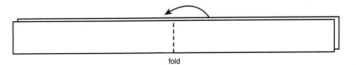

fold

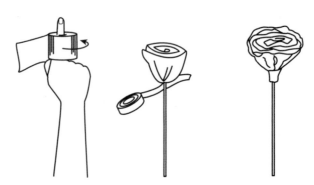

Gifting Glitches

When making a stained glass vase out of a bottle, glue, and tissue paper, be sure to only paint a small area of the vase at a time and add strips of paper as you go along. Also, don't make the glue so runny that it drips off the bottle and is too messy to work with. If you get glue on your fingers, wash them to keep the paper from sticking to your fingers instead of the bottle. If you'd like to create a stained glass effect without the mess of glue and paper, you can buy stained glass paint at a craft store and paint areas of color onto the wine bottle.

Put on Your Easter Bonnet

Decorative Easter bonnet for the door.

(© Robert Schroeder)

Straw hats used to be a tradition for Easter Sunday. You may not want to wear one, but these decorated straw hats look lovely on a door or as a bedroom decoration.

Time frame: One to two hours

Level: Moderately easy

What you need:

> Spring silk flowers
>
> Wire cutters or sturdy scissors (to cut the flowers apart)

143

Present Tense

Statice (pronounced *STAT–is*) is a dried branch of tiny white flowers, similar to baby's breath. It is used in arrangements or as decoration and nicely complements the larger, more colorful dried and silk flowers. Statice is sturdier than baby's breath and holds up better in permanent projects. It can be sprayed with clear acrylic spray or hair spray to help keep the flowers from drooping or falling off.

Glue gun

Straw hat

Baby's breath or *statice*

Matching ribbon

Wire

1. Cut the silk flowers into small clumps. Using a glue gun, glue bunches of flowers around the rim of the hat as shown.

2. Place the baby's breath or statice in between the silk flowers. Glue them onto the hat, pushing them down to make sure they catch.

3. Glue a ribbon band around the middle of the hat as shown. Make a homemade bow out of the remainder of the ribbon, following the directions in Chapter 3, "Wrapping It Up."

4. Attach the bow to the bottom of the hat with wire.

Hop This Way

Hop this way Easter bunny sign.

(© Robert Schroeder)

Make sure the Easter bunny goes to all of your friends' houses this year. Show the Easter bunny the way to the front door by creating this cute bunny trail sign. Paint several at a time to give to your family and friends.

Time frame: One to two hours

Level: Moderately easy

What you need:

> Bunny foam stamp
>
> Yellow, white, blue, green, and red acrylic paints
>
> Paintbrushes
>
> Piece of slate (You could find this in nature in mountainous areas or buy finished slate at a craft store.)
>
> Varnish
>
> Drill with masonry bit or glue gun
>
> Wooden stake
>
> Two bolts

1. Paint the bunny stamp white and stamp it onto the left side of your slate. Paint a yellow trail leading into the distance with a sign that points to the trail. Paint the words "Bunny Trail" in blue above the trail.
2. Paint some green bushes and colorful Easter eggs along the trail.
3. Paint a layer of varnish over the sign and allow it to dry.
4. Drill a small hole in the top and bottom of the slate with the masonry drill bit. Place the slate sign over the stake and drill through the wooden stake. Bolt the slate to the wooden stake. If your slate is thin, you could glue it to the stake with a glue gun. If your slate is heavy, you could give this gift without the stake attached to it. The recipient could simply lean the sign against the house, a gate, a step, or even a pot of flowers. Or, you could buy slate in a craft store that has holes already drilled in the top with a piece of cord or leather attached for hanging purposes.

Hopping Down the Bunny Trail

If you ask kids what they like most about Easter, they'll probably say the arrival of the Easter bunny. If you're still hopping down the bunny trail, you owe it to yourself to check out these fun Easter gifts for kids.

Egg Dyeing Smock

Help the kids and adults on your list keep their clothes spotless by making them these cute bunny-stamped smocks.

145

The Gift of Knowledge

It is generally agreed that Easter received its name from Eostre, an Anglo-Saxon goddess of spring. Eostre symbolized the rebirth of the day at dawn and the rebirth of life in the spring. Christians celebrate Easter as the resurrection of their savior, Jesus Christ, which occurred during Passover. The Jewish feast of Passover, or Pesach, commemorates the memory of the deliverance of the Jews from Egypt and celebrates the advent of the Messiah as foretold by the prophets.

Time frame: Two to three hours plus seven days to set

Level: Moderately easy

What you need:

> Plain white or beige pillowcase
>
> Scissors
>
> Piece of cardboard
>
> Bottle of *textile medium*
>
> Pink, orange, and green craft paints
>
> Paintbrushes
>
> Disposable cups or bowls
>
> Foam bunny stamp
>
> Foam carrot stamp
>
> Squeezable fine-tipped black or purple fabric paint

1. Wash the pillowcase with detergent but without using fabric softener. Cut a large hole (approximately 10 inches) in the center of the short end of the pillowcase for the head, and two smaller holes (approximately 6 inches) in each side of the pillowcase for the arms (close to the end with the hole for the head).

2. Place a piece of cardboard under the working area of the smock.

Present Tense

Textile medium is a liquid helper that transforms acrylic paints into washable fabric paint. The advantage of this product is that, if you already have the colors you need, you don't have to go buy the same colors in fabric paint. Just add one part textile medium to two parts acrylic paint to make a paint that's washable and flexible. Be sure to wash the unpainted fabric first without using fabric softener. Then allow the painted material to dry for seven days. Heat set the painted area by placing it on an ironing board and putting a cloth over the area. Using an iron set to the fabric temperature, iron over the area for 20 seconds. Wash the material in mild soap when necessary. See the manufacturer's directions on the textile medium you use.

3. Mix the textile medium with pink paint in a disposable cup or bowl, using approximately ¼ cup of paint to ⅛ cup of medium. Stir well.

4. Use the paintbrush to paint the mixture onto the bunny stamp. Carefully position the stamp on the bottom edge of the smock and apply gentle pressure. Remove the stamp, being careful not to smudge the design. Repeat across the bottom of the apron, leaving room in between bunnies for the carrot stamp. Stamp one bunny on the top center of the smock or use your own design.

5. Repeat step 4 using the orange and green paint on the carrot stamp. Stamp a carrot in between each bunny on the bottom and on each side of the bunny on the top.

6. Use the black or purple fabric paint to write "Happy Easter" across the top of the smock.

7. Allow the smock to dry for seven days. Place it on an ironing board and cover it with a piece of cloth. Press the area with an iron for approximately 20 seconds to set the paint. The smock can now be washed as necessary.

Present Tense

You might want to include this egg-dyeing smock in a basket with Easter egg dye and an Easter egg holder. Older kids would enjoy a Psanky egg-making kit that teaches them how to make beautifully designed eggs out of wax and dye based on the Ukrainian art form (Psanky). You can buy these kits in most craft stores or order them on the Internet.

Fuzzy Friends

Surprise the kids on your gift list by making these cute and cuddly Easter pets to decorate their Easter baskets. You might want to give them a box of the leftover supplies so they can create their own fuzzy animals.

Time frame: Half to one hour

Level: Easy

What you need:

One bag of assorted pompoms (Be sure yellow, white, and orange pompoms are included in the assortment, or buy them separately.)

Tacky or fabric glue

Scissors

One piece each of yellow, orange, white, and pink felt

Bag of plastic eyes

Pack of pipe cleaner that includes orange

Bag of plastic hollow Easter eggs (the ones that snap apart)

1. For the bunny: Glue two white pompoms together. Cut two hind legs and two bunny ears out of white felt. Glue these to the pompom body. Glue two small eyes to the head.

Present Pointers

You may want to consider buying extra pompoms for this fun and easy project: Glue pompoms onto an old glove to make puppets. Design a different animal for each finger. A great last–minute gift!

2. For the chick: Glue two yellow pompoms together. Cut a triangular beak out of orange felt and glue it to the face. Glue on two plastic eyes. Use an orange pipe cleaner for the feet: Make a circle out of the middle of the pipe cleaner and glue it to the bottom pompom. Bend the ends of the pipe cleaner into two circles. Pinch the circles in half to form "V" shaped feet.

3. For the duck: Glue two white pompoms together. Glue a smaller orange pompom on the mouth area. Cut feet out of orange felt and glue them to the body. Glue two eyes onto the head.

4. Place your pompoms in hollow, snap apart, plastic Easter eggs. Put the Easter eggs and leftover supplies in a gift basket and present it to the kids on your list.

Papier-Mâché Easter Eggs

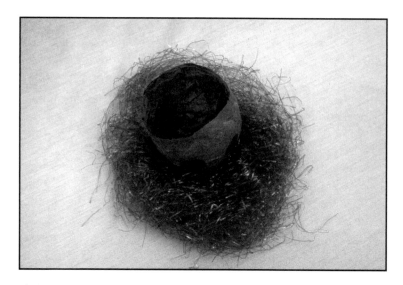

Decorative Easter eggs made from paper and paint.

(© Robert Schroeder)

If you don't mind a little mess, papier-mâché is a relatively easy medium for creating unusual homemade items. These handcrafted Easter eggs filled with goodies will brighten up any Easter basket.

Time frame: Two to three hours plus overnight to dry

Level: Moderately easy

What you need:

Newspapers

Five-inch balloon(s)

Shallow bowl

¾ cup flour

½ cup water

Small wrapped candies

Masking tape

Colorful craft paints

Paintbrush

Clear acrylic finish spray

1. Cover your work area with newspapers or a plastic tablecloth.

2. Decide how many eggs you want to make and blow up the balloon(s). Tie a knot in the end(s).

3. In a shallow bowl, make a paste from the flour and water. The paste should be thick enough to thoroughly coat a piece of newspaper without dripping off. If the paste is too runny, add more flour; if it's too stiff, add more water.

4. Tear or cut a newspaper into one-inch strips. Dip the strips into the flour mixture and run your fingers down the strip to remove excess paste. Paste the strip onto the balloon in a vertical direction, going from the knotted end to the top and back down again. Repeat this process until the balloon is covered. Do not cover the knot of the balloon. Keep a one-inch "hole" in this area to insert the candies. Next add strips horizontally until the balloon is covered with a ¼-inch layer of newspaper. Press the strips to the balloon and rub a layer of the paste over the top to smooth any wrinkles. Allow the egg to dry overnight.

5. When the egg is dry, carefully pop the balloon and pull it out through the hole. Fill the egg with wrapped candies and seal the hole with masking tape.

6. Paint the egg with colorful craft paints and allow it to dry. Spray the egg with clear acrylic finish spray and allow it to dry thoroughly. The kids could keep the egg to reuse as a decoration for Easter by carefully removing the tape to get to the candies, or they could crack the egg open by hitting it against a hard surface (such as concrete).

The Gift of Knowledge

The Mexicans celebrate Easter by making these fanciful confetti Easter eggs to share with their friends and family. They save their eggs throughout the year and dye or spray paint them bright colors. The inside of the egg is filled with confetti. The tradition is to conk each other with the eggs, releasing the confetti into the air.

Confetti Conkers

Dyed Easter eggs are a standard for Easter celebrations. You might want to try these fun confetti eggs to share with the tots.

Time frame: One to two hours

Level: Easy

What you need:

>   Needle or nail
>
>   One dozen eggs
>
>   Easter dye or spray paint
>
>   Confetti
>
>   White glue
>
>   Tissue paper
>
>   Egg carton

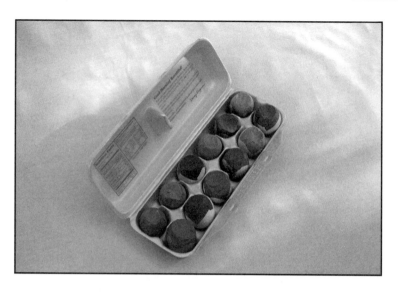

Box of Mexican confetti conkers.

(© Robert Schroeder)

1. Holding the egg over the sink, make a hole in the pointed end of the egg using the needle or nail. Carefully enlarge the hole until it has about a ½-inch opening.

2. Shake the egg out of the shell into a sink. Rinse the egg's shell and allow it to dry.

3. Dye or spray paint the egg a bright color. Allow it to dry. Place confetti inside the egg, and cover the hole by gluing a strip of tissue paper over it. Repeat this procedure with the remaining eggs. Place the finished eggs in the egg carton and wrap them in tissue paper.

4. The Mexican tradition is to crack the egg on or near a friend to release the confetti into the air. (Keep these eggs out of the reach of infants or toddlers.)

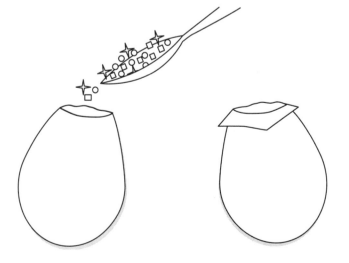

Filling the eggs with confetti.

(© Melissa LeBon)

Tempting Treats

What would Easter be without a basket full of chocolate goodies? Please the chocolate lovers on your list by making these delicious homemade candies and eggs.

Exquisite Eggs

Making homemade candy Easter eggs.

(© Melissa LeBon)

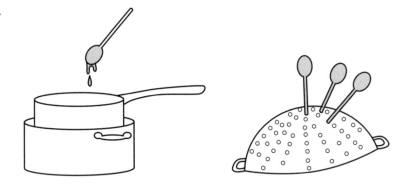

The Easter bunny won't find any eggs as good as these on his bunny trail. Be the first to make homemade coconut, butter cream, and peanut butter eggs for your family and friends.

Time frame: Two to three hours plus overnight to harden

Level: Moderately difficult

What you need:

> Mixer or large food processor

For butter cream eggs:

> One stick (½ cup) butter
>
> 8 ounces cream cheese
>
> 2 pounds powdered sugar
>
> ½ teaspoon vanilla extract

For peanut butter eggs:

> 12 ounces peanut butter
>
> 4 ounces cream cheese
>
> 1-pound box of powdered sugar

1 teaspoon vanilla extract

¼ teaspoon salt

For coconut cream eggs:

½ stick (¼ cup) butter

8 ounces cream cheese

2 pounds powdered sugar

1 teaspoon vanilla extract

½ cup grated coconut

To make into eggs:

Cookie sheets

Waxed paper

1 pound melting chocolate

Paraffin shavings (optional)

Double boiler

Colander with holes (not slits) in the bottom

Wooden skewers

1. In a mixing bowl or food processor, mix the butter or peanut butter and cream cheese until blended. Add the remaining ingredients (for the flavor you're making) and blend approximately three minutes or until thoroughly mixed.

2. Refrigerate the mixture overnight. Using your hands, shape pieces of the mixture into small eggs. Place the eggs on a cookie sheet covered with waxed paper. Refrigerate for several hours until hardened.

3. After the eggs have hardened, place the chocolate pieces in the top of a double boiler or two pans that fit inside each other. Fill the bottom pan with about one inch of water. Melt the chocolate on medium-low heat until thoroughly melted. Do not allow the chocolate to get too hot; otherwise, it will scorch. Once melted, turn the chocolate down to

Present Pointers

You can make delicious peanut rolls using the recipe for butter cream eggs. Just roll the butter cream mixture into small balls instead of egg shapes. Dip the eggs into the melted chocolate and then roll them in crushed peanuts until completely covered. Allow this to harden in the refrigerator overnight. Placed in a pretty box or container, these make lovely gift at any time of year.

low. The chocolate should stay hot without bubbling. If desired, shave some paraffin wax into the chocolate mixture (about two tablespoons) to make the eggs glossy.

4. Turn the colander upside down on a piece of waxed paper. Remove the eggs from the refrigerator and place one on a wooden skewer. Dip the egg into the chocolate mixture until it is thoroughly coated. Stick the end of the skewer into one of the holes of the colander until it hardens (about two minutes). Once it hardens, remove the egg from the stick and return it to the cookie sheet. You can reuse the skewers for the rest of the eggs. Repeat this step until all the eggs are coated. Place the coated eggs in the refrigerator for a couple hours until hardened. Store the eggs in the refrigerator in a plastic container between layers of waxed paper until you're ready to eat them or give them as a gift.

Chocolate Bunnies

Make your friends an Easter gift that they'll want to bite the head off of! Homemade Easter bunnies are easier to make than you'd think.

Time frame: Two to three hours

Level: Moderately easy

Present Pointers

You can use different colors of chocolate to make features or accents on your Easter candies. For example, you can drizzle pink and yellow melted chocolate on a dark chocolate Easter egg or paint eyes, a nose, and a mouth on a white chocolate bunny using melted colored chocolate and a new, small paintbrush.

What you need:

Double boiler

1 pound dark chocolate melting pieces

1 pound white chocolate melting pieces

1 pound colored chocolate melting pieces (yellow, pink, or green)

Candy bunny molds

1. Place one inch of water in the bottom pan of the double boiler. Place one type of the chocolate pieces (dark, white, or colored) in the top pan. Melt on medium heat for about five minutes until all the pieces are melted.

2. Pour the melted chocolate into the molds and allow them to chill in the refrigerator for about two hours. Repeat steps 1 and 2 until you have three colors of molded chocolate.

3. Remove the chocolate from the molds and store it in a plastic container between layers of waxed paper until ready to serve or give as a gift.

The Gift of Knowledge

Many symbols of Easter originated in ancient times. Lambs, chicks, bunnies, and other baby creatures were associated with spring and represented the birth of new life. The Easter rabbit and Easter eggs were symbols of fertility. In pagan times, eggs were colored with bright colors to represent the sunlight of spring. Romans, Gauls, Persians, and Chinese all dyed and painted Easter eggs and used them in spring festivals to represent the rebirth of life. The Christian symbol of the egg is the rebirth of man rather than nature. The white lily, a symbol of the Resurrection, is an official Easter flower.

Edible Basket

Place your homemade Easter goodies in this edible chocolate Easter basket. Just fill the basket with some Easter straw and arrange your candies inside.

Time frame: Two to three hours

Level: Moderately easy

What you need:

> Small round casserole dish (about three-inch diameter)
>
> Tinfoil
>
> Vegetable oil
>
> Double boiler pan
>
> 1 pound melting chocolate
>
> Plastic zip-close bag

1. Turn the casserole dish upside down. Cover the dish with tinfoil, turning up the ends where the chocolate will drip. Lightly grease the foil with vegetable oil.
2. Place one inch of water in the bottom of a double boiler. Place the melting chocolate in the top of the double boiler and melt the chocolate over medium heat.

3. Slightly cool the chocolate, (about two minutes), and then pour the melted chocolate in a sturdy zip-close bag. Make a hole about ¼ inch wide in one corner of the bag. Squeeze the chocolate through the hole onto the prepared casserole dish. Make lines across the dish horizontally and then vertically until the dish is coated with a chocolate grid.

4. Allow the chocolate to dry until firm.

5. Lift up the casserole dish, turn it over, and gently pry the basket from the foil lining.

6. Fill the basket with Easter basket straw and arrange homemade candies inside.

Passover Symbols

Passover is a sacred holiday that commemorates the liberation of the Jewish people from enslavement by the Egyptian Pharaoh Ramses II. This eight-day event begins each year on the fifteenth night of the Jewish Month of Nisan (a spring occurrence).

A traditional dinner gathering known as a Seder is held in the home. Seder is the Hebrew word for "order," and a certain order is followed during this ceremony. Family and friends recall the story of Passover as recorded in the Book of Exodus. According to the account, Moses led the Jews out of slavery in Egypt after a series of plagues caused chaos in the Egyptian Empire. The tenth and final plague, the killing of the first-born child, claimed the son of Ramses II. The legend states that Jewish families were instructed to mark their doorways with the blood of a sacrificed lamb. The angel of death *passed over* these households and spared the lives of the first-born children inside.

Several traditional ceremonies are key components of the Seder: preparing the Seder plate, eating specific symbolic foods, filling Elijah's cup, asking the four questions, reclining on a pillow, hiding the *Afikomen,* and playing music.

Precious Plate

This plaster Seder plate would make a beautiful centerpiece for a traditional Passover dinner. A Seder plate is a symbolic centerpiece that holds the following five items:

➤ **Charoset.** A mixture of chopped apples, walnuts, cinnamon, and wine that represents the mortar the Hebrews used when assembling the Pharaoh's bricks.

➤ **Karpas.** An herb (usually parsley) that symbolizes springtime. It is dipped in salt water to represent the tears of the Jewish people during enslavement.

➤ **Beritzah.** A baked or roasted egg that symbolizes mourning for the suffering and deaths of the Jewish people over the ages.

➤ **Zeroa.** A shank bone that symbolizes the sacrificial lamb offering that the Jews made to God. The blood of this lamb was applied to the doorways of the Jewish dwellings to alert the Angel of Death to *pass over* their homes and spare the life of their first born.

➤ **Maror.** Bitter herbs to represent the bitterness of the slavery the Jewish people have suffered throughout history.

Present Tense

The **Afikomen** is a piece of matzo that gets hidden by the father or the leader of the Seder. The child who finds it gets a small gift or treat. The matzo represents the Jewish people's haste to leave Egypt—they were unable to allow the yeast in their bread dough to rise. They took the raw dough on their journey and baked it into flat crackers (matzo) in the hot desert sun.

Time frame: Two to three hours plus two days to dry

Level: Moderately difficult

What you need:

Newspaper or plastic cloth

Stepping stone mold

Bag or box of plaster (at least five pounds)

Water

Putty knife

Toothpick

Bags of polished glass pieces

Sponge

Steel wool

Paintbrush

Clear acrylic finish spray

Piece of felt for bottom of plate

Glue gun

Five or six three-inch glass flower pots

1. Cover your work area with newspapers or plastic. Place the stepping stone mold on the covering. Pour the plaster powder into the mold to about two thirds of the depth. Add water according to the directions on the plaster bag or box (usually about three parts plaster to one part water). Mix the water into the plaster with the putty knife. Use a toothpick to burst any holes that appear on the surface. Smooth the top of the plaster with the knife.

2. Place the glass pieces in a design around the border of the plaster plate. Form the Hebrew letters for Pesach (Passover), shown in the following figure, in the center of the plate using glass pieces.

3. Allow the plate to set for about 15 minutes. Gently wipe the glass pieces with a moist sponge to remove any excess plaster.

4. Do not move the mold until it has hardened overnight.

5. Carefully pry the plate from the mold. Gently rub the plaster finish with steel wool to smooth the surface. With a paintbrush, brush away any plaster particles that exist. Spray the plate with clear acrylic finish spray and allow it to dry. Spray the plate with a second coat of the finish spray and allow it to dry overnight.

6. Lay the plate on top of the piece of felt and trace around the felt with a magic marker. Cut the felt to fit the plate and glue it to the bottom of the plate using a glue gun. Place five or six glass pots on the plate to hold the Seder foods (see the preceding descriptions of Seder plate items).

Hebrew letters of Pesach depicted on the Seder plate.

(© Melissa LeBon)

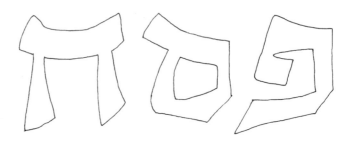

~~Mary Ann~~
Becky
~~Sara~~
~~Shirley~~

A personal note...

Thinking of you Basket

Get Well Jelly Bean Candy Pills

Chicken Soup

~~Monday~~
Wednesday

Tea Bags / Cups

flower planter   Card

candle   Baby sitter anything
                                          need

list of neighbors / phone #'s

Chicken Soup for the Soul Book
                                    bookmark
fruit   w/quote

phone card 10.00

body lotion Bath/Body Works Kohls - stress   8.50

mints

A personal note...

The Gift of Knowledge

Most Seder dinners include wine or grape juice "toasts" that represent the four stages of the Jewish people's exodus from Egypt: 1) freedom, 2) deliverance, 3) redemption, and 4) release. It is thought that a visit from the prophet Elijah occurs on this night. A beautiful silver cup filled with wine or juice is placed on the table to refresh him. A child is sent to open the door for Elijah and let him in.

Awesome Afikomen

Please your friends who celebrate Passover by making them this classic Afrikomer (matzo bag) for Seder dinner. You might want to include a special prize with your gift for the lucky child who finds the hidden matzo.

Time frame: Two to three hours

Level: Moderately easy

What you need:

>Piece of fabric 20 × 12 inches

>Straight pins

>Sewing machine or needle and thread

>Ironing board and iron

>Shoelace or cord

>Large safety pin

>Glue

>Gold trim

>Gold glitter

>Box of matzo

>Small gift

1. Fold the material in half with the right sides of the material together. Use the folded edge as the bottom of the bag and pin the two side edges together. Using a ½-inch seam, stitch the pinned edges with a sewing machine or a needle and thread. Remove the pins.

2. Using an iron, press a ¼-inch seam around the top of the bag toward the wrong side of the bag. Fold this pressed edge down again to the wrong side of the bag, forming a one-inch casing along the top. Press the casing down and pin it in place to prepare for sewing. The pressed casing should be seen on the wrong side of the material (which at this point is still on the outside since it hasn't yet been turned right side out).

3. Stitch the casing using a ¼-inch seam around the bottom of the casing. Leave a two-inch opening on one side of the casing to insert the cord. Reinforce the stitching at each end of the opening by reversing over the original stitching. Remove the pins from the casing.

4. For the drawstring, use a shoelace or cut a piece of cord that is double the width of the bag plus eight inches.

5. Secure a safety pin on the end of the lace or cord and thread the cord through the opening around the casing to the other side. Tie a secure knot in the two ends of the cord. Do not resew the opening because the cord will be pulled through the hole.

6. Turn the bag right side out. Glue or sew gold trim around the top of the bag. Write the word "Afikomen" on the center of the bag in glue. Sprinkle gold glitter over the glue and allow it to dry. Shake the excess glitter off the bag. Place a piece of matzo in the bag and add a small gift for the child who finds it.

Kosher Treats

It's traditional to eat only unleavened bread (matzo) for Passover, but you don't have to give up all sweets. Make these Kosher treats for your family and friends from matzo meal and crackers.

Passover Macaroons

Time frame: One to two hours

Level: Moderately easy

What you need:

Mixing bowl or mixer

One 14-ounce package of sweetened flake coconut (5⅓ cups)

⅔ cup granulated sugar

6 tablespoons matzo meal

¼ teaspoon salt

Four egg whites

1 teaspoon almond extract

Cookie sheets

Cooking spray

Cooling racks

1. Preheat oven to 325°F. In a large bowl (or a mixer on low speed), mix the first four ingredients. Stir in the egg whites and almond extract and mix well.

2. Prepare two cookie sheets by lightly greasing them with cooking spay and sprinkling them with a dusting of matzo meal. Using a tablespoon, drop the mixture onto the sheets one inch apart.

3. Bake them in a 325°F oven for about 20 minutes or until golden brown. Remove from cookie sheets immediately and allow them to cool on cooling racks.

Present Pointers

You might want to present your macaroons in a tin decorated with a Passover theme. Buy a gold or silver cookie tin in a craft or discount store. Make a gold Star of David (see Chapter 6, "Hanukkah Happenings") and glue it onto the lid of the can. Line the can with blue plastic wrap and layer the macaroons into the can. Place a piece of plastic wrap in between each layer to keep them from sticking together.

Chocolate-Covered Matzo Crackers

Time frame: One to two hours

Level: Moderately easy

What you need:

Double boiler

1 pound of Kosher-for-Passover melting chocolate

Box of matzo crackers

Tongs

Cookie sheets lined with waxed paper

Blue plastic wrap

Curling ribbon

1. Place one inch of water in the bottom of the double boiler and bring it to a boil over medium heat. Place the chocolate into the top pan. Heat on medium heat until it begins to melt and bubble.

2. Turn down the heat to medium low. Break the crackers into sections. Using tongs, dip the crackers into the melted chocolate and lay them on top of the prepared cookie sheet to dry. Wrap the crackers in blue plastic wrap and tie with matching curling ribbon.

The Gift of Knowledge

At a Seder, the youngest child at the table traditionally asks the following four questions, and the eldest at the table answers them:

➤ *Why do we eat only matzo on Pesach (Passover)?* To remind us that the Jews had no time to bake their bread when they left Egypt.

➤ *Why do we eat bitter herbs at our Seder?* To remind us of the bitter and cruel way the Pharaoh treated the Jewish people when they were slaves in Egypt.

➤ *Why do we dip our foods twice tonight?* We dip bitter foods into Charoset to remind us how hard the Jews worked making bricks in Egypt; we dip parsley into salt water to remind us of the tears of Jewish slaves.

➤ *Why do we lean on a pillow tonight?* To be comfortable and to remind us that once we were slaves, but now we are free.

Spring Fling

Celebrate the arrival of spring by making these natural gifts that even Eoster (the goddess of spring) would be proud of.

Birdhouse Wind Chime

Give this special wind chime to the bird lovers on your gift list. They'll love the country look of the chime and will enjoy the soft sounds created by a gentle breeze.

Time frame: Two to three hours

Level: Moderately difficult

Springtime wind chime.

(© Robert Schroeder)

What you need:

Piece of wood, 18 × 3 inches

Crackle paint base coat spray (white)

Crackle paint top coat spray (green)

"Welcome" stencil

White and rust-colored stencil paints

Stencil brushes

Watering can stencil

Hammer

Seven nails with large rounded heads

Cord

Two wooden candle cups (⅝-inch hole)

Two four-inch clay pots

Two large wooden buttons

Three small, metal birdhouses

1. Spray the board with white base coat crackle paint and allow it to dry. Lightly spray the board with green crackle paint and allow it to dry.

2. Center the "Welcome" stencil on the board and fill in the stencil areas with white stencil paint. In the same manner, stencil a rust-colored watering can on each side of the "Welcome" stencil. Allow this to dry.

3. Hammer five nails equally spaced on the bottom edge of the board. Hammer a nail on either side of the top edge of the board. Tie a 22-inch piece of cord from one of the top nails to the other to form a hanger.

4. Make bells out of the clay pots: First tie a large knot on the end of a 12-inch piece of cord. Thread the cord through an upside down wooden candle cup, catching the knot in the cup. Make another large knot about three inches up to catch in the hole of the clay pot. Thread the cord (what's above the knot) through the hole in the clay pot and then through a large wooden button (see illustration). Tie the cord in a double knot onto the second nail in the bottom of the wooden board. Make a bow out of the ends of the cord. Repeat with the other pot, tying it to the fourth nail. You should have two clay pots that ring like bells.

5. Tie the metal birdhouses onto the remaining nails with cord. Make bows out of the ends of the cord. Your finished project should be a welcome sign with a birdhouse—clay pot bell—birdhouse—clay pot bell—birdhouse tied onto nails underneath it (see photo).

Basket of Bulbs

Deliver the promise of spring to your loved ones by making up this lovely basket of spring flowers. The best part about this gift is that the bulbs can be replanted when the flowers die so they can grow again next spring. (Just cut off the flower, dig out the bulbs and plant them in a garden in the spring or fall.)

Time frame: One to two hours

Level: Easy

What you need:

Three to four clay pots of bulb flowers (I recommend tulips, daffodils, crocuses, hyacinths, grape hyacinths, or lilies.)

Large rectangular basket big enough to hold four pots (found at craft or discount stores)

Bag of Spanish moss

Homemade bow

1. Place the pots in the basket. Cover the pots with Spanish moss.
2. Place a matching homemade bow on the basket.

Present Pointers

If you can't find an appropriate basket for your pots of bulb flowers, you might want to buy a rectangular wooden plant box and spray paint it with crackle paint. You could also paint the box with craft paint and stencil ivy or flowers on the box.

Box of Tulips

A spring bouquet that won't fade away.

(© Robert Schroeder)

Give your friends a box of flowers that they won't have to take care of. These country wooden tulips make great spring or Easter gifts.

Time frame: Two to three hours plus overnight to dry

Level: Moderately easy

165

What you need:

Wooden tulips (approximately three × two inches)

Pink, yellow, mint green, white, and forest green craft paints

Paintbrushes

Wooden dowels

Clear acrylic finish spray

Drill with drill bit that matches the size of the end of the dowels

Glue gun

Unfinished wooden vase in a spring shape (butterfly, bunny, Easter egg; see photo)

Flower arrangement foam block

One bunch of dried baby's breath

Spanish moss

1. Paint one tulip pink, one mint green, and one yellow. Paint each dowel forest green and allow it to dry. Spray each piece with clear acrylic finish spray and allow everything to dry.

2. Drill a hole in the bottom of each tulip. Squeeze glue into the holes and twist in the dowels.

3. Paint the vase with white craft paint and allow it to dry. Paint a green border around the edges of the box as shown. Spray with clear acrylic spray and allow it to dry overnight.

4. Glue a block of flower arrangement foam into the vase. Add the tulips and arrange baby's breath in between them. Cover the top of the vase with Spanish moss.

The Least You Need to Know

➤ You can create a special Easter celebration for friends and family by making homemade Easter decorations and gifts.

➤ You don't have to act your age. You can hop down the bunny trail with your favorite tots by making them homemade gifts.

➤ Celebrate Passover with special, handmade symbolic gifts that commemorate this holiday.

➤ Spring is a rebirth of life that can be celebrated with a nature gift that comes from the heart.

Chapter 9

Fall Fun

In This Chapter

➤ Easing the transition back to school with these cool gift ideas

➤ Creating spooky Halloween treats

➤ Decorating friends' homes for Halloween

➤ Making unique Thanksgiving gifts for the host or hostess

For kids, Labor Day signals the end of summer and the beginning of a new school year. As a parent, you may be sad to see the school buses fueling up, or you may be secretly rejoicing to return to your old routine. Either way, you can make the transition easier with these clever back-to-school gifts.

And don't forget: Once school starts, Halloween and Thanksgiving are right around the corner. You'll want to check out the ideas in this chapter to enhance your holiday celebrations.

School Daze

If the kids in your life have the back-to-school blues, this would be the perfect time to cheer them up with a special gift to commemorate the new school season.

Crayon Creations

Kids will be tickled pink with this easy-to-make apron that transforms into a carryall. This apron would be a perfect gift for a new kindergarten student.

Time frame: One to two hours plus one week to set the paint

Level: Moderately easy

*A handy apron that folds
into a carryall.*

(© Robert Schroeder)

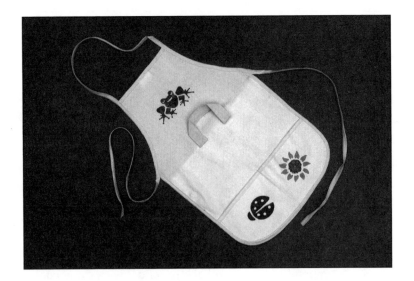

What you need:

> Child's-size apron/carryall (found at craft stores)
>
> Green, red, black, yellow, and orange craft paints (Or, you could use fabric paints to avoid using the textile medium and waiting for the paint to set.)
>
> Foam plate
>
> Textile medium (if not using fabric paints)
>
> Piece of cardboard
>
> Paintbrushes
>
> Foam stamps (*Chunky Stamps*): frog, ladybug, sunflower
>
> Iron and ironing board
>
> Clean cloth or piece of material
>
> Pack of crayons
>
> Watercolor paint set

1. Wash and dry the apron without using fabric softener.
2. Place a dollop of green, red, black, yellow, and orange craft paint (about the size of a quarter) on a foam plate. Add half as much textile medium to each color and mix well. Place a piece of cardboard under the apron for a firm working surface.

3. Paint the frog stamp with the green paint. Carefully center the stamp on the top front of the apron and press down to make a frog imprint.

4. Paint the body of the ladybug stamp red and the head black. Press the stamp down on the left pocket to make a ladybug.

5. Paint the petals of the sunflower yellow and the inside orange. Press the stamp down on the right pocket to make a sunflower. Add a few dots of black in the center of the flower as shown.

6. Allow the apron to set for one week. (You can avoid this step by using fabric paints.) Put the apron on an ironing board, and place a clean cloth or piece of material on top. Iron over the material for 20 seconds on each stamped image to set the paint and make it machine-washable. (See the manufacturer's instructions on the textile medium.)

7. Place a pack of crayons in one pocket of the apron and a watercolor paint set in the other pocket.

You might want to present your gift in a gift bag along with a coloring book and construction paper.

Present Tense

Chunky Stamps are trademarked stamps made out of raised foam over a foam base. You can use these stamps with poster paint, craft paint, fabric paint, or stamp pads to create vivid designs. These stamps differ from rubber stamps in that they are much cheaper, they're easier for kids to use and clean up, and they can create simple designs with a variety of mediums. There are other trademarked names for these stamps, but I like the quality and design of the Chunky Stamps.

School Supplies

Kids will love this personalized pen and pencil case that'll keep their book bag clean and protect their pens and pencils at the same time.

Time frame: One to two hours

Level: Moderately easy

What you need:

Foam lizard stamp (for a boy) or flower (for a girl)

Black, green, pink, and yellow craft paints

Paintbrushes

Acrylic pencil box

Packs of crayons, pens, pencils

Erasers

1. For a boy's box, paint the lizard stamp green and stamp it onto the acrylic box in the right-hand corner. For a girl's box, paint the flower pink with a yellow center and a green stem and stamp it onto the right-hand corner. Allow this to dry.

2. Using a fine-tipped brush and black paint, paint the child's name on the box.

3. Fill the box with crayons, pens, pencils, erasers, and so on.

College Survival Kit

A welcome college survival kit.

(© Robert Schroeder)

If you know a student who is heading off to college, you can help ease the transition by sending him or her this welcome survival kit.

Time frame: One to two hours

Level: Easy

What you need:

Shower tote

Tissue paper

Shampoo and conditioner

Razors

Moisturizer

Soap

Toothpaste and toothbrush

Brown craft paper or cardboard box

Arrange the toiletries in the shower tote. Place the filled tote in a cardboard box to ship.

Present Pointers

You could also make a food gift for a college student that contains soups, hot chocolate, microwavable popcorn and macaroni and cheese, granola bars, homemade cookies, and wrapped candies in a plastic candy dish. A large soup or coffee mug would also be a welcome addition.

Halloween Hauntings

Why not make this year's Halloween celebration a magical one that brings out the little kid in you?

Whether you go all out for Halloween and throw a huge costume party or spend a leisurely evening walking with your trick-or-treaters, you can't help but have a good time on this spooky occasion. Catch the Halloween spirit by making some of these special gifts for your friends and family.

Trick or Treat Bag

A trick-or-treat bag that takes the wear and tear.

(© Robert Schroeder)

Send the kids out to trick-or-treat in style with this Halloween treat bag that can be used year after year.

Time frame: Two to three hours

Level: Easy

What you need:

> Piece of cardboard
>
> Canvas bag
>
> Foam Stamps (I used bats, pumpkins, and candy corn.)
>
> Foam or paper plate for paints
>
> Black, orange, green, yellow, and white craft paints
>
> Paintbrushes

1. Place a piece of cardboard inside the canvas bag to keep the paint from seeping through to the other side.
2. Pour a small dollop of each color paint on the foam or paper plate. Paint the bat stamp black and stamp on the upper-left and upper-right corners of the bag. Paint the pumpkin stamps orange and green and stamp them in the lower-right corner. Paint the candy corn stamps orange, yellow, and white and stamp them in the lower-left corner.
3. Using the black paint and a fine-tipped paintbrush, paint the word "Trick" across the top of the bag and the word "Or" underneath it. Paint the word "Treat" down the middle of the bag as shown.

The Gift of Knowledge

Every year on October 31, kids in the United States dress in costumes and ring doorbells to collect treats from their neighbors. We've come to accept the tradition of trick-or-treating, but most of us don't know how this tradition came about. According to the History channel, trick-or-treating probably dates back to the early All Souls' Day parades in England. Poor people would take to the streets and beg for food during the parade. The wealthy citizens were encouraged to give them pastries called "soul cakes" in exchange for prayers for their dead relatives. This practice, called "going a-souling," was eventually taken up by children. They visited the houses in their neighborhoods and received ale, food, and money for their efforts.

Come In for a Bite

A clever welcome to a Halloween bash.

(© Melissa LeBon)

Invite your friends in for a bite with this cute bat decoration and then make some extra ones to give as Halloween gifts to your friends and neighbors.

Time frame: Two to three hours including drying time

Level: Moderately easy

What you need:

Unfinished wooden bat

Wooden stake

Black and white craft paints

Paintbrushes

Glue gun

Clear acrylic finish spray

1. Paint the wooden bat and the wooden stake black and allow them to dry.
2. Highlight the areas on the wings with white paint and paint two eyes and a mouth on the head as shown. Allow this to dry.
3. With white paint, paint the words "Come in …" on one wing and the words "for a bite!" on the other wing. Allow this to dry.
4. Using a glue gun, glue the bat to the stake. Spray the project with clear acrylic finish spray and allow it to dry.

Halloween Messages

A crafty Halloween greeting.

(© Robert Schroeder)

These block messages will look perfect in a window or on a shelf decorated for Halloween. Make several sets to give to your friends and family for a Halloween treat.

Present Pointers

You might want to present your Halloween message blocks in a cardboard box painted orange and stamped with Halloween stamps. (You could use the stamps from the Halloween trick-or-treat bag to make this box.) The box can be reused on Halloween night to hold candy treats. Consider making the trick-or-treat bag and placing the blocks inside as a gift for a family with kids.

Time frame: Two to three hours plus overnight to dry

Level: Easy

What you need:

Newspapers

18 unfinished miniature wooden blocks (Approximately 1-inch blocks work well.)

Orange spray paint

Black craft paint

Fine-tipped paintbrush

Clear acrylic finish spray

1. Cover a work area in the garage or outside with newspapers. Place the blocks on the newspapers and spray paint orange the three sides that are showing. Allow this to dry. Turn the blocks over and spray paint the remaining side. Allow it to dry.

2. Using the black paint and a fine-tipped paintbrush, paint the letters spelling "Happy Halloween" and "Boo!," one letter on each block. Allow this to dry.

3. Spray the blocks with clear acrylic finish and allow them to dry overnight.

Spooky Spider Costume

Don't let Halloween night pass you by without playing dress-up with your favorite trick-or-treaters. This black widow spider is a perfect costume for any age and can be made from items you may already have at home. Consider giving a gift of a costume to the kids you know who can't decide what they want to be. You could suggest the idea and if they like it, help them assemble the ingredients. (Their parents will be grateful, too!)

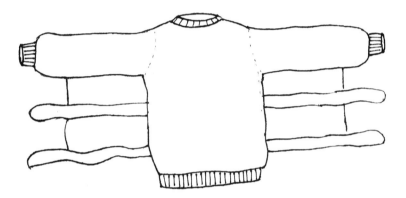

An easy-to-make, spooky Halloween spider.

(© Melissa LeBon)

Time frame: Two to three hours

Level: Easy

What you need:

Three pairs of black tights

Newspaper or tissue paper

Black turtleneck

Black stretch pants or sweat pants

Black stocking cap

Black makeup for nose and cheeks

Reflective tape (optional)

Gifting Glitches

Some of the best Halloween costumes are homemade. If you decide to make a costume for a lucky trick-or-treater, you might want to follow these safety guidelines: 1) Be sure the costume materials are inflammable and don't drag on the ground, 2) Never put something bulky over a kid's face that obstructs his or her vision when trick-or-treating, 3) Don't make the costume too heavy or tiring to wear or carry around, and 4) Place reflective tape on the costume (especially darker materials) so that cars can see the trick or treater coming.

Present Pointers

You can make the spooky spider into an octopus by changing the color of the outfit to purple and adding an extra set of purple stockings. Finish it off with a purple stocking cap and purple makeup. Be sure to have cold cream on hand to remove the makeup. Or, you could change the color to green to make a creepy crawler.

1. Cut the legs off of the tights. Make six spider legs by stuffing the legs of the tights with newspaper or tissue paper. Turn the raw ends of the legs inward and sew the ends of the legs shut using a sewing machine or needle and thread.

2. Sew the legs along the side seams of the turtleneck (under the arms). Equally space three legs on either side under the arms and sew them onto the seam (see illustration). When the child raises his or her arms, there should be four arms on each side, including his or her arm.

3. Put the turtleneck and black pants on the child and pull a black stocking cap over the head covering the hair. Use makeup to create a spider face (see illustration). Place reflective tape on the costume if it will be worn at night for trick-or-treating.

Halloween Hanging

Adding a touch of country to your Halloween décor.

(© Robert Schroeder)

Your friends will hang around if you give them this cute Halloween garland to decorate their homes.

Time frame: Three to four hours

Level: Moderately difficult

What you need:

    Orange material

    Scraps of green and brown calico material

    Polyester fill

    Embroidery needle

    Orange embroidery thread

    Drill

    Three metal Halloween cookie cutters

    Wire

    Three green and three brown wooden beads

1. To make the pumpkins: Cut two pieces of orange material, one five × five inches and one three × three inches. Cut two strips of green calico material 2 × ½ inch and two strips of brown calico material 2 × ½ inch to form the leaves.

2. Place a ball of polyester fill approximately 3½ inches in diameter on top of the 5 × 5-inch square of orange material. Thread the embroidery needle with an eight-inch-long piece of orange embroidery thread. Gather the material up around the ball of filler, and hold it together with your fingers. Stitch the top of the ball as shown to keep it together. Place one green and one brown leaf on top of the thread, and catch them in a knot at the top. Tie the remaining thread into a bow on top.

3. Repeat step 2 with the smaller piece of material, using a ball of filler approximately two inches in diameter.

4. Drill a hole in the top and bottom of each cookie cutter. (You might want to start the hole with a hammer and nail to accommodate the drill bit.) Cut a piece of wire approximately 18 inches long. Place a large knot in the bottom of it and thread the objects in the following order: a wooden bead, a cookie cutter, a wooden bead, the larger pumpkin, a wooden bead, a cookie cutter, a wooden bead, the smaller pumpkin, a wooden bead, a cookie cutter, a wooden bead. You should be able to poke a hole with the wire in the bottom of the pumpkins and thread it through to the top of them. If your wire isn't sturdy enough to do this, thread an embroidery needle onto it to string the pumpkins.

5. Cut four strips of the green and brown calico material approximately 10 inches long and two strips approximately 5 inches long. Put a knot in the center of the smaller strips and thread them onto the top of the hanging. Using the longer strips, make a loop in one with a knot on the end of it and thread the loop onto the top of the hanging. Tie the remaining 10-inch pieces of calico material onto the hanging above each cookie cutter.

6. Make several knots in the top of the wire and form a loop on the top for hanging purposes.

Cute Creepy Crawler

These easy-to-make spiders will capture the kids' imaginations. Make them to give to your favorite trick-or-treaters, but be sure to save some to crawl across your front door on Halloween night.

Time frame: Half to one hour

Level: Easy

What you need:

> Pack of pipe cleaners
>
> Scissors
>
> Large pompoms (approximately three inches in diameter)

Tacky glue

Plastic eyes

Piece of red felt

Bag of spider webs

An easy-to-make Halloween decoration.

(© Robert Schroeder)

1. Twist two pipe cleaners together to form an "X." Twist a third pipe cleaner onto the "X" to form six legs that are connected in the center. Cut a pipe cleaner in half and wrap it around the junction of the three pipe cleaners. Form a circle with the ends of this pipe cleaner to make a base for the pompom. Separate the pipe cleaners and make an "L" on the end of each to form the legs. Spread the legs out so that they stand on their own (see illustration).

2. Glue a large pompom onto the circle you made from the half a pipe cleaner to form the body of the spider (see illustration).

3. Glue plastic eyes and a mouth made out of red felt onto the body. Stick the spider on a gauze spider web.

Present Pointers

You might want to assemble the materials needed to make Halloween spiders and give them to a child for a gift. Include a sample spider and enough supplies for them to create their own creepy crawlers. Present this gift in a plastic jack-o-lantern that can be reused to store their Halloween treats.

Making a spiffy spider.

(© Melissa LeBon)

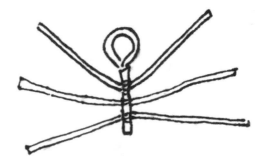

We Give Thee Thanks

One thing Americans have in common is the celebration of Thanksgiving. Whether your Thanksgiving holiday involves football games, parades, feasting, visiting relatives, or a combination of all these activities, it should be a special time to spend with those you love.

In a way, Thanksgiving is the official kickoff to the winter holiday season. Once Thanksgiving arrives, Christmas, Hanukkah, and Kwanzaa can't be far away. So take the time before the rush of the busiest holiday season of all to celebrate the gift of friends and family. You might want to try making some of these unique Thanksgiving mementos to show how much you care.

Sharing the Bounty

The *first Thanksgiving feast* was a cooperative effort between the pilgrims and their neighbors—Native Americans. The pilgrims might not have made it through the winter without the help of their fellow human beings. Bring that spirit of generosity and cooperation to your Thanksgiving celebration by sharing your dinner with someone less fortunate.

Time frame: One to two hours

Level: Easy

Present Tense

The **first Thanksgiving feast** was held in Plymouth Colony in the fall of 1621. The Pilgrims, who had sailed from England on the Mayflower, made landfall on December 11, 1620. They experienced a devastating first winter and lost 46 of their 102 members. Fortunately, the fall harvest of 1621 was a bountiful one. The remaining colonists and 91 Native Americans, who had helped the Pilgrims through the winter, decided to celebrate with a Thanksgiving banquet. Governor William Bradford sent men hunting after wild ducks and geese. We don't know if there was turkey at the first Thanksgiving celebration, but we do know that the Pilgrims had venison. Since there was a shortage of flour there was no pumpkin pie, but there was boiled pumpkin, wild berries, watercress, dried fruits, and seafood.

What you need:

> Covered plastic containers (You can buy the new disposable kind or wash take-out containers.)
>
> Plastic flatware and paper napkins
>
> Extra turkey dinners

Remember the elderly and homeless in your neighborhood by making a few extra plates of food and delivering them to those in need.

You could also invite a friend or neighbor to your dinner who would otherwise be spending Thanksgiving alone. You'll be surprised how much these guests will enrich your holiday experience.

It's All in a Nutshell

Express thanks to your loved ones by making them these Thanksgiving favors.

Time frame: Half-hour

Level: Easy

Present Pointers

You might want to give your Thanksgiving guests a gift of appreciation. Make up a sheet of paper for each guest that says, "I'm thankful for ...." Leave the papers around the party area with lots of pens and have people write their sentiments on the papers. Let the guests take their papers home with them.

What you need:

Unshelled walnuts

Nutcracker

Small fork or knife

Small pieces of paper

Pen

White glue or glue gun

Tinfoil

1. Carefully crack the walnut shells in half with a nutcracker. Discard any shells that don't crack into two even pieces.

2. Remove the nutmeats and scrape out the shell with a small fork or knife.

3. Write a special message on a piece of paper, fold it up, and place it inside the shell. Glue the two shell halves back together and wrap them in foil. Place a nut on each guest's plate. Have a nutcracker handy to open the walnuts.

Toss the Turkey

These turkey beanbags are easy to make and are lots of fun to toss around the house. They're perfect for keeping the young ones occupied while the turkey's in the oven.

Time frame: One to two hours

Level: Moderately easy

What you need:

Canvas garden glove

Felt scraps

White glue or glue gun

Plastic eyes

Dried beans

Needle and thread or sewing machine

1. Place the glove on a flat surface. Cut pieces of felt into the shape of feathers and glue them onto each side of the fingers.

Present Pointers

You can make a homemade target for the beanbags by turning a cardboard box upside down and cutting out different-size holes. Assign a point value for each hole, and try to accumulate points by throwing the beanbags into the holes.

2. Make a beak and comb out of red felt and glue them onto the thumb. Glue on plastic eyes and allow the glove to dry.

3. Fill the glove with dried beans, leaving a little room at the bottom so it's not overstuffed.

4. Turn the cuff of the glove inside. Thread a needle and make small stitches, closing the bottom of the glove. You also could sew this seam with a sewing machine.

Papier-Mâché Gourds and Pumpkins

Use papier-mâché to make decorative gourds and pumpkins for a Thanksgiving centerpiece. These gourds look nice in a horn of plenty basket with raffia or Spanish moss layered on the bottom. This is a great gift for a harried hostess.

Time frame: Two to three hours plus overnight to dry

Level: Moderately difficult

What you need:

Newspaper

One bag of five-inch balloons

Shallow bowl

Mixing spoon

¾ cup flour

½ cup water

Popcorn kernels (optional)

Orange, yellow, green, brown, and black craft paints

Paintbrushes

Clear acrylic finish spray

Green and brown felt

Scissors

Glue gun

Basket

Raffia or Spanish moss

1. Cover your work area with newspaper or a plastic tablecloth. Blow up the balloons and tie knots in the ends of them. You'll need at least six balloons.

185

2. In a shallow bowl, make a paste out of ¾ cup of flour and a little less than ½ cup of water. The paste should be thick enough to thoroughly coat a piece of paper without dripping off. If the paste is too runny, add more flour. If it's too dry, add a bit of water.

3. Tear or cut the newspapers into one-inch-wide strips. Dip the strips into the paste mixture and run your fingers down the strip to remove excess paste. Be sure the paper has an even coating of paste. Paste the strip of paper onto the balloon in a vertical direction, going from the knotted end to the top and back down again. Repeat this procedure several times until the balloon is evenly covered with strips. Be sure to leave a small "hole" where the knot of the balloon protrudes so it can be pulled out when dry. If you like a bumpy texture to your gourd, add a few kernels of popcorn between the layers of newspaper.

4. Add strips around the balloon horizontally until it is covered with a ¼-inch layer of paper. Press the strips to the balloon to keep the shape intact. Rub some extra paste around the strips to smooth them out. Add more popcorn kernels to form bumps on the gourds, if desired.

5. Make stems for the top of the gourds by twisting several layers of paper together like a snake and dipping them into the paste. Allow the stems to dry.

6. Let the gourds dry overnight. Carefully pop the balloons and pull them out. Glue a piece of the twisted stem into the hole of each gourd.

7. Paint the gourds bright green, orange, yellow, white, and black. Paint the stems brown Allow them to dry overnight.

8. Spray with a coating of clear acrylic finish spray and allow the gourds to dry. Make leaves out of green and brown felt and glue them to the top of the gourds.

9. Place the gourds in a basket filled with raffia or Spanish moss.

Present Pointers

A basket of real gourds makes a lovely fall centerpiece to give to a friend or neighbor. Pick out nicely shaped and colored gourds from a farmer's market or grocery store and wash and varnish them. If desired, you could paint faces on them with acrylic paints. Place them in a wicker basket filled with Spanish moss or raffia. Some colored silk leaves look nice placed in between the gourds.

Hand Towel Ring

A trendy, stamped tea towel and holder.

(© Robert Schroeder)

This lovely tea towel holder is a perfect gift for the host of your Thanksgiving dinner.

Time frame: Two to three hours

Level: Moderately easy

What you need:

> Cotton hand towel
>
> Orange, green, and brown craft paints
>
> Foam plate
>
> Textile medium
>
> Paintbrushes
>
> Foam stamps of a pumpkin and leaf
>
> Raffia
>
> Glue gun
>
> Small grapevine wreath
>
> Orange and rust-colored dried straw flowers
>
> Statice or baby's breath
>
> Cord

1. Wash and dry the cotton towel without using fabric softener. Iron the towel if necessary.

2. Place small dollops of orange, green, and brown craft paint on a foam plate. Add the textile medium to each color (using half as much as the amount of the paint) and mix each color well with a paintbrush.

3. Paint the pumpkin stamp orange with a green stem. Stamp the pumpkin in the bottom middle of the towel.

4. Paint the leaf stamp brown and stamp a leaf on the top of either side of the pumpkin (see photo).

5. Make a bow out of the raffia, and glue it onto the grapevine wreath with a glue gun. Glue straw flowers down each side of the wreath with a clump of statice or baby's breath in between.

6. Tie a five-inch piece of cord to the top of the wreath for hanging purposes. Hang the hand towel from the wreath.

Door Décor

A stylish door decoration for Thanksgiving.

(© Robert Schroeder)

Your friends will welcome their guests in style if you make them this lovely eucalyptus and silk flower arrangement for their front door. These are so easy to make that you might want to make one for your own door at the same time.

Time frame: One to two hours

Level: Easy

What you need:

Six strands of brown and green *eucalyptus*

Wire

Small decorative broom

Bunch of fall-colored silk flowers

Glue gun

Statice

Raffia

1. Gather the strands of eucalyptus into a bunch and wire them to the top of the broom so they hang down vertically from the top (see photo).

2. Separate the silk flowers into small bunches. Using a glue gun, glue the flowers onto the top of the broom, over the eucalyptus. Glue statice in clumps in between the flowers.

3. Tie a raffia bow around the handle of the broom to finish it off.

Present Tense

Eucalyptus is a form of evergreen tree found chiefly in Australia and used widely as timber. The tree yields a potent, aromatic oil used in medicine. It helps the respiratory tract by drying phlegm and combating sinusitis. It has also been used for asthma, tuberculosis, and bronchitis. A small drop of eucalyptus oil rubbed onto the soles of the feet or diffused into the air is said to be a fever reducer. Psychologically, eucalyptus clears the mind and is thought to have a cleansing effect reminiscent of being outdoors.

Fall Shadowbox

Celebrate Mother Nature's bounty by creating this decorative nature shadowbox for your friends and family. Part of the fun of making this gift is searching for the ingredients!

Present Pointers

You might want to add some miniatures to your fall shadowbox. You can find a wide assortment of tiny, fall-like objects (such as pumpkins or scarecrows) that would fit perfectly in the compartments along with your natural fall treasures.

Time frame: One to two hours

Level: Easy

What you need:

Unfinished wooden shadowbox

Sandpaper

Oak stain

Paintbrushes

Varnish

Dried seed pods

Miniature pine cones

Outdoor treasures such as unusual rocks, small pieces of wood, bunches of berries, acorns, and so on

Dried flowers (You could either dry your own flowers by hanging them upside down by bunches until dry or purchase these from a craft store.)

Glue gun

1. Sand any rough edges off the wooden shadowbox. Paint the box with oak stain and allow it to dry. Paint the box with a coat of varnish and allow it to dry.

2. Take a walk in a wooded area and look for natural seeds, acorns, unusual rocks, and so on. Using a glue gun, glue the objects into the little compartments. Glue some dried flowers on the shadowbox to fill in the compartments and add color.

The Least You Need to Know

➤ You can prepare kids mentally for a new school year by making it an occasion to celebrate.

➤ You'll make the most of Halloween if you check out the spooky gifts and decorations in this chapter.

➤ Don't be afraid to share the bounty of your Thanksgiving dinner with the homeless or those who may be alone for the holiday.

➤ Show your friends that you're thankful for them by making them a host/hostess gift they'll display year after year.

Part 3

Special Gifts for Special People

In the following chapters, you'll learn that lots of special occasions in people's lives are perfect for giving homemade gifts. For example, you'll find age-appropriate gifts for the kids on your birthday list and ideas for that special aunt who has everything. If you have a new baby in your life, you'll want to check out the ideas in Chapter 11, "New Kid on the Block," for baby shower gifts and new-baby presents. Finally, the anniversary chapter will take you step by step through the process of making a symbolic anniversary gift for the happy couple.

In this part, you'll learn how to put a new twist on giving traditional gifts for special occasions. Now that you've been bitten by the gifting bug, don't waste any time—turn the page to get started on your next project!

Chapter 10

Birthday Bash

In This Chapter

➤ Making creative birthday gifts for the preschoolers in your life

➤ Creating birthday surprises for the school-age kids on your gift list

➤ Treating teens to homemade birthday treasures

➤ Designing special birthday gifts for young adults

➤ Fashioning gifts that reflect the tastes of the older (and hopefully wiser) generation

---

Get bit by the birthday bug this year and vow to make homemade gifts to celebrate the special events in the lives of your loved ones. Whether the recipient is just a kid or only a kid at heart, you'll find some great ideas for birthday gifts in this chapter. Don't let a busy schedule staunch your creative talent. Most of the gifts here are easy to make and won't take a bite out of your time. Feel free to jump right in and gain a reputation for being the "clever one" at birthday time.

Preschool Presents

If you've ever been around preschoolers, you know they're a whirlwind of constant motion. They don't stop long enough to really enjoy a toy before moving on to their next activity. A perfect gift for a preschooler should be colorful, simply designed, and able to withstand constant wear and tear. With that in mind, you might want to try your hand at the following gifts for tots.

Handy Puppets

A colorful puppet that withstands any amount of play.

(© Robert Schroeder)

Soar away with their imaginations by creating this bluebird of happiness for your favorite preschoolers. This puppet is easy to make and stands up to hours of playtime.

Time frame: One to two hours plus overnight to dry

Level: Moderately easy

What you need:

    Scissors

    Two pieces of blue felt

    Pins

    Sewing machine

    Blue thread

    One piece of white felt

    One piece of yellow felt

    Fabric glue

    Fabric paint

1. Cut a piece of blue felt in half. Put the two pieces together and round off the top to form the mouth (see illustration).

2. Cut a circle out of another piece of blue felt that is five inches in diameter. Pin the circle to the rounded ends of the body of the bird as shown. Sew a ½-inch seam around the mouth, being careful not to sew through the body of the bird.

Trim the seam and cut slits on the bias (material outside the seam) to keep the seam from puckering.

3. Close the mouth and sew the two side seams up to the already sewn mouth. Reinforce the seams on the ends by reversing over them a couple times so your puppet stays together.

4. Turn the puppet right side out. Cut a four-inch square out of the yellow felt to make the beak. Glue the beak onto the mouth so that a small triangle of beak sticks out of the middle of the mouth (see illustration).

5. To make the wings, cut two triangles out of the white felt that are 6 × 6 × 4 inches. Notch the one six-inch end of the wing as shown. Glue the wings onto the back side of the puppet.

Present Pointers

You can use your imagination and create other animals using this basic hand-puppet design. You might want to try making a pink fish with green fins and a tail or a yellow snake with a forked tongue and striped body.

6. Cut two rectangles out of the white felt that are two × four inches. Notch one of each of the two-inch sides as shown to form a tail. Glue the tails onto the ends of each side of the puppet.

7. Decorate your puppet with fabric paint. Paint two eyes on the top of the face of the puppet as shown. Allow the puppet to dry overnight.

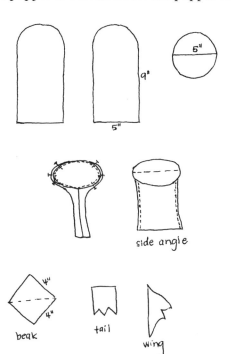

Steps to sewing and creating details on your puppet.

(© Melissa LeBon)

Coloring Book Cover

A colorful and handy coloring book cover.

(© Robert Schroeder)

Kids won't be bored if they have this handy coloring book cover with them on a trip, in a car, in a waiting room—or any time you want them to play quietly.

Time frame: Three to four hours

Level: Moderately difficult

What you need:

> Piece of quilted material, 40 × 30 inches
>
> Scissors
>
> Straight pins
>
> Sewing machine
>
> Thread
>
> Wide trim or rickrack
>
> Matching piece of material, 21 × 12 inches
>
> Iron and ironing board
>
> Coloring book
>
> Pack of crayons

1. Fold the 40 × 30-inch quilted material in half. Cut two rectangles that are 20 × 15 inches long.

2. Place the rectangles, finished sides together, on a flat surface. Pin them together to prepare for sewing. Sew along the edges, using a ½-inch seam and leaving a 3-inch opening on one side for turning the material right side out. Remove the pins and turn the book cover right side out. Stitch the opening together.

3. If desired, sew or glue rickrack or trim around the edges of the book cover. Cut two pieces of trim eight inches long. Sew a piece of trim on both sides of the book cover to allow the cover to be tied together.

4. Place the 21 × 12-inch material on an ironing board. Using an iron, press a ½-inch hem (the wrong sides of the material should be together) on both 21-inch ends of the material. Sew the pressed hem on either side. Fold the material in half lengthwise with the right sides together. Sew each side. Turn the pocket right side out. Mark off one-inch slots for the crayons and sew through the material as shown. Pin the material to the bottom of the inside book cover and sew around the sides and bottom edge.

5. Place a piece of trim along the inside spine of the book cover to hold the coloring book in place. Sew the top and bottom edge of the trim to the cover.

6. Insert the coloring book inside the cover. Place a crayon in every slot.

Present Pointers

If you decide to make a coloring book cover, you also might want to try making the place mats in Chapter 6, "Hanukkah Happenings." The material required for both projects is the same size, and the directions are similar. You're basically making what could be a place mat for the front cover of the coloring book.

The Gift of Knowledge

To know them is to love them. As a natural part of growing up, human beings pass through stages of development that have been studied by psychologists throughout the ages. Whether or not it affects your choice of a gift for the people in your life, it might be helpful to know the major developmental goals of various age groups. You can research these goals on the Internet by key-wording developmental theories, or check the library for books on growth and development.

School-Age Surprises

It's fun to buy presents for school-age kids. They're into everything and especially enjoy presents that allow them to use their imaginations and manual dexterity. They can write (in varying degrees), draw, paint, and follow directions, so your gift options are numerous! You might want to consider the following birthday surprises for this age group.

His or Hers Aprons

They'll go buggy over this cute apron.

(© Robert Schroeder)

School-age kids love to use messy mediums such as paint and clay. Help them protect their clothing from splatters with these cool canvas aprons. But don't stop there—buy them some paints, paper, and stamps so they can make their own masterpieces.

Time frame: One to two hours plus seven days for paint to set if using textile medium

Level: Moderately easy

What you need:

> Canvas apron
>
> Squeeze fabric paint
>
> Green, blue, yellow, black, orange, and red craft paints (Or, you could use fabric paint and omit the textile medium.)
>
> Foam plate

Textile medium

Several bug or reptile foam stamps

Paintbrushes

Clean cloth or piece of material

Iron and ironing board

1. Wash and dry the apron without using fabric softener.

2. Using the squeezable fabric paint, paint the word "Bugs ..." on the top front of the apron. Then paint the word "Everywhere!" on the middle center (see photo).

3. Place a dollop of each color of paint on the foam plate. Add half the amount of textile medium to each pool of paint and mix well. Or, use fabric paints and omit the textile medium.

4. Take a bug stamp and paint it with appropriate colors. Begin at the top and stamp bugs all around the lettering on the apron. You can use your imagination or follow the pattern shown in the picture.

5. Allow the paint to set for seven days. Place a clean cloth or piece of material over the stamps and iron over them for 20 seconds to set the paint and make the apron machine washable. If you chose to use fabric paints, you can omit this step and simply allow the apron to dry.

Present Pointers

If you decide to make a bug apron for a kid's birthday, you might want to include a bug-catching kit with the gift. The kit should have a bug net, a plastic box with ventilation, tweezers, a magnifying glass, and an insect guide. Be sure to warn the kids about bugs that sting or bite and help them set up a cozy environment in the box for their specimens. Remind them to set their bugs free at the end of the day so they don't end up with a box of dead bugs.

King or Queen for a Day

A crown fit for a king or queen.

(© Robert Schroeder)

What kids wouldn't want to be treated like royalty on their birthdays? Make them feel like a king or queen for the day by fashioning a *birthday crown* for their heads.

Time frame: Half hour

Level: Easy

What you need:

Nine-foot decorative garland

Six 12-inch pieces of matching curling ribbon

Six 20-inch strands of different-colored curling ribbon

Scissors

Piece of parchment paper

Fine-tipped marker

Three 12-inch pieces of curling ribbon

Gift bag

Tissue paper

Confetti

Matching bow

Present Tense

The tradition of making a **birthday crown** may have started ages ago in Europe, when birthdays were first celebrated. It was feared that people who were celebrating birthdays were especially vulnerable to evil spirits. To help keep them from harm, friends and relatives would visit the birthday person and bring him or her well wishes, good thoughts, and in some cases, presents. It was originally thought that only kings were important enough to have a birthday party, which may explain the tradition of a birthday crown. Eventually, children were included in birthday celebrations. The Germans celebrated the first children's parties and called them kinderfeste.

1. Wrap the garland into approximately a seven-inch circle. Tie the six 12-inch pieces of foil ribbon into bows around the crown to hold it together.

2. Tie the six 20-inch pieces of ribbon on one end of the crown, knotting them in half (see photo). Curl the ribbon with a pair of scissors.

3. Grant the birthday celebrant three wishes. Using a fine-tipped marker, write down several categories of wishes to fulfill on a piece of parchment paper. For example, you could grant a "Restaurant of your choice" wish, a "Favorite meal" wish, a "Movie of choice" wish, a "Toy of your choice" wish, a "Stuffed animal of choice" wish, and so on. Sign your name and add "Grantor of Wishes" underneath your signature. Roll up the parchment paper and tie it with the three 12-inch pieces of curling ribbon. Curl the ends of the ribbon with scissors.

4. Place the crown and scroll in a gift bag filled with tissue paper and add a sprinkle of confetti to the top. Tie a matching bow on the handles.

Step on It

Kids usually need a boost to reach the bathroom sink or a garment in their closet. This step stool can be decorative and useful at the same time.

Time frame: One to two hours plus overnight to dry

Level: Moderately easy

A useful and decorative kids' stool.

(© Robert Schroeder)

What you need:

Unfinished wooden stool

Sandpaper

White craft paint

Paintbrush

Bear, honeycomb, and bee stencils

Masking tape

Brown, purple, yellow, pink, and green stencil paints

Stencil brushes

"Welcome Friends" stencil

Clear acrylic finish spray

1. Sand any rough edges off the stool.
2. Paint the entire stool with white craft paint and allow it to dry.
3. Place the bear, honeycomb, and bee stencils in the middle of the top of the stool. Tape them in place with masking tape. Carefully paint the stencil area with the appropriate colors. (I used brown for the bear, yellow and purple for the bees, pink and brown for the honeycomb, and purple for the bear's outfit.) Remove the stencils and allow the stool to dry.

4. Place the "Welcome" stencil above the bear stencil and the "Friends" stencil below the bear stencil. Tape in place and paint the stencil area green or a color of your choice. Remove the stencils and allow the stool to dry.

5. Spray the entire stool with clear acrylic finish spray, and allow it to dry overnight before wrapping or using.

Gifting Glitches

If you decide to make a step stool for a kid, be sure to choose a sturdy design. I noticed that some of the stools I looked at would tip over if you stepped on only one end. Also, be sure the stool is reinforced with a wooden piece connecting the legs underneath it to keep it from wobbling.

Terrific Teens

The teenage years can be wonderful and difficult at the same time. It's harder to find the perfect gift for teenagers because their tastes and interests are so diverse. Hopefully, these handmade presents will give you some ideas for your teenager.

Scrunchies

Simple handmade pony-tail holders.

(© Robert Schroeder)

Girls with long hair can never have enough scrunchies (hair holders). Make a bunch of them from your leftover fabrics or check the remnant box at a fabric store.

Time frame: One to two hours

Level: Moderately easy

Present Pointers

You might want to place the scrunchies, some barrettes, a comb, a brush, and a mirror in a plastic cosmetic case to complete your gift.

What you need:

Scissors

Scraps of material

Sewing machine

Thread

½- to 1-inch-wide elastic

Safety pin

1. Cut a piece of material to 16 × 4 inches. Fold the material in half with the right sides of the material together to form a tube that's 16 × 2 inches.

2. Sew the tube together leaving a ¼-inch seam along the length (16 inches) of the tube. Turn the tube right side out.

3. Cut a piece of elastic approximately eight inches long. Pin the safety pin onto the end of the elastic, and use the pin to thread the elastic through the tube. Gather the tube around the elastic. Pull the ends of the elastic out of the tube and sew them together using a ½-inch seam.

4. Pull the ends of the tube together to cover the elastic. Turn each raw end of the tube inward about ¼ inch. Pull one end of the tube over the other end, overlapping them by about ¼ inch. Sew a line down the overlapped edges to keep the ends together. Reinforce the stitches by sewing over the first line.

Sports Equipment Crate

A stenciled wooden crate to stash sports equipment.

(© Robert Schroeder)

The sports enthusiast will appreciate this decorated wooden crate to stash his or her sports equipment. You might want to make two or three so they can be stacked in a room.

Time frame: Two to three hours plus two nights to dry

Level: Moderately easy

What you need:

> Two to three wooden crates
>
> Sandpaper
>
> Oak stain
>
> Paintbrush
>
> Sports stencils
>
> Stencil paint
>
> Stencil brushes
>
> Clear acrylic finish spray

1. Sand any rough edges off the crates with sandpaper. Paint the crate with oak stain. Allow it to dry overnight.

2. Place the sports-related stencils on the crate and stencil in the appropriate colors. (I used a pattern of stencils on either side of the crate.) Allow the stencils to dry.

3. Spray the crate with clear acrylic finish spray and allow it to dry overnight before using it or giving it as a gift.

Captured Memories

Assembled materials for scrapbook gift.

(© Robert Schroeder)

Present Tense

Scrapbook packs are tablets or packs of paper used in scrapbook making. The papers are acid free and contain print designs, backgrounds, cutouts, and patterns for enhancing a scrapbook or photo album.

Get your favorite teenager into the scrapbooking craze. Kids accrue many happy memories on their way to adulthood and will appreciate a new scrapbook and scrapbook packs to keep their mementos safe.

Time frame: One to two hours

Level: Easy

What you need:

> Scrapbook
>
> Scrapbook filler
>
> *Scrapbook pack*
>
> Scissors
>
> Pack of fine-tipped markers
>
> Storage box

Gather all the materials and place them in a storage box. The teen can keep his or her mementos in the box in between working on the scrapbook.

You might want to include a book on the art of scrapbooking with your gift.

Young Adults

My daughter, Melissa, is a young adult with her first apartment. I never have any trouble thinking of something she could use. Many times, young adults are out on their own for the first time and finally appreciate the little things you do for them. If you're stuck for ideas, take a look at these unique birthday gifts.

Birthstone Baubles

Creating beautiful beaded jewelry.

(© Melissa LeBon)

You can check the list of months and birthstones (see sidebar) to find out your recipient's birthstone. Buy beads in a craft store that resemble that particular stone and string them on bead elastic to make a mood bracelet.

The Gift of Knowledge

The following is a list of birthstones and their meanings for each month of the year:

January: Garnet—constancy, faith, loyalty, and strength

February: Amethyst—deep love, happiness, and humility

March: Aquamarine—continual happiness and constancy in love, or Bloodstone—endows courage, wisdom, vitality

April: Diamond—brilliance, constancy, purity

May: Emerald—spring, rebirth, hope, peace, and tranquility

June: Moonstone—pensiveness and intelligence, good luck, or Pearl—beauty, faithfulness, wisdom, and wealth

July: Camelian—courage, joy, friendship, and peace, or Ruby—beauty, clarity, daintiness, dignity, love, and happiness

August: Peridot—happiness, discourages disloyalty

September: Sapphire—calmness, constancy, hope

October: Opal—confidence, happiness, hope, innocence

November: Topaz—divine goodness, eager love, fidelity

December: Lapis Lazuli—ability, cheerfulness, nobility, and truth, or Turquoise—earth, happiness, good health

Scented Lights

Keep their new digs smelling great by making the young adults on your list this potpourri vigil light.

Time frame: Half hour

Level: Easy

A lovely scented vigil light.

(© Robert Schroeder)

What you need:

> Bag of potpourri
>
> Mason jar
>
> Vigil candle holder and candle
>
> Raffia bow
>
> Glue gun
>
> Statice and dried flowers to match potpourri

1. Place the potpourri in the Mason jar.
2. Place a candle in the candle holder, and rest it on the lip of the jar. Tie a raffia bow around the neck of the jar.
3. Using a glue gun, glue dried flowers and statice around the bow (see photo).

Spool Hanging

This whimsical spool hanging brings back memories of yesteryear. Make several of these hangings to give as gifts throughout the year.

Time frame: One to two hours

Level: Moderately easy

Add a touch of country décor.

(© Robert Schroeder)

What you need:

>Three unfinished spools (you can buy these in a craft store)
>
>Wooden or dough heart
>
>Oak stain
>
>Paintbrush
>
>Clear acrylic finish spray
>
>Red, yellow, and brown yarn
>
>Calico material for bow
>
>Drill
>
>Two small pinecones
>
>Four two-inch pieces of cinnamon stick
>
>Wire (heavy duty)

1. Stain the wooden spools and a wooden heart with oak stain. Allow them to dry and spray with clear acrylic finish spray.
2. Wrap each spool with a different color of yarn.
3. Make a bow out of a 12 × 1-inch strip of calico material.
4. Drill a hole in the top of the heart and through the pinecones and cinnamon sticks.

5. Make a knot in one end of a 20-inch piece of heavy-duty wire. Thread the items in the following sequence: wooden heart, spool, pinecone, two pieces of cinnamon stick, spool, pinecone, two pieces of cinnamon stick, spool, calico bow. Twist the ends of the remainder of the wire together to form a loop at the top.

Middle Adults

This age group isn't over the hill; they're just trying to ease their way down the other side. Some middle-agers are a sandwich generation—feeling the pressure to help teenage and young-adult kids on one hand and aging parents on the other. A perfect gift for this age group would be a gift of pampering—perhaps something that ensures a tranquil sleep …

Simmering Sleep

Ingredients for a perfect pampering gift.

(© Robert Schroeder)

Many people agree that herbs and spices have medicinal benefits. Why not make some of these special simmering bath bags for the adults on your guest list. Wrap the herbal bath bags in a gift bag with an *aromatherapy* candle and scented soaps.

Time frame: Half to one hour

Level: Moderately easy

What you need:

> White organdy material (a translucent, thin material with a tight enough weave to hold salt)
>
> Mixing bowl

Spoon

3 cups Epsom salts

2 cups baking soda

1 cup table salt

3 drops of green food coloring

1 cup fresh mint or ½ cup dried mint

½ cup chopped bay leaves

2 teaspoons vanilla extract

Ribbon

Aromatherapy candles

Scented soaps

Gift bag

Tissue paper

Present Tense

Aromatherapy is the use of the sense of smell to influence physical and mental states. The scents and essences of various plants and flowers are extracted and used in several ways. These methods include using scented massage oils, preparing aromatic baths, and inhaling simmering or burning plant essences.

1. Cut the organdy cloth into a six-inch square.

2. In a bowl, mix the Epsom salts, baking soda, table salt, food coloring, mint, bay leaves, and vanilla extract. Spoon about ½ cup of the mixture onto the organdy material.

3. Gather up the ends of the cloth and tie them together with a thin piece of ribbon. Knot the ribbon and tie the ends into a bow.

4. Place the finished bags, candles, and soaps in a gift bag layered with tissue paper.

Stained Glass Votive

A shining, stained glass vigil light.

(© Robert Schroeder)

They won't have to go to church to enjoy the beauty of stained glass if you make them this colorful candle holder. Tell them to burn a candle in this at night to fully appreciate its beauty.

Time frame: Two to three hours plus two nights to set up

Level: Moderately easy

What you need:

> Mosaic adhesive
>
> Bag of assorted plastic stained glass pieces
>
> Rounded glass vase
>
> Tile grout
>
> Popsicle stick
>
> Sponge
>
> Votive candle

1. Using mosaic adhesive, glue the stained glass pieces onto the glass vase. You can make a definite pattern on the vase or place the pieces randomly. Either way looks nice. Allow this to set overnight.

2. Mix the grout according to manufacturer's directions. Using a Popsicle stick, spread the grout all over the stained glass, filling in the cracks. Allow this to set for about 10 minutes, and then wipe it lightly with a damp sponge to remove the grout from the tops of the stained glass pieces. Allow the grout to set overnight.

3. Place a candle in the middle of the finished vase.

Terrific T's

You don't have to be a designer to make these terrific T-shirts to give as birthday gifts. Think of your friend's most relaxing place or activity, (in this case it was a garden), and tailor a message to his or her tastes. You may want to change the message on this shirt to "Gone Fishing," "Out to Lunch," "Ski Bum," and so on. Consider using one of the many transfers available in craft stores and moving on to freehand after you get the knack of painting on fabric.

Time frame: Two to three hours plus overnight to dry

Level: Moderately easy

"Meet me in my garden" T-shirt.

(© Robert Schroeder)

What you need:

Light colored T-shirt (50 percent cotton, 50 percent polyester works best)

Ironing board and iron

Iron-on transfer

Scissors

Straight pins

Piece of cardboard

Squeezable fabric paint

1. Wash and dry the T-shirt without using fabric softener. Press to remove any wrinkles.

2. Preheat the iron to the appropriate setting for your fabric; do not use steam. Cut the design out of the transfer paper, leaving about a one-inch border. Pin the design to the shirt, ink-side down. Press with the iron for about 10 seconds. Remove the iron and then press again for 10 seconds. Don't wiggle the iron or the transfer will blur. Lift one corner to see if the design is transferred; if not, repeat the ironing process.

3. Insert a piece of cardboard into the shirt. Pin the area to be painted to the cardboard to prevent wrinkles in your design.

Gifting Glitches

Don't make a long, continuous line when using squeezable texture fabric paint, or you may develop cracks in your design. You can fill in larger areas of a design by adding a bit of water or paint extender to the paint and using a brush to apply it. Try practicing techniques on a piece of paper before beginning your design on fabric.

4. Paint the T-shirt with squeezable fabric paint using the following techniques: Paint right from the bottle so the applicator tip touches the fabric surface. Allow the paint to seep into the fibers by squeezing and dragging the tip along the design. You can brush on fabric paint mixed with extender or water to fill in large areas or add shading to your design by painting a darker color over a light one where light would hit the object. You can make dots or teardrops on your project by squeezing the bottle quickly, barely touching the fabric and then lifting the bottle up. Make a dot and drag the bottle to the side to make a teardrop.

5. Allow the T-shirt to dry overnight. After 72 hours, the T-shirt can be washed when necessary. Turn the garment inside out and use warm water in a gentle cycle.

The Least You Need to Know

➤ Preschoolers are a bundle of energy and enjoy playing with toys that are colorful and durable.

➤ Most school-age kids enjoy experimenting with new craft mediums and would appreciate the gift of craft materials.

➤ You can make the perfect gift for a teenager if you research his or her hobbies and interests.

➤ Young adults in their first apartments need everything and would appreciate a practical homemade gift.

➤ Great gifts for adults can be pampering or whimsical in nature.

New Kid on the Block

There's no feeling on earth like the excitement of having a baby. After enduring nine long months of being pregnant, the couple receives an incredible gift that makes all the waiting and preparation worthwhile. This is truly a time to celebrate and treat the occasion like the special event that it is. Whether you're invited to a baby shower, a christening, or just want to make something special for the new baby, you'll want to check out this chapter.

Showered with Baby Gifts

Baby showers are a fun way to celebrate the imminent arrival of a new bundle of joy. They also help get the couple started with some of the equipment necessary for taking care of an infant.

Pregnancy is an emotional time for first-time parents-to-be. A creative handmade gift for the mommy-to-be would be a thoughtful way to say, "I care about you." You might want to try your hand at some of the projects in this chapter and pair a homemade gift with a practical gift (such as a box of diapers, baby booties, blankets, and so on).

Angels from Heaven

A heavenly baby shower favor.

(© Robert Schroeder)

Edna Rumbold of Kempton, Pennsylvania, makes these lovely little angels to sell in her gift shop, D.E.A.R. Creations. They're easy to make and would be a perfect favor for a baby shower.

Time frame: One to two hours

Level: Moderately easy

Present Pointers

If you decide to make clay pot angels for baby shower favors, you might want to make matching centerpieces for the table. Just use a larger clay pot for the body and a Styrofoam ball covered with pink crepe paper for the head. Make the wings and halo larger to fit the pot, and paint facial features onto the ball with craft paint or markers.

What you need:

Two-inch clay pots

Pink and blue craft paints

Paintbrushes

Clear acrylic finish spray

Glue gun

Wooden doll heads (You can buy bags of these in a craft store with or without painted faces.)

Spanish moss

Fine-tipped black marker

Pink stencil paint

Pink stencil brush

Eight-inch piece of lightweight wire

Gold foil ribbon

Tacky glue

Natural color raffia

Pink and blue satin ribbon

Lace

1. Paint the clay pots blue and pink and allow them to dry. Spray the pots with clear acrylic finish spray and allow this to dry.

2. Using a glue gun, glue the wooden doll heads onto the bottoms of the painted clay pots. The upside-down pot forms the body of the angel.

3. Glue clumps of Spanish moss onto the top of the heads with a glue gun to form hair. If your heads don't have facial features, make two eyes and a mouth on them with a fine-tipped black marker. Use two smudges of pink stencil paint to make rosy cheeks.

4. Make circles out of the wire pieces to form halos that are 1½ inches in diameter. Leave the remaining six-inch tail of wire on each halo to twist around the raffia wings. Glue the gold ribbon onto the wire circles and the upper two inches of the tails with tacky glue. You should have wire circles with six-inch tails and the circles, and a two-inch length of wire should be covered with gold ribbon.

5. Form the raffia into thick bows (wings) and wire them together with the uncovered ends of the halo wire. Glue the raffia wings onto the back of each angel with a glue gun. The halos should protrude from the back of the heads.

6. Make small bows from the blue or pink ribbon, and glue them onto the front of the angels at the neck. Glue lace on the bottom of the angel bodies.

Steps to making a heavenly angel.

(© Melissa LeBon)

Baby Bear

A baby shower favor they'll want to keep.

(© Robert Schroeder)

The parents-to-be will "bearly" know how to thank you if you make these cute knick-knacks to grace the package of a baby present. You can mix up the pink and blue colors or make them one color if you know the sex of the baby.

Time frame: One to two hours

Level: Easy

What you need:

Wooden bear cutout (I found these at craft store.)

White, pink, and blue craft paints

Paintbrushes

Four miniature wooden blocks (You could also use square wooden beads with the holes turned to the inside.)

Fine-tipped black marker

Glue gun

Clear acrylic finish spray

Thin pink or blue satin ribbon

Small pink or blue satin rose

1. Paint the bear white, two of the blocks blue, and two of the blocks pink. Allow them to dry. Make a face on the bear using the fine-tipped marker.

2. Using the fine-tipped marker, draw the letter "B" on both blue blocks and draw "A" and "Y" on the pink blocks. Allow the blocks to dry.

3. Glue the blocks together, spelling out the word "Baby" on the front. Glue the white bear onto the top of the blocks. Spray the entire project with clear acrylic finish spray and allow it to dry.

4. Make a tiny bow out of the ribbon and glue it onto the neck of the bear. Glue a tiny ribbon rose onto the middle of the bow.

Gifting Glitches

Do's and don'ts for baby showers:

➤ **Do** get together with the family and friends of the parents-to-be and decide on a time, budget, menu, and guest list.

➤ **Don't** get stuck planning and organizing the shower yourself. "Many hands make light work."

➤ **Do** check with the parents-to-be about a guest list. Decide whether co-workers and neighbors will be included.

➤ **Don't** forget to make the shower special by making one of the shower gifts in this chapter.

➤ **Do** plan some games and prizes as entertainment for your party. For example, you could give prizes to the person who has been a parent for the longest/shortest period of time, the person who traveled the farthest to get to the shower, or the person who has known the couple the longest.

Light Up Their Lives

A votive that resembles a bassinet would make a great gift, as well as party favor, for your next baby shower. You could place either candy or a candle in the glass holder.

Time frame: One to two hours

Level: Easy

What you need:

    Eyelet lace

    Tacky glue or glue gun

Glass votive (I used a two-inch glass flower pot from the craft section of a discount store.)

Blue or pink satin flowers

Thin blue or pink ribbon

A votive candle or candies

Netting (optional)

A votive light to signify the light of their lives.

(© Robert Schroeder)

Gifting Glitches

Avoid giving heavily scented candles or potpourri to a pregnant friend. Consider making your own votive candles out of unscented bees-wax sheets. Place them in a pastel-colored gift bag along with this votive and a nice picture frame for the baby's picture.

1. Cut a piece of eyelet lace large enough to cover a votive candle holder. With tacky glue or a glue gun, glue the top of the lace to the top of the candle holder.

2. Glue pink or blue flowers around the top of the lace. Make a small bow out of the satin ribbon, and glue it onto the side of the votive.

3. Place a votive candle in the holder or place the candies in a piece of netting. Draw up the ends and tie a bow around the gathered ends with the satin ribbon and place in the holder.

Waiting in Luxury

Take care of the mommy-to-be by making her this basket of pampering items to help get her through her final months. You might want to get together with some mutual friends to make this basket really special.

Time frame: One to two hours

Level: Easy

What you need:

> Soaps and bath salts
>
> Candles
>
> Body lotions
>
> Soothing CD
>
> Gift certificate to a beauty salon
>
> Wicker basket
>
> Crepe paper filler
>
> Shrink-wrap
>
> Pink and blue homemade bow (See Chapter 3, "Wrapping It Up," for instructions.)

Gather the goodies and place them in a wicker basket filled with pastel crepe paper filler. Add some shrink-wrap and a bow to finish off your gift.

Life's Necessities

A basket of necessities for the newborn would be a perfect shower gift. There are so many little things that babies need—you shouldn't have any trouble filling this basket.

Time frame: One to two hours

Level: Easy

What you need:

> Baby bottles
>
> Baby booties
>
> Baby socks
>
> Onesies
>
> Rattles
>
> Baby bowl and spoon

Present Pointers

Consider going in together with some friends to make a baby basket and include a gift certificate to a baby specialty store in your area.

Baby drinking cup

Stuffed animals

Wicker basket

Pastel colored tissue paper filler

Shrink-wrap

Homemade bow (See Chapter 3 for instructions.)

Gather the baby supplies and place them in a basket filled with pastel-colored filler. (You might want to try making your own paper filler using a paper shredder and construction paper.) Add shrink-wrap and a bow for the finishing touch.

There's a New Kid in Town

Once the baby is born, he or she becomes another potential recipient of a homemade gift from you! Be up to the challenge by checking out these fun gifts for babies.

Noah's Ark

A perfect baby bedroom hanging.

(© Robert Schroeder)

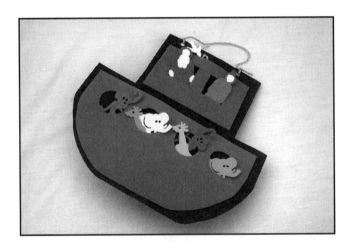

Noah's ark is a common decorating theme for a baby's room. This cute wall hanging would be perfect for the nursery.

Time frame: Two to three hours

Level: Moderately easy

What you need:

Black, brown, green, blue, and white foam sheets

Scissors

Pencil and ruler

Bottle cap

Foam sheet glue or glue gun

Hole puncher

Eight-inch piece of yarn or cord

Pack of foam animals (found in bags in craft stores)

1. Begin by cutting the ark: Round off the two bottom corners of a piece of black foam sheet (12 × 12 inches) to make the shape of the boat.

2. Cut two rectangles that are two × five inches out of the top right and left corner (see illustration). You should have a black piece of foam sheet shaped like an ark.

3. Cut a rectangle that is 10½ × 5½ inches out of the brown foam sheet. Cut another brown rectangle that's four × six inches. Round off the bottom two edges of the larger rectangle to match the rounded edges of the black ark. Using a bottle cap, trace four holes in the top upper section of the rectangle. Cut the holes out to form windows. Cut out two squares in the smaller foam sheet to form windows (see illustration).

4. Glue the two pieces of brown foam sheet onto the black ark along the sides and bottom only. Leave the top open to insert the foam animals. With a ruler and pencil, draw lines approximately ¼ inch apart on the ark to represent wooden boards.

5. Punch two holes in the top of the ark. Tie a piece of cord or yarn through the holes to hang the ark.

6. Follow the illustrated pattern to cut out Noah and his wife. Add the beard, hands, and hair as shown. Make a dove out of white foam sheet and attach it to the top of the ark.

7. Insert the animals, Noah, and his wife into the ark.

Steps to making a Noah's ark hanging.

(© Melissa LeBon)

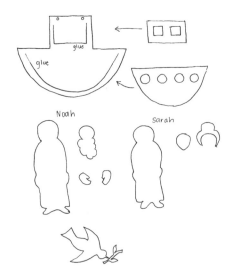

Quilted Quickie

If you like giving quilted gifts but don't want to spend the time sewing the seams yourself, you should check out this quilted wall hanging for a baby's room. No one will know how easy it was to make.

Time frame: Two to three hours

Level: Moderately easy

An easy-to-make wall hanging for baby's room.

(© Robert Schroeder)

What you need:

One *panel* of a quilted mural that is finished on both sides (I chose Noah's ark, but other baby designs are available.)

Scissors

Pins

Four yards of double-fold bias quilt binding in a matching color

Sewing machine

Thread

Wooden dowel

Cord

1. Trim any uneven edges off the panel. Pin the *double-edge seam binding* onto the edges of the panel. Bend the binding around the corners, using one continuous piece of binding (see illustration). Sew the binding to the panel, using about a ¼-inch margin on the inside of the binding.

2. Make five five-inch-long flaps out of the binding and sew them onto the top of the mural, spacing them equally along the top. Be sure to sew the raw edges of the tabs onto the wrong side of the mural. The tabs will hold the dowel.

3. Slide the dowel through the tabs. Tie a piece of cord from one end of the dowel to the other for hanging purposes.

Present Tense

Quilted panels can usually be found in fabric stores and discount stores that sell material from a bolt. The panels are prequilted and portray a seasonal mural or design that's ready to be used in projects. You might want to buy panels for different holidays and make banners or flags for your entranceway. **Double-edged seam binding** is a material edging that can be sewn onto the edges of the quilted material to finish them off. The binding comes in different colors and has two finished edges that cover the front and back of the unfinished edge.

Turning the corners when
sewing seam binding onto
a panel.

(© Melissa LeBon)

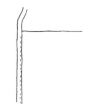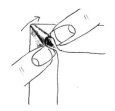

Rub a Dub Dub, Some Fun in the Tub

Make bathtime fun time for the new kids in your life. Assemble a variety of bath toys in a plastic tote or net bag that allows for easy drainage.

Time frame: One to two hours

Level: Easy

What you need:

Rubber ducky

Sponge toys

Squirting toys

Bathtub decals

Net bag or plastic tote

Washcloth mitt

Baby wash

Baby lotion

Soft baby towels

Plastic baby bathtub

Present Pointers

Bathtub decals are foam shapes that stick to the walls of a tub or shower when wet. You can buy these in most toy or discount stores or make your own out of foam sheets. You can also buy packs of precut foam shapes in a craft store that would be perfect for telling a bathtime story.

Gather the bath toys. Place the toys in the net bag or plastic tote, and put them in the plastic baby bathtub with the rest of the bath supplies.

A Teddy Bear Hug

Send a bear hug to a new arrival by making him or her this cute heart-shaped wreath to hang on the door or bedroom wall.

Time frame: Two to three hours

Level: Moderately easy

A bear hug for a special baby.

(© Robert Schroeder)

What you need:

Wire

12-inch extruded foam heart

Tacky glue or fabric glue

10 yards of pink or blue satin ribbon (depending on the sex of the baby)

Glue gun

Spray of silk or plastic baby's breath

White or pastel colored silk roses or flowers

Small stuffed animal (I used a teddy bear made out of chenille fabric that I found in a fabric store.)

Straight pins or anchoring pins

1. Take a piece of wire and wrap it around the top of the heart. Form a loop out of the ends of the wire for hanging purposes.

2. Place a line of tacky or fabric glue on the back right side of the heart. Glue one end of the ribbon down and wrap the pink or blue satin ribbon in and out of the heart until the entire wreath is covered with ribbon. Glue the other end of the ribbon to the back of the heart, overlapping the first end. Be sure to keep the ribbon tight as you wrap it to avoid gaps. Make a homemade bow out of the remainder of the ribbon (see Chapter 3 for instructions).

3. Using a glue gun, glue a spray of baby's breath onto the right side of the heart. Glue a sprig of flowers on top of the baby's breath. You may have to use fine wire to hold the flowers in place, depending on the size of your flowers. Wire the bow onto the bottom of the wreath.

4. Using the straight pins, anchor the stuffed animal onto the bottom of the heart as shown.

The Gift of Knowledge

It is thought that the teddy bear got its name from the American president Theodore Roosevelt. In 1902, Teddy Roosevelt participated in a hunting trip in Mississippi and re-fused to kill a bear that was caught in a trap. The incident was illustrated by a Washington Post cartoonist who dubbed the cartoon "Drawing the line in Mississippi." People started calling toy bears "teddy bears" in affection for the president.

Love Bear

An unusual frame for a newborn's picture.

(© Robert Schroeder)

This wooden teddy bear can accent a display shelf or bookcase in the newborn's room. You might want to make an extra one for the grandparents while you're at it.

Time frame: One to two hours

Level: Easy

What you need:

Three-inch clay pot

Small wooden heart

Blue or pink craft paint (depending on the sex of the baby)

Paintbrushes

Wooden-carved teddy bear (I found this item in a craft store; you could also use a stuffed bear.)

Oak stain

Clear acrylic finish spray

White glue

Baby picture

Pen

Scissors

Glue gun

Black fine-tipped marker

Lace ruffle

1. Paint the clay pot and the wooden heart pink or blue, depending on the sex of the baby. Stain the bear with the oak stain. Allow it to dry.
2. Spray each piece with clear acrylic finish spray and allow it to dry.
3. Glue the wooden bear to the bottom of the clay pot. Place the wooden heart on top of the baby picture and trace around it with a pen. Cut the photo along the traced lines. Glue the picture onto the wooden heart. Glue the wooden heart onto each side of the bear's hands with a glue gun. The bear should be sitting on the upside-down clay pot, holding the wooden heart.
4. Draw eyes on the bear with the black marker.
5. Using a glue gun, glue a lace ruffle on the clay pot for a finishing touch.

Storytime

A durable baby book.

(© Robert Schroeder)

Experts agree it's beneficial to start reading to your children at an early age. This durable, material book will delight both parents and baby.

Time frame: Two to three hours

Level: Moderately difficult

What you need:

> Quilted material
>
> Scissors
>
> Pins
>
> Sewing machine
>
> Thread
>
> Three different-colored pieces of felt, each at least 14 × 6 inches (Buy felt from a bolt in a fabric store to make seven-inch-long pages, or you could modify the size of the book to fit a standard square of felt.)
>
> Decorative-edge scissors
>
> Foam stamps
>
> Craft paint
>
> Paintbrush
>
> Squeezable fabric paint

1. Cut out two rectangles of quilted material to 18 × 8 inches. Pin the rectangles together with right sides touching. Sew around the perimeter of the material, leaving a four-inch opening on one side to turn the material.

2. Remove the pins and turn the cover right side out. Sew the opening. Sew around the perimeter of the cover to make a decorative edge.

3. Cut three pieces of felt to 14 × 6 inches using decorative-edge scissors.

4. Using foam stamps, stamp two simple objects, one on each side of the front of each piece of felt. You might want to use a theme of fruits, animals, toys, or mix them up. Allow the stamps to dry. Paint the name of the object under each stamp using squeezable fabric paints. Allow this to dry. Turn the felt pages over and repeat this process on each side of the back of the felt. Allow this to dry.

5. Lay the three pieces of felt on top of each other. Center the pieces on the inside of the quilted cover. Sew down the center of the felt, catching all three pieces of felt and the quilted cover in the seam. Reinforce the seam by sewing over it. If you like to embroider, you might want to embroider the child's name on the front of the cover.

God Bless This Baby

A christening is a rite of initiation into the Christian faith. If you're invited to a baby's baptism, you might want to check out these homemade mementos.

Lacey Keepsake Boxes

A baby can accumulate many cherished items from birth to his or her christening day. You might want to make him or her these pretty keepsake boxes to store baby treasures.

Time frame: Two to three hours

Level: Easy

What you need:

> Stack of three lacey keepsake boxes (These can be found in craft stores.)
>
> Pink or blue thin satin ribbon (depending on the baby's sex)
>
> White thin satin ribbon
>
> Glue gun
>
> White satin roses

Present Pointers

Enhance your gift of a keepsake box by buying the baby a gold cross or charm on a chain and placing it inside the box.

Fancy keepsake boxes for baby.

(© Robert Schroeder)

1. Weave the ribbon in and out of the holes in the lacey boxes. Alternate blue and white or pink and white ribbon, according to the sex of the baby. Repeat this process on the lids. Tie each end of ribbon into a tiny bow.

2. Glue white satin roses and a small white bow on the lid of the largest box.

Baby Bands

Cute headbands for a baby girl.

(© Robert Schroeder)

Any baby girl will look stunning in these cute baby headbands. Make one for her christening and several more to give as a gift.

Time frame: Half hour

Level: Easy

What you need:

>*Elastic baby headband trims* (or trims and elastic thread)

>Scissors

>Needle and thread

>Iron and ironing board

>Embroidered appliqué

1. Cut a piece of elastic baby headband trim to approximately 16 inches. (If you can, measure the baby's head and add an inch.)
2. With the wrong sides together, sew the ends of the headband trim together, making a ½-inch margin. Press open the seam of the band. Hand-stitch the matching appliqué onto the opened seam. The seam ends should not be on the inside, pressing against the baby's head. The opened seams should be covered by the appliqué on the outside.

Present Tense

Elastic baby headband trims can be found with the other trims and laces in a fabric, craft, or discount store. The trims are easy to use because they're elasticized and come in different colors that can be paired with matching embroidered appliqués. The trims I used were made by Wrights.

If you can't find elastic baby headband trims, you could use a soft, nonelastic trim and make it stretchy by sewing elastic thread by hand down the middle. Gather the trim around the elastic thread and sew the ends together as described in step 2.

Christening Day Memorabilia

Immortalize a baby's christening day by making him or her this attractive plaque that commemorates the important event. You might want to include this gift with a silver baby cup and/or spoon engraved with the baby's name and christening date.

Time frame: Two to three hours plus overnight to dry

Level: Moderately easy

Present Pointers

A gift of baby headbands would be perfect paired with a baby comb and brush set. Place the items in a gift bag and clip some baby barrettes onto the handle. Add a bow to finish the effect.

What you need:

Computer

Good-quality paper

Scissors

Wooden plaque

White glue

Varnish

Paintbrush

1. Using a large-size calligraphy font, type "[the name of the baby] was christened on [date] at [name of church]." Then type "God bless [baby's name]."
2. Print the message on good-quality paper.
3. Cut the paper to fit the wooden plaque, and glue it onto the plaque with white glue. Allow this to dry.
4. Paint a thin layer of varnish over the certificate and plaque and allow it to dry. Paint a second coat of varnish on the plaque and allow it to dry overnight.

The Least You Need to Know

➤ With a little thought and advance preparation, you can make memorable favors and gifts for baby showers.

➤ Celebrating the birth of a new baby with a homemade gift has never been easier.

➤ You might want to pair a homemade baby gift with a practical gift (like diapers).

➤ You can immortalize the rite of a baby's christening with a commemorative gift.

Spanning the Years from Paper to Gold

The honeymoon may be over, but hopefully the wedding anniversaries will keep adding up for the couple. If all goes well, their love will grow for each other with every year that passes. A caring and trusting relationship develops between a couple over the years, and there are many reasons to celebrate another year together. If you know someone who's celebrating an anniversary, you might want to check out these gifts from the heart.

Years One Through Five of Marital Bliss

The first five years of a couple's life are the toughest. They find out how compatible they are as soulmates and try to make adjustments where necessary. Help them remember the good times and why they decided to get married in the first place by making them a special anniversary gift.

Paper Presents

A whimsical paper gift box.

(© Robert Schroeder)

It's not hard to think of something for the first anniversary, which is represented by paper. A gift certificate to the movies and dinner would be an excellent gift. You also might want to consider books or magazine subscriptions. Whatever you decide, you'll want to present your gift in this lovely paper box.

Time frame: Two to three hours plus two days to dry

Level: Moderately easy

What you need:

> Funny papers or other colorful paper
>
> Small bowl
>
> White glue
>
> Thick paintbrushes
>
> Heart-shaped cardboard box or any sturdy cardboard box
>
> Varnish
>
> Crepe paper filler
>
> Colorful ribbon

1. Cut or tear the funny papers into strips that are approximately five × three inches.
2. In a small bowl, mix ½ cup of glue with about 2 tablespoons of water. Using a paintbrush, spread the glue onto a small area of the box, and glue a strip of paper down. Smooth the paper out with your hands. Continue this process until the box is covered inside and out with several layers of funny paper strips.
3. Paint a thin layer of glue over the entire box. Allow the box to dry overnight.

4. Paint a layer of varnish over the box and allow it to dry overnight.

5. Place some crepe paper filler in the box and add your gift certificate. Tie the box together with a colorful ribbon and make a bow on top.

Present Pointers

You can make paper boxes out of any kind of paper. You might want to try customizing them to the taste of the recipient. For example, you could use cutout dolls for a kid's box (and add some cutouts inside the box for the child to enjoy), or you could use wrapping paper, maps, photos, or pictures cut out of magazines. You can buy already-made cardboard boxes at a craft shop or use a sturdy gift box or shoebox. Add a handle to the lid by cutting out a piece of leather and securing it to the top of the box with brackets or small bolts. You can also use bits of leather for hinges and fasten them in the same manner as the handle. Use a hole punch to make holes in the leather to accommodate the fasteners.

Cotton Covers

Cotton is the symbol for anniversary year two. Combine the tradition of cotton with a homemade soup kit, which is ideal for a cozy, intimate celebration. These easy-to-make cotton bags are perfect slipped over a gift of homemade soup ingredients. You can buy the soup mix or make it yourself using the following recipe.

Time frame: Two to three hours

Level: Moderately easy

What you need:

For the cotton bag:

      Cotton muslin remnants

      Straight pins

      Sewing machine or needle and thread

      Colorful yarn or cord

      Yarn needle

Food-related stencils (such as mushrooms, peas, carrots, and so on)

Stencil paint

Stencil brush

Fine-tipped black magic marker

For the soup mix:

1½ cups lentils or mixed dried beans

¼ cup beef bouillon

1 tablespoon celery flakes

½ teaspoon dried basil

1 teaspoon dried parsley

½ cup dried vegetable flakes

For assembly:

Sealable plastic bag for soup mix

White poster board

Stapler

1. Cut a 16 × 8-inch rectangle out of the cotton muslin. Fold down and pin a ½-inch flap on both 8-inch sides of the material, keeping both wrong sides of the material in the hem touching. Using a sewing machine or needle and thread, stitch a hem into the two eight-inch sides.

2. Fold the rectangle in half with the right sides together (the hem folds should be seen on the wrong side). Pin the material together. Stitch up both sides of the bag with a sewing machine or needle and thread. The folded section will be the bottom of the bag.

3. Turn the bag right side out. Using a yarn needle and colorful yarn or cord, make a line of stitches around the top of the bag about one inch from the top (see illustration). Pull the yarn through the bag and leave about five inches on either end. Make a knot in each end of the cord so it doesn't pull out of the bag.

4. Using food-related stencils and stencil paint, stencil a design on the bottom front of the bag. Write the words "Soup for Two" on top with a fine-tipped black marker.

5. Assemble the ingredients for the soup mix. Pick through the beans or lentils to check for any foreign objects that can occur in packaged beans, such as tiny pebbles. Place the ingredients in a sealable plastic bag. Cut the poster board to form a cuff on the top of the plastic bag. Write a list of the ingredients and the directions (see the following instructions) for making the soup on the poster board and staple it to the bag.

6. Place the bag of soup mix in the muslin bag and seal by pulling the two ends of the yarn together and tying a bow.

Directions for the soup:

Place a beef bone, soup mix, and six quarts of water in a Dutch oven or heavy stock pan. Bring this to a boil and skim off any foam that develops on top of the water. Cover and cook on low for two to three hours or until the lentils or beans are tender.

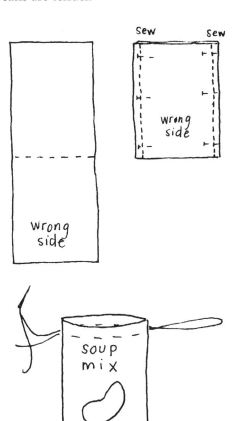

Steps to sewing a muslin bag.

(© Melissa LeBon)

The Gift of Knowledge

Most people are aware that the twenty-fifth wedding anniversary is silver and the fiftieth is gold, but few know that the second anniversary is cotton and the tenth is tin. Check this list the next time you celebrate an anniversary:

Year	Traditional	Modern	Alt Modern
1	paper	plastics	clocks
2	cotton	cotton/calico	china
3	leather	leather	crystal and glass
4	flowers	linen/silk/nylon	appliances
5	wood	wood	silverware
6	candy/iron	iron	wood
7	copper/wood	copper/wood/brass	desk set
8	bronze/pottery	bronze/appliances	linens
9	pottery/willow	pottery	leather
10	tin	aluminum	diamond
15	crystal	glass	watches
20	china	china	platinum
25	silver	silver	silver
30	pearl	pearl	pearl
35	coral	coral/jade	jade
40	ruby	ruby/garnet	ruby
45	sapphire	sapphire	sapphire
50	gold	gold	gold
55	emerald	emerald/turquoise	emerald
75	diamond	diamond/gold	diamond

Memories Preserved in Leather

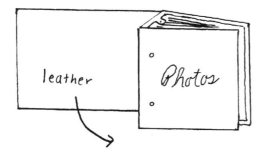

A gift of leather for a third anniversary.

(© Melissa LeBon)

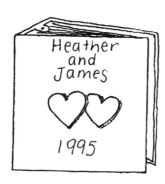

Leather is the gift of choice for a third anniversary. Surprise the couples on your list with a customized photo album to keep the photos of their previous years together protected.

Time frame: One to two hours

Level: Easy

What you need:

Small photo album, approximately six × six inches

Piece of leather, approximately 15 × 6 inches (found in craft stores)

Glue gun

Fine-tipped black permanent marker

Contrasting color of precut leather shapes of hearts or flowers

1. Lay the photo album in the middle of the leather. Close the album and pull the leather over one side. Form a flap with the excess leather (about 1½ inches inside the front cover). Do the same with the back cover.

2. Using a glue gun, put a layer of glue around the perimeter and inside the front of the album. Glue the leather to the front of the album and allow it to dry. Place glue down the spine of the album and the perimeter and outside the back of the album to glue on the leather. Glue the inside flaps on the front and back of the album.

3. Write the couple's names on the front of the album using a permanent marker.

4. Glue a contrasting color of leather shapes (hearts or flowers) on the front of the cover.

Flower Power for Year Four

A lovely floral arrangement preserved in a frame.

(© Robert Schroeder)

Surprise the lucky couple with a gift of their favorite flowers, pressed and preserved in a frame. You can find these flowers in nature or buy a bouquet at the grocery store or florist for this project.

Time frame: Two to three hours to assemble plus two to three weeks to press

Level: Moderately difficult

What you need:

Waxed paper

Fresh flowers

Flower press or two to three heavy books and weights (Bricks work well as weights.)

Picture frame

Lace doily

Ribbon (optional)

White glue

Gifting Glitches

In some areas of the country, national parks in particular, you're not allowed to remove anything from the countryside. The flower you decide to pick may be on the endangered list and could cost you a hefty fine. Be aware of the rules and regulations of the area you hunt for wild flowers and natural artifacts.

1. Place a sheet of waxed paper inside a heavy book. Arrange the flower, keeping it as flat as possible, on the paper and place a second sheet of waxed paper on top of the flower. Close the book and add weight to the top. Follow this step with the remainder of your flowers using different sections of the book or separate books for pressing. If you have a thick flower, you might want to put a layer of paper towels in between the flower and waxed paper to protect the book.

2. Allow the flower to press for one to two weeks, depending on the thickness of the flower. I'd check the progress after one week. The flower should be pressed flat with no moisture remaining.

3. When the flowers are ready, open up the picture frame. Place a doily on the open area. Arrange your pressed flowers into a design on the doily. You might want to make a bouquet of flowers and add a small satin bow at the base. Carefully glue the flowers to the doily.

4. Reassemble the frame. You may want to present your gift to the couple with a fresh bouquet of the same type of flowers you pressed.

Wood 'n' You

A wooden gift is appropriate for year five. This lovely wooden birdhouse on a stand will grace an entranceway for many years to come.

Time frame: Three to four hours plus two nights to dry

Level: Moderately difficult

A quaint decoration for the front entranceway.

(© Robert Schroeder)

What you need:

Sandpaper

Wooden spindle

Heavy wooden base, approximately 12 inches square (Check scrap boxes at home improvement stores or lumber mills or have wood cut to these dimensions.)

Small wooden base (approximately six inches square)

Wooden birdhouse

Oak stain

Paintbrushes

Varnish

Drill with ½-inch drill bit

Two screws (approximately four-inch)

Screwdriver

Glue gun

Spanish moss

Silk flowers

Raffia

1. Sand any rough edges off the spindle, bases, and birdhouse. Stain the pieces with oak stain and allow them to dry overnight. Brush a coat of varnish onto the wooden pieces and allow them to dry overnight again.

2. Drill a hole through the middle of the larger wooden base and another hole about one inch into the bottom of the spindle. Screw the wooden base onto the bottom of the spindle. Drill a second hole through the middle of the smaller wooden base and another hole about one inch into the top of the spindle. Screw the smaller wooden base onto the top of the spindle.

3. Using a glue gun, glue the bottom of the birdhouse onto the top base. Be sure to use lots of glue to keep the birdhouse sturdy.

4. Using a glue gun, glue Spanish moss to the top of the birdhouse. Glue silk flowers on top of the moss.

5. Make a bow out of the raffia and glue it onto the top of the birdhouse.

Present Pointers

If you decide to make a birdhouse on a spindle, you might want to decorate it with a seasonal scene. You could add brightly colored birds and pastel-colored flowers for the spring, a scarecrow and colored leaves for the fall, a pair of lovebirds and daisies for the summer, or holly and poinsettias for the Christmas season. Try wrapping some ivy and miniature lights around the spindle for a lovely evening effect.

The Way to Their Hearts Is Through Their Stomachs

Help the couple avoid the seven-year itch by celebrating years six through ten of their loving relationship with a delicious homemade gift.

Fudge Fantasy

Candy is a must for year six. Fudge is surprisingly quick and easy to make. However, I wouldn't let anyone know that you didn't spend the night slaving over a hot stove to make this delicious treat.

Time frame: One to two hours plus overnight to set

Level: Moderately easy

What you need:

Large heavy saucepan

For the chocolate fudge:

¾ cup margarine

3 cups sugar

⅔ cup evaporated milk

12-ounce bag chocolate chips

7-ounce jar marshmallow whip

1 teaspoon vanilla extract

For the peanut butter fudge:

1 tablespoon butter

1¾ cup sugar

½ cup evaporated milk

1 cup peanut butter

1 cup marshmallow whip

To assemble:

Two heart-shaped cake pans

Waxed paper

Butter-flavored cooking spray

Two pieces of cardboard

Tinfoil

Pink plastic wrap

Curling ribbon

1. To make the chocolate fudge: Combine the margarine, sugar, and evaporated milk in a heavy saucepan. Bring to a rolling boil, stirring constantly. Continue boiling five minutes over medium heat, stirring constantly. Check to see if the fudge is ready by placing a teaspoon of the mixture in a cup of cold water. If it forms a soft ball, it's ready. If not, continue to cook and check again in a minute.

Remove from heat and stir in chocolate chips, marshmallow, and vanilla. (You should make the chocolate fudge first and put it in the prepared pan to cool in the refrigerator for an hour before making the peanut butter fudge.)

2. To make the peanut butter fudge: Melt butter in the pan. Add the sugar and milk and boil two minutes, stirring constantly. Check to see if the fudge is ready by placing a teaspoon of the mixture in a cup of cold water. If it forms a soft ball, it's ready. If not, continue to cook and check again in a minute. Remove from heat and add peanut butter and marshmallow whip.

3. Prepare the heart-shaped pans by lining them with waxed paper and thoroughly spraying the waxed paper with butter cooking spray.

4. Pour half of the chocolate fudge into one prepared pan and half into the other pan. Allow this to chill for one hour in the refrigerator.

5. Pour half of the peanut butter fudge on top of the chocolate fudge in one pan and half on top of the chocolate fudge in the other pan. Allow this to set up overnight in the refrigerator.

6. Cover a piece of cardboard with foil. Invert one heart-shaped pan on top of the cardboard, allowing the fudge to fall out. Remove the waxed paper from the fudge. Cover the cardboard with plastic wrap and tie with a bow. Repeat this step for the second heart. If you only want to make one heart fudge, you can cut each recipe in half.

Gifting Glitches

Making fudge is a simple process, but there are a few glitches you want to avoid:

➤ Be sure to cook your fudge over medium/low heat (after it boils the specified amount of time). Cooking it at too high a heat will scorch it and give the end product a burnt taste. You'll know you've scorched the fudge if the cream-colored mixture of butter, sugar, and milk turns a brownish color.

➤ Be sure to cook your fudge to a soft ball stage. You can use a candy thermometer and cook it to the appropriate temperature (234°F) or drop a teaspoon of the mixture into a cup of cold water and see if it forms a soft ball.

➤ When cutting fudge, run the knife under hot water occasionally for a few minutes and wipe it with a paper towel. A hot knife makes a smooth edge on the cut fudge.

Cookie Cutter Creation

A unique cookie cutter decoration.

(© Melissa LeBon)

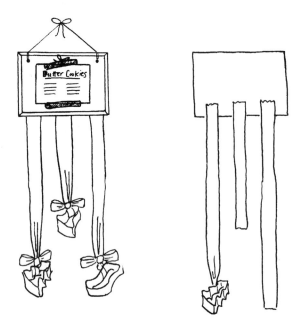

Copper represents anniversary year number seven. The cooks on your anniversary list will appreciate this gift of copper cookie cutters accompanied by a favorite cookie recipe.

Time frame: One to two hours

Level: Easy

What you need:

      Computer or paper and marker to write out recipe

      Cookie recipe

      Unfinished wooden sign

      White glue

      Two cinnamon sticks

      Varnish

      Paintbrush

      Drill or hammer and nail

      Cord

Pieces of material

Glue gun

Six copper cookie cutters

1. Using a computer and a calligraphy font, type your favorite cookie recipe and print it out on a piece of paper. (Or you could hand-print the recipe onto a piece of paper.) Glue the recipe onto the sign using white glue. Glue a piece of cinnamon stick on the top and bottom of the recipe. Put a coat of varnish over the sign and allow this to dry overnight.

2. Drill two holes in the upper-right and upper-left corners of the sign. (If you don't have a drill, you could make the holes with a hammer and nail.) Thread cord through the top two holes and tie the ends into a bow on top.

3. Cut two pieces of material into 18 × 2-inch rectangles, and one piece into a 10 × 2-inch rectangle. Using a glue gun, glue one end of each of the material strips onto the back bottom of the sign, equally spaced (see illustration), placing the shorter piece in the middle.

4. Loop two cookie cutters onto the end of each piece of fabric and tie into a loose knot. Tie an eight × two-inch piece of fabric into a bow on top of each knot.

Present Pointers

If you're hand–delivering your gift, you might want to make some cookie dough from the cookie recipe to include with your present. Roll the cookie dough into logs and refrigerate until hard. Wrap the logs in plastic wrap and then tinfoil. The dough can be rolled out and cut into cookies with the cookie cutters or sliced and baked for no-fuss homemade cookies. Most cookie dough can also be frozen for up to two months.

Bronze, the traditional gift for the eighth anniversary, is a particularly elusive metal. Most of us don't even know what it is—is it a combination of brass and iron, copper and tin, just rusted tin? With your indulgence, I've elected to skip the traditional eighth year bronze anniversary symbol and use the alternate modern symbol: linen. If you're interested, you might want to check out the Present Tense sidebar explaining the unique composition of bronze.

Present Tense

Bronze is a reddish brown alloy consisting mostly of copper and tin. The metal is used in statues, trophies, busts, and other decorative items. Weapons and implements were made out of bronze during the Bronze Age, a stage in prehistory following the Stone Age and preceding the Iron Age.

Lovely Linens

Linen hand towels, which have been replaced over the years by towels made of more practical materials, are making a comeback as a decorative item. They look particularly nice when hand-stamped or stenciled with a welcoming theme.

Decorative linens for the kitchen or bath.

(© Robert Schroeder)

Time frame: Two to three hours plus overnight to dry

Level: Moderately easy

What you need:

Cardboard

Linen hand towels (You can buy these at a craft store.)

Welcome stencils

Stencil paint

Stencil brush

1. Place a piece of cardboard behind the working area of the linen towel. Center the stencil over the bottom middle of the towel. I used a stencil of a house and the words "Welcome Friends," but you could use the couple's initials, seashell stencils, fruit stencils (for a kitchen), or any other appropriate design.

2. Allow the stencils to dry overnight. You may want to present the linens in a gift box with some matching soaps or candles.

Pottery Coffee Break

Unless you take a course in making pottery, you probably won't be using this art form for the people on your ninth anniversary list. But there are masters of the art who produce unusual pottery gifts that you might want to consider for this important anniversary. Pair a lovely vase with a bouquet of flowers or place special coffee mugs with an assortment of gourmet coffees and teas in a gift basket, as I've laid out for you here. You might want to include a note with your gift that says: "Here's a little something to remind you to take a break from your hectic schedules to be with one another."

Time frame: One to two hours

Level: Easy

What you need:

Gourmet coffee and teas

Biscuits

Pottery mugs

Basket

Crepe paper filler

Shrink-wrap

Bow

1. Assemble the coffee, teas, biscuits, and mugs.

2. Place the items in a basket layered with crepe paper filler. Finish off your gift with shrink-wrap and a bow.

Tin for Ten

A perfect gift of tin for anniversary 10.

(© Robert Schroeder)

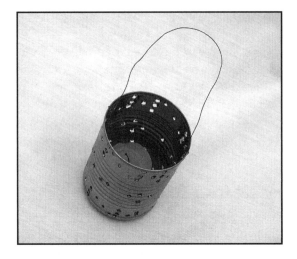

This lovely tin lantern will be a perfect gift to light up the lives of the anniversary couple. You might want to consider making several lanterns in different designs to brighten their porch or deck.

Time frame: Two to three hours plus overnight to freeze the water

Level: Easy

What you need:

Tin cans that have a paper (not painted) label (Soup cans or vegetable cans work well.)

Wide masking tape

Hammer

Nails (different sizes)

Sturdy wire

Wire cutters

Votive candle

1. If your can still has a paper label, soak the can in water to remove the label, and clean the can inside and out.

2. Fill the can with water and freeze it overnight. The ice that forms will keep your can from collapsing when you hammer it.

3. Wrap the masking tape around the outside of the frozen can. Pick an interesting pattern or use one of the illustrated examples and draw the dots onto the tape.

4. Pound in the nails with a quick light blow. Use nails of different sizes to make different holes. Make a hole on opposite sides of the top edge of the can to string the wire for hanging purposes.

Present Pointers

You can make your lantern more decorative by stenciling a pattern on the top and/or bottom of the can. You could also paint the outside of the can with rust-effect paint to hang in a garden.

5. Allow the ice to melt or run hot water over the can to remove the ice. Thread a 10-inch piece of wire through the two top holes. Make a knot in the wire on each end. Remove the tape and insert a votive candle into the bottom of the can.

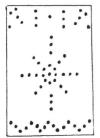 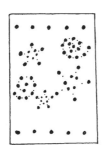 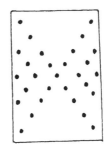

Some designs to use on hanging lanterns.

(© Melissa LeBon)

Marking the Milestone Years

Once a couple gets to 10 years, they pretty much have the marriage thing figured out. They may still have their ups and downs, but they should have developed a sense of security in their relationship. Celebrate their longevity by making them a special gift.

Crystal Clear

Fifteen years of marriage is symbolized by the gift of crystal. And, unless you know how to blow your own glass, you might want to consider giving the couple a pair of glasses from their favorite crystal pattern paired with a bottle of champagne and tray of fancy hors d'oeuvres.

Time frame: One to two hours

Level: Easy

What you need:

Set of crystal glasses

Bottle of champagne or sparkling cider

Foil bags

Tray of hors d'oeuvres

1. Wrap the crystal glasses and champagne in foil bags.
2. Order a tray of appetizers from a local gourmet food store, grocery store, or caterer for a prearranged evening when the couple will be home. (Be sure to arrange a time to deliver your present when they can enjoy hot appetizers.)
3. Deliver the tray and gifts and either enjoy an evening together or allow them to savor your gift during a personal celebration. Either way, you come out a winner for thinking of such a thoughtful present.

Simply Silver

Steps to making lovely silk flowers.

(© Melissa LeBon)

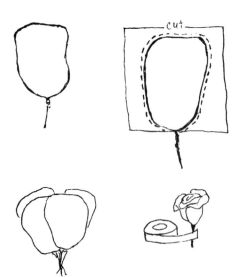

Silver is the metal of choice to celebrate 25 years of wedded bliss. You can purchase a silver vase and place these lovely homemade flowers inside it to brighten up the couple's day. A silver frame would be a perfect complement to this gift.

Time frame: One to two hours

Level: Easy

What you need:

Pipe cleaners that match the material

Scissors

Fabric glue

Silk material (several different colors that blend well)

Wire flower stems (found in craft stores)

Florist tape

Silver vase

Silk ribbon

1. Twist the pipe cleaner into the shape of a flower petal with a one-inch tail on the end. Glue the petal onto the material with fabric glue and allow it to dry. Carefully cut the material around the pipe cleaner.

2. Repeat this step using the same color pipe cleaner and material until you have six to eight petals. Gather the one-inch tails together and wrap them around a wire flower stem. Wrap the tails and wire stem with florist tape to hold them together and cover up the individual tails.

3. Use different-colored pipe cleaners and material to make a bunch of silk flowers following steps 1 and 2. You might want to change the shape of the petals for each flower.

4. Place the flowers in a silver vase and tie a silk bow onto the top of the arrangement.

Golden Accents

Making it to a 50-year anniversary is really special. The couple may decide to throw a big party and renew marriage vows. You'll want to be there for them and give them this lovely memento of their wedding day.

Time frame: One to two hours, time to collect and develop pictures

Level: Easy

What you need:

Wedding photo of the couple

Photo from their fiftieth wedding anniversary

Gold leaf frame with two windows

Gold confetti

Gold gift bag

1. Find a copy of the couple's wedding picture, and place it in one side of the frame.
2. Take a picture of the couple at their fiftieth anniversary celebration and have it developed. Insert it into the other side of the frame. Place the gift in a gold gift bag with gold confetti sprinkled inside.

The Least You Need to Know

➤ You can make traditional gifts that symbolize the first five years of anniversary celebrations.

➤ Start a tradition by making homemade gifts that celebrate a milestone in a couple's married life.

➤ Sometimes a store-bought gift is the perfect gift to pair with a handmade greeting or memento.

➤ Silver and gold are in order for the special twenty-fifth and fiftieth wedding anniversaries.

Part 4
Showing You Care

If you know a kid who spends too much time in front of the TV or video games, you'll want to check out this section. You'll find ideas for interactive gifts that will take kids back to the simple pleasure of creating a work of art or pursuing a hobby.

You'll also find the perfect gift for that favorite teacher, business associate, or hired helper on your gift list. Don't just give them a gift certificate for Christmas; learn how to present it in a unique and thoughtful way!

You'll also want to read this section for gift ideas for friends who are on the mend. You've gotten this far, so keep reading. This section is the icing on the cake!

Chapter 13

Parent-Approved, Kid-Tested Gifts

In This Chapter

➤ Exploring nature with a little buddy

➤ Getting a child started on a special hobby

➤ Learning the art of sculpture together

➤ Sharing the craft of making gifts from paper

Most kids today have more electronic toys and gadgets than they know what to do with. As a result, many of them spend their free time surfing the Internet, playing video games, listening to CDs, and watching movies. Some parents and parenting experts worry about exposing children to violence in video games and movies and are advocating a trend away from media and back to wholesome kid activities.

If you know a kid celebrating a special event in his or her life, why not try making an old-fashioned, homemade gift that will take him or her back to simpler times. Don't just make the gift, though; pick up some extra ingredients and spend some time with the child creating a special project. Hopefully, this gift of your time and energy will be appreciated much more than another electronic gadget.

Gifts from Nature

Remember when kids used to run outside after school to meet their friends for a game of basketball or a tour on their bikes? Reading for pleasure and working on hobbies have also been replaced by interacting with electronic media. Kids expect to be constantly entertained, but at times they find that even their video games have become boring and repetitious. Spending some time with kids at this age can make a big difference in their lives.

If you're a nature buff, you'll want to try these easy projects that celebrate the great outdoors. Gather the kids around you and spend some time outside making these great gifts together.

Earthly Delights

Mother Nature tamed.

(© Robert Schroeder)

A *terrarium* is a wonderful way to bring Mother Nature indoors. You'll want to spend some time with a special kid picking and choosing the artifacts for this project.

Time frame: Two to four hours

Level: Easy

What you need:

> Clear glass bowl, acrylic box with lid, or jar with wide mouth opening
>
> Gravel
>
> Spanish moss
>
> Potting soil
>
> Digger
>
> Small plants, moss, ferns (Succulents and cacti do well.)

Sticks, stones, shells, and other objects from nature

Spray bottle filled with water

Lid for container or plastic wrap to cover the container

1. Cover the bottom of the container with about three inches of gravel. Add a one-inch layer of Spanish moss and three inches of potting soil.

2. Using a digger, dig a small hole in the soil for each plant. Push the plants into the holes root first and cover with a layer of soil. Be sure the roots are firmly pushed into the soil. If your terrarium is a jar, you might want to use a pair of tongs for this step.

3. Arrange the other objects, such as rocks, sticks, bark, shells, and so on, on top of the potting soil around the plants.

4. Spray the terrarium with a mist of water from the spray bottle. Cover the terrarium with a lid or plastic wrap.

Advise your recipient to place the terrarium in a window that receives indirect sunlight and to spray it once a week with a mist of water.

Gifting Glitches

Shells are homes for sea creatures. If you find a shell on the beach with a live creature inside, it's best to return it to the sea. If you keep the shell, it will probably develop an odor that's not worth dealing with. Also, creatures like seahorses and starfish are becoming endangered, and live ones should be left in their habitat.

Present Tense

A **terrarium** is a place or enclosure for keeping land, animals, plants, and so on. Terrariums can be created to grow plants, to provide a home for an animal (such as a lizard, turtle, or frog), or to display wildflowers, rocks, shells, and other nature artifacts. You might want to consider using a fish tank with a lid to hold small creatures. Be sure to set your creatures free if they experience adverse effects from being confined.

Sand Candles

Using Mother Nature's resources.

(© Robert Schroeder)

You could make these candles with your kids at the beach or assemble them at home by bringing in your own sand. Either way, they'll be a big hit and will light up your evenings together.

Time frame: Two to three hours plus overnight to harden

Level: Moderately easy

What you need:

> Dishpan
>
> Sand
>
> Water
>
> Digger
>
> Seashells or other artifacts
>
> Frying pan
>
> Box of paraffin wax
>
> Tin can
>
> Colored wax pieces
>
> Candle wicking
>
> Toothpicks
>
> Paintbrush

1. Fill the dishpan with sand and smooth out the top until it's level. Add water to the sand and mix it with the digger until the sand is firm enough to make a hole in it without the sides crumbling. Using the digger or your hands, make a hole in the sand that is the desired size of the candle you'd like to make. I'd recommend making the hole approximately four inches by three inches.

2. Place seashells in the bottom of this hole.

3. Fill the frying pan with one inch of water and heat over medium heat. Break four blocks of wax into small pieces and place them in a tin can. Place the tin can in the pan of water and heat the wax on medium high heat until it is melted. Add colored pieces to the wax until the desired color is obtained.

Gifting Glitches

Whenever you make homemade candles, be sure to be extra careful with the wax. A small amount of spilled wax on a stove can start a fire. Keep some sand on hand when melting the wax to douse a fire. Be sure to clean up any spills immediately before they harden onto a surface. Also, never throw unused wax down a drain.

4. Dip a five-inch piece of wicking into the wax to coat and allow it to dry until stiff. Place the wick in the sand hole you dug in step 1. Holding the top of the wick over the hole, slowly pour the melted wax into the hole. Be sure the wick is centered and meets the bottom of the hole. If you want the bottom of the hole area to be the top of your candle, before adding the hot wax, push about ½ inch of wick on the bottom through the sand with your finger to form the wick. Poke any air bubbles that form in the candles as you pour the wax with a toothpick and add more wax where necessary.

5. Allow the wax to cool for several hours without moving the sand. Dig your candle out of the sand, and brush any excess sand off the candle with a paintbrush. Your candle will have a sandy texture and will contain the fruits of your walk on the beach.

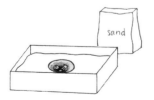  

The steps to making sand candles.

(© Melissa LeBon)

Gifts of Hobbies

If you help to get kids started on a hobby, they'll always have something to occupy their time (and their minds) when they're bored. Their parents will thank you!

Coin Collecting

A fun way to save for the future.

(© Robert Schroeder)

Here's a gift that kids will enjoy now and appreciate later when their coins increase in value. Teach kids the value of money by getting them started with a coin collection.

Time frame: One to two hours

Level: Easy

What you need:

Coin collection books (You might want to include a state quarter collection map of the United States.)

Coin collection book of values

Coins to start the collection

Magnifying glass

Storage box

1. Gather the books, coins, and magnifying glass and place them in a storage box.

2. Spend some time with the child looking at coins and explaining how to find rare ones.

If this gift was a hit, you might want to check out starting a stamp collection for the child in the future.

Pen Pals

The ingredients to start a pen-pal correspondence.

(© Robert Schroeder)

Help the kids in your life correspond with other kids in distant places by introducing them to the pen-pal connection. Assemble the materials listed below to get them started on designing their own stationery.

Time frame: One to two hours

Level: Easy

What you need:

Pen-pal list

Paper

Envelopes

Textured scissors

Fine-tipped markers

Stickers

Stamps (You might want to choose a theme for the stamps you buy, such as animals, nature, holidays, landscapes, geometric designs, and so on.)

Stamp pads

Glitter pens

Storage box

Homemade bow

1. Check your school system or a local library for a possible list of pen pals. Be sure to put your own name on the recipient's pen-pal list.
2. Assemble the supplies listed and place them in a plastic storage box. Wrap the box with a homemade bow.
3. Spend some time designing stationery and envelopes with the recipient, and get this new pen pal started on writing to people on the list.

It's Fun to Read

It's never too late to get a kid hooked on reading. This gift of appropriately aged books and supplies will get a child started off on the right foot.

Time frame: One to two hours

Level: Easy

What you need:

Books

Book light

Book markers

Storage bin

Check your local library or school for an age-appropriate reading list. Purchase the books and place them in a storage bin with a book light and book markers. Spend some time reading to a smaller child.

Bring Out the Artist

Michelangelo would approve of these hand-sculpted gifts that you can make with the kids in your life. Clay or play dough is a versatile medium that can be sculpted into almost any shape. You might want to sign up both of you for a class in pottery if you and your young friend enjoy these projects.

There are also lots of gifts that you and a small buddy can make out of recycled paper. You might want to keep a box handy to collect used gift wrappings and old newspapers for these projects.

Dough Cactus

An easy-to-care-for cactus.

(© Robert Schroeder)

This cactus looks great on a kid's bedroom shelf. They're easy to make and bring out the creativity in child and adult sculptors.

Time frame: Two to three hours plus overnight to cool and dry

Level: Moderately easy

What you need:

    Aluminum foil

    Mixing bowl

    2 cups flour

    1 cup water

    1 cup salt

    Toothpicks

    Cookie sheet

    Cooking spray

Gifting Glitches

Some do's and don'ts of sculpting with dough: Don't make your sculpture too large. It will be difficult to bake and arrange in a pot. Do make a second batch of dough and make cutout shapes using cookie cutters. Do store any leftover dough in a tightly sealed baggie for future use. Don't leave your creations where small children or pets can reach them.

Green paint

Paintbrush

Clay pot

Spanish moss

Raffia

1. Make a form for your cactus by shaping crumpled pieces of aluminum foil into a cactus shape. A cactus around six inches high and four inches wide fits nicely into a four-inch pot.

2. In a mixing bowl, mix the flour, water, and salt, working out any lumps with your hands. If the mixture is too thin (watery) add more flour. If it's too thick, add water. The dough is perfect if it doesn't stick to your fingers and is easy to shape into objects.

3. Spread the dough about ¼-inch thick over the foil shape covering all the foil areas with dough. Make a sturdy base out of about one-inch-thick dough around the bottom of the cactus to enable it to stand up on its own. Break toothpicks into thirds and stick the toothpicks at irregular intervals in the dough to simulate cactus needles.

4. Place the cactus standing up on a cookie sheet sprayed with cooking spray.

5. Bake the cactus at 350°F for approximately 20 minutes or until it's firm to the touch and golden brown. Baking time will depend on the size of the cactus.

6. Remove the cactus from the oven and allow it to cool overnight.

7. Paint the cactus green and allow it to dry. Fill the clay pot to within two inches of the top with Spanish moss or crumpled newspaper. Place the cactus in the pot and press down firmly. Spread a one-inch layer of raffia around the base of the cactus to hold the cactus in the pot. If necessary, add extra moss to stabilize the cactus. You could also use sand or gravel to fill the pot. Tie a raffia bow around the top of the pot.

Paper Sculptures

You don't have to spend a lot of money to make these cool paper sculptures. All you need are some recycled papers and a vivid imagination.

Time frame: One to two hours plus several hours to dry

Level: Easy

A sculpted work of art.

(© Robert Schroeder)

What you need:

Newspapers

Markers

Scissors

Stapler

White glue

Foam dish or paper plate

Tissue paper or wrapping paper

Dowel

Glue gun

Drill

Wooden plaque

1. Think of a shape you'd like to make for this project. Draw an outline of that shape onto four layers of newspaper and cut it out (through the four layers of paper). You might want to start with a simple fish, like the one in the photo, or you could copy a coloring book design. Make your design approximately 8 × 10 inches.

2. Staple the edges of the four newspaper cutouts of your design together, leaving a three-inch area unstapled to add stuffing.

3. Crumple newspaper into small balls, and stuff the design to give it dimension (see illustration). Once the design is stuffed, finish stapling the open edge.

4. Mix about ¼ cup of white glue with 2 tablespoons of water on a foam dish or paper plate. Cut or rip pieces of tissue paper or wrapping paper into small strips. Dip the paper strips into the glue mixture and glue them onto the design. Cover the design with at least two layers of paper strips. Allow it to dry overnight.

5. Cut a small hole in the bottom of the fish and glue the dowel into the hole using a glue gun.

6. Using a drill, make a ¼-inch hole in the middle of the wooden plaque. Glue the end of the dowel into the hole. If desired, you could stain and/or varnish the plaque and dowel.

Fortune-Teller

Kids will have fun folding paper into this unique shape and telling the fortunes of their friends and family. They can make this simple fortune-teller, or customize it to fit their tastes by adding decals, stamps, or drawings on the flaps to illustrate the fortunes.

Time frame: Half hour

Level: Easy

What you need:

Piece of paper

Scissors

Fine-tipped marker

1. Cut a piece of paper into a nine-inch square.

2. Fold the paper in half diagonally to form a triangle. Fold in half again, forming a smaller triangle.

3. Unfold the paper and fold in each of the ends to meet in the center crease, forming a square (see illustration). Flip the paper over and turn in those edges to meet at the center, forming another smaller square.

4. Lift up the flaps on the other side and place a thumb and finger in each flap to make a moving square form.

5. With a marker, place the name of a color on each of the four outside squares. Place a number on each of the eight inside triangles.

6. Write a fortune under the flap of each inside triangle.

Here's how to tell a fortune: Ask a person to pick a color from the four outside flaps. Open and close the paper spelling out the color. For example, open once for R, close for E, and open again for D. Have the person pick a number from inside and open and close again that number of times. Have them pick a number again and open up the triangle with the fortune written inside.

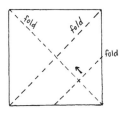 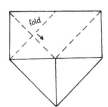

Folding paper into a fortune-teller.

(© Melissa LeBon)

Wallpaper Art

Get the kids on your list involved in the art of making wallpaper refrigerator magnets and jewelry. You can have hours of fun with a young friend with these few simple ingredients.

Time frame: One to two hours plus overnight to dry

Level: Easy

What you need:

> Wallpaper scraps
>
> Scissors
>
> White glue
>
> Cardboard
>
> Varnish
>
> Paintbrush
>
> Glue gun
>
> Magnets or jewelry forms: pins, earrings, barrettes

Present Pointers

If you decide to make wallpaper art, you might want to check out wallpaper borders for a great selection of designs. You also can usually find cheap wallpaper remnants in home-decorating stores. Most craft stores sell the magnets, jewelry forms, and hair clips that are needed for this project. Try putting your wallpaper designs on a wooden plaque for a different effect.

1. Cut a motif out of wallpaper. Glue the wallpaper design onto a piece of cardboard using white glue and allow it to dry. Place something heavy on the design to keep the wallpaper flat while drying.

2. Carefully cut around the design. Paint a coat of varnish on the cut out design and allow it to dry. Paint a second coat of varnish on the design and allow it to dry overnight.

3. Using a glue gun, glue the design onto a precut magnet, jewelry form, or barrette.

The Least You Need to Know

➤ Sharing your creative talents with a child can be a rewarding experience for both of you.

➤ You can spend a beautiful day outdoors making crafts with a small buddy.

➤ Sculpted gifts are easy and fun to make with a favorite kid at your side.

➤ You can make beautiful gifts out of recycled materials.

MISS SMITH

Chapter 14

Appreciation with a Capital A

In This Chapter

➤ Making gifts for the special teachers in your life

➤ Creating unique gifts for co-workers and business associates

➤ Honoring a special boss

➤ Preparing personalized gifts for the hired helpers who make your life easier

If there's a special teacher your kids keep raving about, a business associate you can count on to rescue you in a jam, or a hired helper who gets the little things done in your life, you'll want to check out this chapter. Say thank you to these special people by taking the time to make them a handmade gift. If a monetary gift is in order for a hired helper, you might want to enclose it with one of these easy-to-make customized gifts.

Talented Teachers

Show the special teachers in your life that you appreciate all they do for your kids. This year, forget the scarf set and handcraft teacher gifts that will stand out on their desks.

Teachers Rule!

Remind the kids who's the boss at school by making these cute ruler magnets for the teachers in your life.

A clever way to show teacher appreciation.

(© Robert Schroeder)

Time frame: Two to four hours including drying time

Level: Easy

What you need:

Unfinished wooden ruler (Can be found in craft stores.)

Oak stain

Paintbrushes

Unfinished wooden apple cutout (Can be found in craft stores.)

Red craft paint

Black fine-tipped marker

Clear acrylic finish spray

Green felt

Scissors

Glue gun

Thin gingham ribbon

Magnet sheet

1. Stain the wooden ruler with oak stain, and paint the apple with red craft paint. Allow these to dry.

2. Using a black fine-tipped marker, write the words "Teachers Rule" on the apple. When dry, spray each piece with clear acrylic finish spray and allow it to dry.

3. Cut two leaves out of the felt. Glue the leaves onto the top of the apple.

4. Cut a piece of gingham ribbon the length of the ruler. Glue the ribbon onto the bottom edge of the ruler.

5. Glue the wooden apple onto the side of the ruler. Make a bow out of the ribbon and glue it onto the bottom of the apple.

6. If your magnet has a sticky side, stick the magnet onto the back of the ruler. If not, glue the magnet onto the ruler using the glue gun.

Present Pointers

You might want to personalize your teacher's magnet by writing his or her name on the ruler. You could also drill a hole in the ruler and string it with wire or cord for hanging on a peg or Christmas tree.

A+ Teacher

Giving the teachers in your life an A+.

(© Robert Schroeder)

You'll get an A+ if you take the time to make this gift for your kid's favorite teacher.

Time frame: One to two hours

Level: Easy

What you need:

   Wooden clothespin with spring mechanism

   Miniature blackboard (Can be found in craft stores.)

   Oak stain

   Paintbrush

   White fine-tipped fabric paint (in a squeezable bottle)

   Clear acrylic finish spray

   Natural color raffia

   Glue gun

   Magnet sheet

1. Stain the clothespin and the wooden frame of the blackboard with oak stain and allow them to dry.
2. Write the words "A+ Teacher" on the blackboard using white fabric paint. Allow it to dry. Spray the project with clear acrylic finish spray and allow it to dry.
3. Make a small bow out of the raffia. Glue the bow onto the top of the blackboard with a glue gun.
4. If the magnet sheet is self-sticking, stick the magnet onto the back of the clothespin. If not, use a glue gun to glue the magnet onto the clothespin.

Book Lovers Gift Bag

Most teachers are book lovers. You can please a teacher on your gift list by giving him or her this "food for thought" gift bag.

Time frame: One to two hours

Level: Easy

What you need:

   Homemade caramel popcorn (see recipe)

   Sealable bag for popcorn

   Gift certificate to local bookstore

   Gourmet iced teas or hot chocolate mix

   Gift bag

Crepe paper filler

Bow

For Carmel Crunch recipe:

2 quarts of popped popcorn (Remove any unpopped kernels.)

1⅓ cups pecans

⅔ cup almonds

1⅓ cup sugar

1 cup margarine

½ cup corn syrup

1 teaspoon vanilla extract

1. To make the Carmel Crunch: Mix popcorn and nuts in a single layer on a greased cookie sheet.
2. Combine the sugar, margarine, and syrup in a heavy saucepan. Bring it to a boil over medium heat, stirring constantly. Continue boiling, stirring occasionally, for 10 to 15 minutes until the mixture turns a light caramel color.
3. Remove from heat; stir in vanilla. Pour over popcorn and nuts and mix to coat well. Spread to dry and break into pieces. Store in a sealed container.
4. Place the crunch in a sealable plastic container or large zip-close bag.
5. Assemble the remaining goodies and place them in a gift bag filled with crepe paper filler. Add a bow for a finishing touch.

#1 Associate

Celebrate Bosses' Day or Secretaries' Day in style or just reward a special assistant or employee by making him or her a special present. Choose from the following easy-to-make ideas.

Desk Waterworks

Running water has a therapeutic effect on people and can be a welcome addition to a hectic office scene. Make a waterfall or water fountain for the special co-worker in your life and complement the gift with this homemade matching desert garden.

Time frame: Two to three hours plus overnight to dry if using tile

Level: Moderately difficult

Calming the office atmos-phere.

(© Robert Schroeder)

What you need:

> Do-it-yourself mosaic water fountain kit
>
> Seven-inch diameter clay pot saucer
>
> Sand
>
> Potting soil
>
> Digger
>
> Small cacti plants (two or three varieties)
>
> Decorative rocks that match the water fountain rocks (Can be found in craft stores.)
>
> Raffia bow

1. For the water fountain: I found several varieties of do-it-yourself waterfall and water fountain kits in craft and discount stores. These kits contain everything you need to make a completed water project (including the tiles, rocks, water pump, and so on). I would recommend buying a kit and following the moderately difficult directions carefully. If you don't have time to make your own waterfall, you can purchase a premade water fountain and pick out some interesting rocks to place in the fountain.

2. For the desert garden: Fill the clay saucer with a ¾-inch layer of sand and a ¾-inch layer of potting soil. Mix the two layers together with a digger.

3. Make a small hole in the soil mixture for each plant. Firmly press the plants in the holes root-first and cover the roots with soil. Water each plant with enough water to dampen the soil around the roots (about ¼ cup). Cover the top of the soil with the decorative rocks.

4. Tie a matching raffia bow around the saucer for a finishing touch.

Present Pointers

Bringing the sounds of nature indoors has a soothing effect on people. The sound of running water in a desktop waterfall can calm a hectic office setting. You might want to make an organic garden effect on your waterfall by adding some small potted plants around the edges and placing specially selected gemstones in the water. If your fountain is too small to accommodate plants, consider making a terrarium to place nearby.

#1 Boss Sign

A great gift for a great boss.

(© Marilee LeBon)

Show your boss your appreciation by making him or her this quaint wooden sign expressing your feelings.

Time frame: One to two hours plus overnight to dry

Level: Easy

What you need:

 Unfinished hanging wooden sign

 Oak stain

 Paintbrushes

 Two wooden stars

 Three tiny wooden hearts

 Blue, white, and black craft paints

 Glue gun

 Fine-tipped paintbrush

 Clear acrylic finish spray

1. Paint the wooden sign with oak stain and allow it to dry. Paint the three hearts blue and the two stars white and allow them to dry. You can use other colors of paint for this step if desired.
2. Glue the stars on the top-left and bottom-right corners of the sign. Glue the three small hearts on the bottom right corner of the sign.
3. Using a fine-tipped paintbrush, paint the words "#1 Boss" on the sign. Allow it to dry. Spray with clear acrylic finish spray and allow it to dry overnight.

Hired Help

Is there someone in your life who does the things you can't get to yourself? Show this person how much you appreciate his or her service by giving a hand-crafted gift.

Baby-Sitter's Bag of Tricks

Help the baby-sitters in your life keep the kids entertained by making them this bag of tricks. They'll be the most popular baby-sitters on the block when they show up with these toys for the tots.

Time frame: One to two hours

Level: Moderately easy

Keeping the kids entertained.

(© Robert Schroeder)

What you need:

Material or canvas tote (See Chapter 3, "Wrapping It Up," to learn how to make your own material gift bag, or you can purchase a tote from a craft store.)

Squeezable fabric paint

Coloring books

Crayons

Markers

Construction paper

Storybooks

Water colors/paintbrush

Stickers

Stamps and stamp pads

Book of mazes or hidden words

Curling ribbon (optional)

1. Buy a canvas tote bag or make the material gift bag listed in Chapter 3. Use a bottle of squeezable fabric paint in a contrasting color to the bag to write the baby-sitter's name and the words "Bag of Tricks" on the front of the bag. Allow the paint to dry.

2. Assemble the art supplies and books and place them in the material bag or canvas tote. If using a canvas tote, tie the handles together with curling ribbon and curl the ends for a finishing effect.

The Gift of Knowledge

You might want to check this baby-sitter's guide if you employ a baby-sitter:

➤ Write down the family name, the names of the children, the house address, the number of the nearest relative and/or neighbor, emergency numbers, and the phone number where you will be.

➤ Write down any special instructions about diets, medications, bedtimes, nighttime rituals, and so on.

➤ Walk through the house and familiarize the baby-sitter with exits and deadbolt locks (in the event of a fire), locations of telephones, kitchen equipment (if necessary), baby equipment, and so on. Instruct the sitter to keep windows and doors locked.

➤ Introduce the baby-sitter to the family dog or cat.

➤ If you have a pool, set down rules for its use.

➤ Give specific rules about visitors and phone use. You want to be able to get through to the sitter if necessary.

Loving Nanny

If you're running a household and holding down a job, you know how important the people who keep your life operating smoothly are to the survival of your family. You might want to show your appreciation by making them these special message blocks.

Time frame: Six to eight hours including drying time

Level: Easy

Sending a special message.

(© Marilee LeBon)

What you need:

Unfinished wooden blocks

Antique white craft paint

Paintbrush

Heart stencil

Red, blue, green, and yellow stencil paints

Stencil paintbrushes

Flower stencil

Letter stencils

Gift certificate

1. Buy enough blocks to spell out "We Love [person's name]" and add two blocks for the heart and flower design. Paint the tops and sides of each block white and allow them to dry. Turn the blocks over and paint the remaining sides. Allow them to dry.

2. Place the heart stencil over one side of one of the blocks. Stencil the heart with red stencil paint. Place the flower stencil on a block and stencil in with yellow paint. Place a "W" stencil on one side of a block and stencil with blue paint. Stencil an "E" in green, an "L" in red, an "O" in yellow, a "V" in green, and an "E" in blue. Then stencil the letters of the recipient's name on blocks in alternating colors.

283

3. Set the blocks up where the recipient will see them. Place them near a home-made gift certificate for a day off, if you can arrange it in your schedule, or a dinner for two at a local restaurant.

Special Delivery

A clever way to present a gift certificate.

(© Marilee LeBon)

Anyone who has mail and papers delivered to his or her home knows how important it is to have good delivery people. You can show these special people how much you appreciate their service by making them this special bottle stuffed with a message and gift certificates.

Time frame: Half to one hour

Level: Easy

What you need:

>	Clear bottle with cork or Mason jar with lid

>	Piece of paper

>	Pen or marker

>	Thin ribbon

>	Confetti

>	Gift certificate

>	Self-sticking label

1. If using a recycled jar, rinse it out and soak off the label. If you're using a decorative bottle with a cork, be sure the opening is large enough to insert and retrieve the gift certificates.

2. Write a special message on the piece of paper. For example, you could simply say, "Thank you for the year of wonderful service." Roll the paper into a tube, and tie it with a piece of thin ribbon.

3. Place the paper in the bottle, and add confetti and the gift certificate. Fill out the "To" and "From" sections on the label and place it on the outside of the bottle. Tie another piece of ribbon around the neck of the bottle, and make the ends into a bow.

Here are some ideas for gift certificates:

➤ Video rentals

➤ Restaurant

➤ Movie tickets

➤ Department store

➤ Sporting goods store

➤ Gourmet food store

➤ Bookstore

Present Pointers

A gift of a message in a bottle would be perfect for a birthday present, a gift for a senior citizen, a Mother's Day gift, or just about any occasion. You could add certificates that can be redeemed for your own time or for services for an older couple that may need your help or a young couple starting a family. You could customize this gift to a special season by choosing seasonal confetti and ribbon colors. You could also make your own "To" and "From" gift tag out of a painted wooden shape—a pumpkin for Halloween, an ornament for Christmas, or a decorated egg for Easter.

The Least You Need to Know

➤ You can customize a gift for a teacher by adding a handmade refrigerator magnet or gift tag.

➤ Make the people in your work life feel special by giving them a homemade gift.

➤ Don't just give your hired help a monetary gift; surprise them with a sentimental gift that shows them you care.

➤ Baby-sitters and nannies are the caretakers of your children. Homemade gifts will show them how thankful you are for their services.

Chapter 15

For Those Who Have Everything

In This Chapter

➤ Making special gifts for doting grandparents

➤ Recognizing aunts and uncles in our lives who are like second parents

➤ Creating the perfect gift for retired relatives or neighbors

➤ Learning what to give to the person who has it all

Most of us have people in our lives whom we couldn't imagine living without. Whether your special someone is a favorite aunt or uncle, a doting grandparent, or an adopted retired couple, you'll want to check out the ideas in this chapter to show them how much you care.

Greatest Grandparents

Grandparents have a special place in our hearts. As parents, they nurtured and cared for us when we were little and as grandparents, they continue the tradition by loving our kids. Show these special people how much you love them by making them a unique grandparent gift.

Perfect Present for Pops

Touch a grandfather's heart with these cute hanging hearts that tell him he's special.

Time frame: One to two hours

Level: Moderately easy

A special gift from the heart.

(© Robert Schroeder)

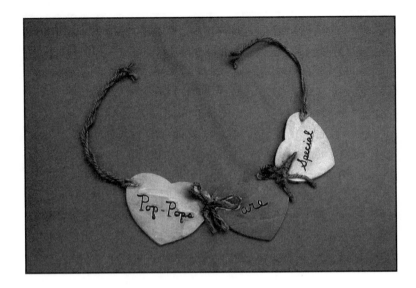

What you need:

> Three unfinished wooden hearts
>
> White and powder blue craft paints
>
> Paintbrushes
>
> Drill with ¼-inch drill bit
>
> Fine-tipped black marker
>
> Clear acrylic finish paint
>
> Cord or yarn
>
> Scissors

1. Paint two of the wooden hearts white and one powder blue and allow them to dry.
2. Drill a hole in the upper-left and -right sides of the three hearts.
3. Write the word "Pop-Pops" (or whatever you call this grandpa) on one white heart. Write the word "Are" on the blue heart and the word "Special" on the other white heart. Spray the three hearts with clear acrylic finish spray and allow them to dry.
4. Cut two pieces of cord or yarn approximately 12 inches long and string them through the left side hole of each white heart. Cut two pieces of cord or yarn approximately six inches long, and connect the two white hearts to the blue center heart. Form a bow in the ends of the cord or yarn that connects the hearts.

Sweet Sachets

A sweet scent for Grandma.

(© Robert Schroeder)

Grandma will love these special *sachets* to sweeten up her clothes drawers or closets. Use several different scents as filler for variety.

Time frame: Two to three hours

Level: Moderately easy

What you need:

> Quilted material (You an use scraps or remnants for this project.)
>
> Scissors
>
> Pins
>
> Sewing machine or needle and thread
>
> Iron and ironing board
>
> Bag of sachet
>
> Lace or decorative trim

Present Tense

Sachets are interesting blends of herbs and flowers that are dried and packaged in bags or envelopes. Some of the common herbs used are parsley, sage, thyme, lavender, basil, salvia, marjoram, mint, sage, and chive.

1. Cut a piece of quilted material 5 × 10 inches. Fold the material in half with right sides together to form a five × five-inch square. Pin two of the open sides together, and sew a ¼-inch seam along the edges, leaving the third seam open to add the sachet.

Present Pointers

Give your grandparents the gift of scent. Include several sachets in a gift basket of aromatherapy candles, room sprays, or bags of potpourri. Add some decorative filler to the basket, and top it off with a handmade bow.

2. Turn the bag onto the right side. Using an iron, press a hem into the two unsewn, wrong sides of the top of the bag.

3. Pour the sachet into the top of the bag. Cut a piece of trim or lace to the width of the bag. Cut a small tab (three inches) of trim or lace to use for a hanging tab. Fold the tab in half and pin the two ends to the center of the bag with the tab facing upward. Pin the piece of trim or lace across the top of the bag. Sew the top opening shut by sewing a seam over the trim and securing ends of the tab in the seam. The loop in the sachet bag is perfect for hanging over a garment hanger.

Happy Handprints

Immortalizing their little handprints.

(© Melissa LeBon)

The grandkids' hands won't stay little forever. Capture their tiny prints in plaster for an awesome grandparent gift.

Time frame: One to two hours plus overnight to dry

Level: Moderately easy

What you need:

    Newspapers or plastic to protect the work area

    Apron to protect clothing

Small bag or box of plaster (The eight-pound box is enough for a stepping stone mold; you can use a four-pound box for smaller molds.)

Water

Mixing bucket

Stick or old spoon to mix the plaster

Popsicle stick or trowel

Plaster mold (stepping stone size or smaller)

Small rubber or plastic glove

Paintbrush

Pieces of decorative glass or marbles

Clear acrylic finish spray

1. Place plastic or newspaper over the work area. Protect clothing with an apron. Mix the plaster according to the directions on the box or bag. Pour the plaster into the mold and smooth the top with a Popsicle stick or trowel.

2. Put a small protective glove on your child's hand. Place the child's hand into the plaster to make a handprint. Remove the glove and wash the child's hand with soap and water. Write the child's name in the plaster with the end of a paintbrush.

3. Place the decorative glass pieces or marbles in a pattern around the handprint. Allow this to dry overnight before moving it.

4. Remove the plaster handprint from the mold and spray with clear acrylic finish spray. Allow it to dry thoroughly.

Awesome Aunts and Uncles

Many kids have aunts and uncles who are like second parents to them, or close family friends they call aunt and uncle. If you have brothers, sisters, or friends who spoil your kids, you might want to make them these special gifts to let them know how much you appreciate their loving care.

Seashell Candleholder

This seashell candleholder may bring back memories of a special time spent combing the beaches together. But even if you buy the shells at a shell shop, this pretty candleholder will be a hit with a favorite aunt or uncle.

The perfect candle accent.

(© Robert Schroeder)

Time frame: One to two hours

Level: Easy

What you need:

Glass jar with lid

White sand (about 1½ cups)

Candle (The candle should be about one inch shorter than the height of the jar. A wider jar could accommodate a thicker candle.)

Bag of small seashells

Ribbon

Glue

1. Fill the glass jar with two inches of sand. Stick the candle in the middle of the jar, pushing it into the sand until it touches the bottom of the jar.

2. Arrange the seashells around the candle inside the jar, filling the jar to two inches below the rim with small seashells. (The top two inches of the candle should be exposed.) If you don't have enough seashells, you might want to add some crystal marbles or decorative glass pieces to the shells.

3. Glue a strip of decorative ribbon around the bottom of the jar. Tie a matching piece of ribbon around the lid of the jar and make a bow out of the ends.

Bay Leaf Hanging

Adding a touch of country to a kitchen shelf.

(© Robert Schroeder)

Bay leaf is a trendy addition to a decorative hanging. These cute country garlands are the perfect thing to hang on a Shaker peg shelf.

Time frame: Two to three hours

Level: Moderately easy

What you need:

> Drill with ¼-inch drill bit
>
> Unfinished wooden heart
>
> Blue craft paint or oak stain
>
> Paintbrush
>
> Wire
>
> Wire cutters
>
> Bay leaves
>
> Yarn needle
>
> Wooden spool
>
> Cinnamon stick

Present Pointers

Country garlands are a new trend in decorating. Try making a hanging out of other materials. You can use wooden spools, seasonal wooden cutouts, pinecones, nuts, cookie cutters, and so on. Any type of ribbon, material, or raffia looks nice tied between the objects. Check out the other garlands in this book (see Chapters 5, 9, and 10).

Stuffed heart (You might want to make your own by following the directions for sachet hearts in Chapter 7, "My Funny Valentine.")

Strips of material

1. Drill a hole in the center top of the wooden heart. Paint the wooden heart and spool blue or stain them with oak stain if preferred. Allow them to dry.

2. Cut a piece of wire so it's 15 inches long. Thread the end of the wire through the hole in the heart and knot the wire. Take a stack of bay leaves (about 20) and make a hole in them with a yarn needle. Thread the leaves onto the wire.

3. Thread the spool onto the wire and make a knot above the spool. Thread more bay leaves onto the wire above the spool and add a piece of cinnamon stick. (You can make a hole in the cinnamon stick with a drill or use the needle to make a hole.)

4. Attach the needle to the wire and thread the stuffed material heart on top of the cinnamon stick. Knot the wire and make a loop out of the top for hanging purposes.

5. Cut six strips of material approximately one × eight inches. Tie the strips onto the hanging above each object and make a bow out of the ends. Make a loop out of one strip and tie it onto the wire loop on top.

Fish Tales

Make up this handy tackle box for the fishermen in your life. Include a disposable camera in the box to take pictures of the big fish they "caught."

Time frame: One to two hours

Level: Easy

What you need:

Lures

Fishing line

Sinkers

Bobbers

Hooks

Bait

Plastic tackle box

Disposable camera

Assemble the preceding fishing supplies, and place them in the tackle box with disposable camera.

You might want to include an instruction video or boat rental with your gift.

Super Senior Citizens

Senior citizens can be the easiest or hardest people on your gift list, depending on their situations and needs. Surprise an older adult with one of these handmade decorative and useful gifts.

Country Garden Sign

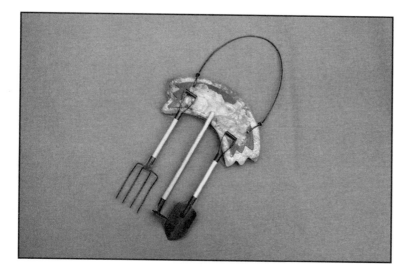

Garden décor with a touch of country.

(© Robert Schroeder)

Make the gardeners in your life this cute sign to hang on a fence or a gardener's rack. You can find these miniature tools and signs with a plain or rusted effect in your local craft store.

Time frame: One to two hours

Level: Easy

What you need:

> Garden theme rub-on transfer
>
> Wooden sign with tin accent
>
> Popsicle stick
>
> Glue gun
>
> Miniature tin and wood garden tools

1. Cut out the rub-on transfer and place the tacky side down on the wooden sign. Carefully rub the transfer with a Popsicle stick up and down and back and forth until the design is transferred to the sign.

2. Using a glue gun, glue the miniature garden tools onto the bottom of the sign.

Gardener's Delight

Time frame: One to two hours

Level: Easy

What you need:

> Garden tools
>
> Seeds
>
> Garden gloves
>
> Painted clay pot
>
> Basket
>
> Raffia filler or Spanish moss
>
> Handmade bow

A perfect accompaniment to a garden sign.

(© Robert Schroeder)

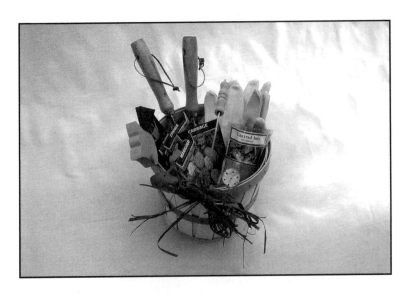

Assemble the gardening supplies and place them in a basket filled with raffia filler or Spanish moss. Top the handle with a handmade bow for a finishing touch.

Practically Whimsical

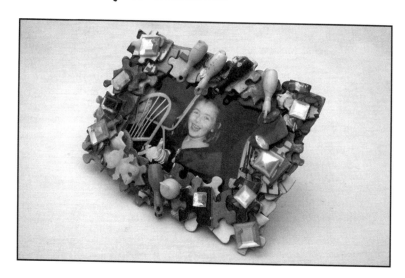

A whimsical frame paired with a practical gift

(© Robert Schroeder)

This cute frame was made by Anne Levine of New York City for her godmother, Jenny. You might want to make one of these simple frames to hold a gift certificate. Putting a favorite picture of you and the recipient in the frame would also be a nice touch.

Time frame: Two to three hours including drying time

Level: Easy

What you need:

Unfinished cardboard or wooden frame

Jigsaw puzzle pieces (Use the old puzzle in your closet that's missing pieces!)

Glue gun

Miscellaneous miniatures or decorative buttons

Clear acrylic finish spray

Picture

Gift certificates

1. Glue the jigsaw puzzle pieces around the frame in a random order and allow them to dry.

2. Choose miniatures or decorative buttons from a craft or discount store that represent the tastes of the recipient, and glue them on the frame on top of the

puzzle pieces. Allow them to dry. Spray the project with clear acrylic finish spray and allow it to dry.

3. Put a picture in the frame, and place the certificates in front of the picture where they'll be noticed.

You can either purchase gift certificates from a store or movie theater or make them yourself for services you'll provide (see the following suggestions). Make the certificates out of copy paper or poster board using textured scissors. List the service or gift on the paper with a fine-tipped magic marker.

Here are some suggestions for certificates:

➤ Transportation to appointments

➤ Special shopping trips

➤ Doing yard work (raking leaves, mowing the lawn, weeding the garden)

➤ Doing light housework (dusting, sweeping, cleaning floors)

➤ Making a hot, home-cooked meal

➤ Doing simple maintenance (putting in screens, cleaning gutters, doing simple household repairs)

➤ Dates for lunch and/or a movie

Here are some great mail-order gift ideas:

➤ Fruit of the month

➤ Flowers of the month

➤ Wine of the month

➤ Gourmet cookies

➤ Gourmet meats and cheeses

Clever Chefs

Share your new recipes with the older generation by making them copies of your favorite concoctions. Make them a hand-painted recipe box, and give them some extra cards to write down their own favorites.

Time frame: Three to four hours, depending on the number of recipes

Level: Easy

What you need:

Unfinished wooden recipe box (Can be found in a craft store.)

Paintbrushes

White craft paint

Pen or fine-point marker

Stencil border (Use a food theme such as fruits, vegetables, breads, pastries, and so on.)

Appropriately colored stencil paints

Stencil brushes

Clear acrylic finish spray

Favorite recipes

Recipe cards

Favorite family recipes for new cooks.

(© Melissa LeBon)

1. Paint the wooden box inside and out with white craft paint. Allow it to dry. Write the word "Recipes" on the top with the fine-tipped marker.
2. Stencil a food-related border around the sides of the box. Allow the box to dry.
3. Spray the box with clear acrylic finish and allow it to dry overnight.
4. Write your favorite recipes on recipe cards, and insert them into the recipe box.

Present Pointers

You might want to create your own cookbook by typing your favorite recipes on a computer. Break down the recipes into categories, and place one or two recipes on each page. You could add some clip art to finish off the project. That way, the next time you want to share a recipe with a friend, you'll be able to pull up the file and print it or e-mail it.

The Least You Need to Know

➤ Grandparents have a special place in our hearts and are the perfect recipients for a homemade gift.

➤ Some aunts and uncles are like second parents. Show them how much you care by making them a special gift.

➤ A homemade gift can be practical or whimsical, depending on the nature of the occasion and the needs of the recipient.

➤ A gift certificate in a handmade frame is the perfect gift for the person who has everything.

On the Mend

Most of us have been hospitalized at one time or another for a short or long term and have experienced the effects firsthand. A feeling of disorientation and a loss of independence go hand in hand with the recovery process. Patients often lose a sense of self-identity and need reassurance from family and friends that they're still part of their lives. If you know someone who is hospitalized or recovering from an illness or injury, you'll want to check out these gift ideas that will lift their spirits.

Gifts That Stimulate the Senses

Two things can happen to a patient who is hospitalized: According to Carol Taylor, R.N., Ph.D., author of *Fundamentals of Nursing,* patients can experience an overabundance of sensory input (sensory overload) or a deprivation of sensory input (sensory deprivation). Gifts for the hospitalized or recuperating people in your life should be geared toward overcoming one of these sensory deficits. Here you'll find something soothing and something stimulating.

Merry Mobile

A gift to brighten a patient's room.

(© Melissa LeBon)

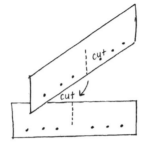

Remind your sick friends and relatives that they're loved and that they've received many get-well wishes by making them this cheerful greeting-card mobile.

Time frame: One to two hours

Level: Easy

What you need:

>   Two strips of cardboard or poster board, 3 × 12 inches
>
>   White craft paint
>
>   Paintbrush
>
>   Sunflower stencil
>
>   Yellow, brown, and green stencil paints
>
>   Stencil brushes
>
>   Scissors
>
>   Yarn or cord
>
>   Hole punch
>
>   Miniature wooden clothespins

1. Paint the two strips of cardboard with white craft paint and allow them to dry. Place the sunflower stencil on one piece of cardboard, and stencil in the flowers with the appropriate colors. Stencil the second piece of cardboard the same way. Allow both to dry thoroughly.

2. Measure a six-inch mark on the strips of cardboard. At the 6-inch mark, cut a vertical slit through the top of one piece of cardboard, 1½ inches long. Cut a vertical strip through the bottom of the second piece of cardboard at the 6-inch mark, also 1½ inches long. Slide one piece of cardboard onto the other, forming an "X" out of them. Tie a piece of cord through the junction, and make a loop on the end for hanging purposes.

3. Using the hole punch or a sharp pair of scissors, make six holes in the bottom of each strip of cardboard. Thread the holes with cord and tie a knot in the end to keep the cord in place. Tie the open end of the cord onto the miniature clothespin.

4. Hang the mobile in the patient's room and pin any cards he or she receives to the mobile using the clothespins.

Present Pointers

Make a card holder for them out of a Pringle's chip can and some yarn. Use a can opener to remove the bottom of the can. Then wrap one end of the yarn through the inside to the outside of the can, forming a vertical loop on the can. Knot the end of the yarn to the inside loop. Continue wrapping the yarn in and out of the can until the entire surface is covered. Tie the last loop of yarn onto the first knot. Slip the get-well cards onto the yarn loops. Add a stick-on bow to the top of the can.

Tranquil Sleep

Help create a tranquil environment for your recuperating friends by making them this basket of stress busters. Don't be surprised if you can't resist making one for yourself at the same time!

Time frame: One to two hours

Level: Easy

What you need:

  Soothing CDs

  Easy-reading material

  Scented bath and body products

Aromatherapy candles

Basket

Helium balloons

Assemble the CDs, reading material, bath products, and candles in a basket. Attach a bouquet of helium balloons to the handle for a finishing touch.

The Gift of Knowledge

Experts agree that hospitalization can create an alteration in the sensory experience of a patient through sensory deprivation or overload. To alleviate this problem: Surround the patient with different colors and an environment that changes. Decrease or eliminate distressing auditory stimuli; use media to keep the patient current and to stimulate his or her senses. Experiment with foods of different tastes, colors, temperatures, and textures. Help the patient savor smells that are pleasant. Expose the patient to different textures and help him or her feel and enjoy them (for example, petting a dog, feeling the petals of a flower, or giving a warm hug). (From *Fundamentals of Nursing* by Carol Taylor, Carol Lillis, and Priscilla LeMone.)

A Stitch in Time

One thing recuperating patients have is lots of time. You might want to help a friend fill some of this time by teaching him or her a new hobby. You can either give the person the supplies and a how-to book, or you can spend the time to get him or her started on one of your own favorite hobbies.

Time frame: One to two hours

Level: Easy

What you need:

How-to book

Supplies to make a project (See the following suggestions.)

Basket

Filler

Homemade bow

A gift of a hobby for a recuperating friend.

(© Robert Schroeder)

Assemble the supplies and place them in a basket filled with filler. Add a homemade bow to the handle to complete your gift.

Here are some suggestions for sharing a hobby:

➤ Knitting: yarn, needles, a pattern book

➤ Making stationery: paper, envelopes, markers, stamps, glitter, glue, stickers

➤ Leather work: leather, leather punch, leather string

➤ Jewelry making: beads, string, closures, tools

➤ Painting: paints, palate, paintbrushes, paper

Gifts That Heal the Heart

Keep your recuperating friends in the loop by making them these simple reminders that they are in your thoughts.

Gifting Glitches

Be sure to check the level of activity that a patient can tolerate before deciding on a gift of a hobby. Some hobbies require more manual dexterity than others and should be avoided in certain cases. Try to spend some time teaching the patient your hobby or helping him or her decide on a new craft. Your time is the most precious gift you can give.

The Missing Piece

A great way to let recuperating friends know you miss them.

(© Robert Schroeder)

Make your friend this missing-piece puzzle to remind him or her to get well and back to your group soon.

Time frame: Two to three hours

Level: Moderately easy

Present Pointers

You might want to include a jig-saw puzzle with your missing-piece card and spend some time with the patient working on it together.

What you need:

>   Poster board
>
>   Scissors
>
>   Picture of a group of friends including the recuperating person
>
>   Glue
>
>   Marker

1. Cut a piece of poster board to fit the picture. Glue the picture onto the poster board. Be sure you get glue on all the surfaces of the poster board.

2. Draw interlocking pieces on the picture that look like a jigsaw puzzle. Be sure to have the recuperating friend's face on one of the interlocking pieces.

3. Cut out the puzzle pieces. Assemble the puzzle, leaving the face of your friend out of the puzzle.

4. Make a card out of the remaining poster board; it should be large enough to accommodate the picture but should have room to write on the bottom. Tape the picture onto the front of the card. Underneath the picture, write "Things just aren't complete without you."

5. Paste the missing puzzle piece on the inside of the card. Using a marker, write "You're the missing piece. Get well soon!"

Spiritual Bouquet

A collage of well wishes.

(© Robert Schroeder)

Don't just tell your recuperating friend that he's in your thoughts—show him how much you care by making him a spiritual bouquet of well wishes.

Time frame: One to two hours

Level: Easy

What you need:

      Several different flower-shaped foam stamps

      Yellow, pink, red, green, and blue craft paints

      Paintbrushes

      Poster board

      Fine-tipped markers

      Hole punch

      Yarn

1. Paint the foam stamps with the appropriate color of craft paint, and stamp flowers over the entire poster board. Allow this to dry.

2. Either write a spiritual message or inspirational saying on each flower or have the recipient's friends and family write a special message on each flower. For example you could write: "You are in our thoughts and prayers," "Things aren't the same without you—get well soon," or "You are missed by all and wished a speedy recovery."

3. Using a hole punch, make two holes on the top of the poster. Thread the yarn through each hole, and tie it in a knot for hanging purposes. Hang the poster in the patient's room.

Gifts That Heal the Body

There's nothing like a home-cooked meal after several days of hospital food. Whether your friend is still in the hospital or recovering at home, a gift of homemade food will put him or her on the mend.

Chicken Soup: The Best Medicine

Chicken soup is a lot easier to make from scratch than you might think. Plus, homemade soup is a lot better than anything you can get in the store. Try out a batch of this chicken soup (recipe courtesy of Mildred Taylor, Pine Grove, Pennsylvania) and be sure to make enough for your family—they won't be able to resist it when the aroma of homemade soup overcomes them. Present your soup in a gift basket with crackers, a new mug and spoon, and a good book or magazine, if desired.

Chicken soup for a speedy recovery.

(© Marilee LeBon)

Time frame: One to two hours to assemble the ingredients plus 1½ hours for the soup to simmer

Level: Moderately easy

What you need:

For Grandma's Never-Fail Chicken Rice Soup:

> One small chicken (three to five pounds)
>
> Stock pot
>
> Water
>
> Small onion, chopped
>
> Three ribs of celery
>
> ½ carrot, diced
>
> ½ cup rice
>
> Two bouillon cubes
>
> Salt and pepper to taste

To assemble:

> Mason jar, flat-sealing lid, and band
>
> Piece of gingham material and ribbon or yarn
>
> Soup mug
>
> Spoon
>
> Crackers
>
> Book or magazine
>
> Basket
>
> Filler

Gifting Glitches

Check the prescribed diet of the patient before making a gift of food. If the person's on a low-fat diet, you can substitute skinless chicken breasts in this recipe for the whole chicken. Use a low-sodium bouillon and eliminate the salt for a low-salt diet.

1. To make the soup: Remove the package of giblets found inside the chicken cavity and discard. Wash the chicken inside and out with cold, salted water.

2. Place the cleaned chicken in a stock pot and cover with water. Bring to a boil and cook for two minutes. Drain the chicken and refill the pot with clean water. Add the chicken, chopped onion, celery, and carrot and bring to a boil. Lower heat to medium-low and simmer, covered, until the meat is tender, approximately one hour.

3. Remove the chicken and allow it to cool.

4. Add rice and bouillon to the chicken broth and simmer, covered, approximately 20 minutes or until rice is tender. Add salt and pepper to taste.

5. Pull the chicken meat from the bones and cut it into small pieces. Add the chicken to the soup and simmer again until hot.

6. Pour the soup into the Mason jar and seal it with the lid. Place a six-inch square of gingham over the lid and tie in place with a matching piece of ribbon or yarn.

7. Assemble the remaining materials listed and arrange them in a basket with filler. Add the jar of chicken soup. Be sure to help the recipient refrigerate the soup if it is not eaten immediately.

A Fruitful Basket

There's nothing like an apple a day to keep the doctor away. Give this basket of fruit to a recuperating friend for an alternative to hospital food.

Time frame: Half to one hour

Level: Easy

What you need:

> Bananas
>
> Apples
>
> Grapes
>
> Pears
>
> Basket
>
> Raffia filler
>
> Bow

Assemble the fruit and place it in a basket filled with raffia. Place a bow on the handle of the basket.

Feel-Good Fishy

Turn the little patient's frowns upside down with this feel-good fishy that will help them get over the bumps and bruises of life. Just put an ice cube in the middle of this fish and place it over a boo-boo.

Time frame: Half hour

Level: Easy

A fish to numb the pain of childhood bumps and bruises.

(© Robert Schroeder)

What you need:

Washcloth

Rubber band

Red felt

Scissors

Fabric glue

Plastic eyes

Ribbon or rickrack

Lollipop

1. Fold the washcloth into a triangular shape. Roll the triangle from the top point toward the two long ends. Fold the roll in the middle and catch the ends in a rubber band (see illustration).

2. Cut a mouth out of the red felt as shown. Glue the mouth onto the front of the fish. Glue two plastic eyes above the mouth.

3. Tie a piece of ribbon or yarn around the rubber band and make a small bow. Stick a lollipop into the tail of the fish.

You might want to include a little note that says, "Put an ice cube in the middle of this friendly fish and place it over a boo-boo to make it feel better." You could include a bag of lollipops with this present if the child is allowed to have sweets.

Steps to making a feel-good fishy.

(© Melissa LeBon)

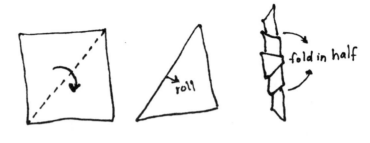

Gifts That Heal the Soul

When a friend is ill, the focus of his or her life changes to accommodate the recovery process. Studies have shown that people recuperate faster when they feel happier, more at peace. You can make a difference in a patient's life by creating a gift that has a healing effect on the soul.

Basket of Blooms

A homemade basket of flowers is a perfect gift for a recuperating friend. The dried flowers don't require any care and will last a very long time.

Time frame: One to two hours

Level: Easy

What you need:

> Flower arrangement foam block
>
> Hanging grapevine basket
>
> Spanish moss
>
> Assortment of dried flowers
>
> Baby's breath
>
> Three yards of matching wired ribbon

1. Place a flower arrangement block inside the hanging grapevine basket. Cover the block with Spanish moss.

2. Arrange the flowers in the basket. Intersperse baby's breath in between the flowers.

3. Make a bow out of the ribbon and attach it to the bottom of the basket. (See Chapter 3, "Wrapping It Up," for directions for making a homemade bow.)

Keep in Touch

People in the hospital usually have a lot of time to catch up on their correspondence. You might want to give a sick friend this gift bag of stationery, pens, and note cards.

Time frame: One to two hours

Level: Easy

What you need:

Tissue paper filler

Gift bag

Note cards

Stationery

Pens

Markers

Stamps

Curling ribbon

1. Crumple tissue paper and place it in a gift bag. Assemble the cards, stationery, pens, markers, and stamps, and insert them into the prepared gift bag. (You might want to make one of the homemade gift bags discussed in Chapter 3 for this project.)

2. Tie *curling ribbon* that matches the tissue paper onto the handles of the bag and curl the ends to form a pompom of ribbon.

Dream Box

Help restore the spirits of a recuperating friend by making this special box of dreams. Tickets to a future event or planned trip will give him or her something to look forward to.

Time frame: Half to one hour

Level: Easy

313

Present Pointers

You'll want to customize the gift certificate for a special event or trip to the tastes of the recipient. Some suggestions for certificates include tickets to the symphony, ballet, or theatre; tickets to a sporting event; tickets to a rock concert; plane tickets to a special location; restaurant reservations; or a planned camping or fishing trip.

What you need:

Silver or gold wrapping paper

Small box (a jewelry gift box works well)

White glue

Glitter (in a contrasting color to the paper)

Small piece of tissue paper for liner

Confetti

Gift certificate or event tickets

Piece of poster board or paper cut to the size of the box

Fine-tipped marker

1. Cut two pieces of silver or gold paper approximately 1½ times the size of the box. Place the box bottom on top of the wrong side of the paper, and pull the ends up around the box. Fold the ends in like you would when wrapping a present, and glue them to the inside of the box bottom. Allow this to dry.

2. Repeat step one with the box top. Write the word "Dreams …" on the top of the box with white glue. Shake a thick layer of glitter over the word and allow it to dry. Shake off the excess glitter.

3. Place a piece of tissue paper in the bottom of the box. Shake some confetti into the box, and add a certificate or tickets to a future event or trip. Using the marker, write the words "… come true!" on the poster board or paper, and place it on top of the tickets or certificates.

The Least You Need to Know

➤ You can help minimize the disorienting effect of a hospital setting on patients by making them gifts that stimulate the senses.

➤ Show sick friends how much you love them by making them special handmade greetings.

➤ Homemade chicken soup and fresh fruit are perfect gifts for a recuperating friend or relative.

➤ Give someone who's on the mend the gift of a dream box.

Resources and Supplies

Books

Carlson, Laurie. *Ecoart.* Charlotte, VT: Williamson, 1993.

———. *Kids Create!* Charlotte, VT: Williamson, 1990.

Chapman, Gillian, and Pam Robson. *Art from Paper.* New York: Thompson Learning, 1995.

———. *Art from Rocks and Shells.* New York: Thompson Learning, 1995.

Conaway, Judith. *Happy Haunting, Halloween Costumes You Can Make.* Mahwah, NJ: Troll Associates, 1986.

Diehn, Gwen, and Terry Krautwurst. *Nature Crafts for Kids.* New York: Sterling, 1992.

Elliot, Marion. *Papier-Mâché Project Book.* Seacaucus, NJ: Chartwell Books, 1992.

Elliot, Marion, and Belinda Hodson. *The Grolier Kids Crafts Funny Face Book.* Danbury, CT: Grolier Educational, 1994.

Hancock, Jim, and David Hancock. *The Grolier Kids Crafts Toy Book.* Danbury, CT: Grolier Educational, 1995.

Morgenthal, Deborah. *Wreaths Around the House.* New York: Sterling, 1994.

Orton, Lyn. *The Grolier Kids Crafts Puppet Book.* Danbury, CT: Grolier Educational, 1993.

Owen, Cheryl, and Anna Murray. *The Grolier Kids Crafts Craft Book.* Danbury, CT: Grolier Educational, 1992.

Robins, Deri, and Maggie Downer. *Easter Fun.* New York: Kingfisher, 1996.

Ross, Kathy. *Crafts for Easter.* Brookfield, CT: Milbrook Press, 1995.

———. *Every Day Is Earth Day.* Brookfield, CT: Millbrook Press, 1995.

Sattler, Helen Roney, and Lee Lothrop. *Recipes for Arts and Crafts Materials.* New York: Shepard Books, 1973.

Solga, Kim. *Make Gifts!* Cincinnati, OH: Northlight Books, 1991.

Stone, Helen. *The Grolier Kids Crafts Papercraft Book.* Danbury, CT: Grolier Educational, 1992.

Taylor, Carol, Carol Lillis, and Priscilla LeMone. *Fundamentals of Nursing.* Philadelphia, PA: Lippincott, 1997.

Waterfall, Jarie Lee. *Nursery Crafts*. Atlanta, GA: Humanics Learning, 1988.

Wright, Lyndie. *Masks*. Franklin Watts, 1990.

Online Resources

The Internet can provide an endless supply of free craft ideas and how-to's. The following Web sites contained quality, easy-to-make craft projects:

- ➤ www.about.com
- ➤ www.baby-shower.com
- ➤ www.childfun.com
- ➤ www.craftideas.com
- ➤ www.craftown.com
- ➤ www.decorating4less.com
- ➤ www.dltk-kids.com
- ➤ www.family.com
- ➤ www.familyplay.com
- ➤ www.family.go.com
- ➤ www.holidays.net
- ➤ www.homeandcrafts.com
- ➤ www.joi.org
- ➤ www.pets.com
- ➤ www.theholidayspot.com
- ➤ www.weddingchannel.com
- ➤ www.yasutomo.com

The following Internet sites sell quality craft supplies:

- ➤ www.craftbarn.com
- ➤ www.dickblick.com
- ➤ www.just4ewe.com
- ➤ www.misterart.com
- ➤ www.bearcountrycandleandsoapsupply.com

Supply Catalogs

Collage
240 Valley Dr.
Brisbane, CA 94005
1-800-926-5524
www.collagecatalog.com

Fine papers and paper products

Craft Catalog
PO Box 1069
Reynoldsburg, OH 43068
1-800-777-1442
www.craftcatalog.com

Art and craft supplies

Dick Blick Art Materials
PO Box 1267
Galesburg, IL 61402
1-800-828-4548
www.dickblick.com

Art supplies

Home Craft
PO Box 24890
San Jose, CA 95154
1-800-301-7377
www.homecraftexpress.com

Supplies for the decorative artist

The Baker's Catalog
PO Box 876
Norwich, VT 05055
1-800-827-6836
www.KingArthurFlour.com

Tools, ingredients, and equipment for home bakers

Utrecht
6 Corporate Dr.
Cranbury, NJ 08512
1-800-223-9132
www.utrechtart.com

Unique Gift Catalogs

Bits and Pieces
One Puzzle Place B8016
Stevens Point, WI 54481
1-800-544-7297
www.bitsandpieces.com

Puzzles and gifts for kids

Flax Art and Design
240 Valley Dr.
Brisbane, CA 94005
1-888-352-9278
www.flaxart.com

Gifts and art supplies

Hearth Song
1950 Waldorf NW
Grand Rapids, MI 49550
1-800-325-2502
www.hearthsong.com

Seasonal and unusual gifts for kids and grown-up kids

Glossary

acrylic paints   Craft paints that clean up easily with soap and water and produce vivid, permanent colors.

afikomen   A piece of matzo that gets hidden by the leader of a Seder celebration. The child who finds it gets a small gift or treat.

annual flowers   Flowers that grow during a specific season and die at the end of that season (such as impatiens, geraniums, begonias, and petunias).

apron carryall   An apron that folds up into a carryall.

aromatherapy   The use of the sense of smell to influence physical and mental states. The scents and essences of various plants and flowers are extracted and used in massage oils, aromatic baths, and simmering pots.

baby's breath   A perennial flower that contains clusters of delicate white flowers and is used in flower arrangements and for decorative purposes.

basket filler   Torn, shredded, or folded material that fills the bottom of a gift basket (such as crepe paper, tissue paper, raffia, Spanish moss, and so on).

bathtub decals   Foam shapes that stick to the walls of a tub or shower when wet.

beeswax sheets   Sheets of wax made from the honeycombs of bees; they can be molded into decorative candles.

beritzah   A Hebrew word meaning a baked or roasted egg. A beritzah is placed on a Seder plate during the Seder dinner.

bulb flowers   Flowers that have a short, underground, tubular stem that can be replanted year after year to produce new growth (such as tulips, daffodils, hyacinths).

bunraku   The name commonly used for the art of puppetry and storytelling.

calligraphy tool   An ink pen or marker used to create intricate letters.

candle wicking   A wand of woven or twisted fiber contained in a candle or lamp.

card stock   Special papers used for making stationery or greeting cards.

charoset   A Hebrew word meaning a mixture of chopped apples, walnuts, cinnamon, and wine. Charoset is placed on the Seder plate during the Seder dinner.

clear acrylic finish spray   A clear, protective spray-on finish for craft projects.

clear glue   Transparent glue that can replace white glue in projects.

crackle paint   Paint that gives objects a weathered or antique look.

craft paints   Water-based paints that provide vivid, lasting colors (similar to acrylic paints).

crepe paper   Decorative paper similar to tissue paper that is used in various craft projects.

crimper   A tool for making shredded, unique-shaped bits of paper that can be used in craft projects.

curling ribbon   Ribbon of different textures and widths that can be curled by running the blade of a pair of scissors swiftly across it.

decorative-edge scissors   Scissors that make a decorative line in the object being cut.

decorative excelsior moss   A form of filler that resembles Spanish moss and comes in different colors.

decoupage   A creative art that involves pasting and varnishing paper cutouts onto objects.

double boiler   Two pans that fit inside each other used for melting or cooking delicate ingredients.

double-edged seam binding   A material edging that can be sewn onto the unfinished sides of material projects.

dowels   Rounded wooden sticks that come in different widths and lengths.

dreidel   A spinning top used at Hanukkah celebrations.

elastic baby headband trims   Soft, elasticized trims that come in different colors and designs.

Elijah's Cup   A ceremonial cup that is filled with wine or juice and placed on the table at the Seder dinner to symbolize the prophet Elijah's visit.

embroidery thread   Floss used in decorative sewing.

Eoster   The ancient goddess of spring.

eucalyptus   A form of evergreen tree found chiefly in Australia that yields potent oil. Its dried branches are used in floral arrangements.

Exacto knife   A sharp-bladed knife used in precision cutting.

extruded foam   Molded Styrofoam shapes used in craft projects.

fabric glue   Adhesive used for gluing objects to material or holding material pieces together.

fabric paint   Machine-washable paint used on fabric.

felt   Fabric made of a composite material that has no raw edges.

florist tape   Green, tacky tape used to wrap wire stems in floral arrangements.

foam block (florist)   A block of porous material (foam) used in flower arrangements.

foam sheet cutouts   Shapes that are precut from foam sheets.

foam sheets   Flexible foam material used in craft projects.

fondue   A dish made from melted cheese or chocolate that is used as a dip.

garden stone   A painted stone (usually slate) that decorates a garden.

gift bags   Decorative bags that hold gifts.

glass etching solution   Acid used to etch stencils into glass.

glass etching stencils   Stencils taped to glass that form the design created by the acid.

glue gun   A tool that dispenses melted glue.

glycerin block   A material that can be cut, melted, and poured into molds to make soap.

grout   A powdered material that can be mixed with water and applied to a mosaic to fill in the spaces between the decorative pieces.

Hanukkah   A sacred Jewish holiday that commemorates the rededication of the temple of Jerusalem under the Macabees in 164 B.C.E.

imani   An African-American term for having faith in the creator, parents, family, community, and the goodness of the struggle for excellence.

karamu   The Kwanzaa feast.

karpas   A Hebrew word meaning the green vegetable placed on the Seder plate during the Seder dinner (usually lettuce or parsley). Karpas represents springtime.

kids' stamps   Thick stamps made of a foam-like material that are easy for children (and adults) to use.

kinara   A ceremonial candleholder that holds seven candles for the African-American celebration of Kwanzaa.

kitchen caddy   A container used for holding kitchen utensils.

kujichagulia   An African-American term for being proud of who you are and what you do in life.

kuumba   An African-American term for being able to express yourself in a creative fashion through music, art, dance, and so on.

Kwanzaa   Swahili for "first," this is an African-American celebration developed by Dr. Maulana Karenga to promote unity and pride in the African-American community.

liquid lead   Thick, black liquid that can be squeezed from a bottle onto a stained glass project to simulate molded lead.

liquid scent   A pleasant-smelling extract used in making candles and soaps that is available in a variety of scents.

magnet sheet A sheet of magnetic material that can be cut to size and used for refrigerator magnets or other magnetic crafts.

maror A Hebrew word meaning the bitter herb (usually grated horseradish) placed on the Seder plate to represent the bitterness of slavery.

material remnants Ends of bolts of material that are packaged and sold at a reduced rate in fabric stores.

matzo A cracker that represents the Jewish people's inability to allow the yeast in their bread to rise in their haste to leave Egypt.

matzo meal A kosher substitute for flour in recipes.

menorah A ceremonial candleholder used during Hanukkah celebrations.

mkeka A woven mat, one of the seven basic symbols of Kwanzaa.

mosaic adhesive The glue that holds mosaic pieces in place.

mosaic sealant A sealer that protects and fortifies a mosaic project.

mosaics Works of art designed from grout and pieces of materials such as glass, stone, or tile.

nia An African-American term for trying to be the best you can be and being responsible for your own actions.

organdy A thin, crisp, transparent, cotton muslin used for dresses, collars, cuffs, and so on.

origami The art of folding paper; it originated in China.

papier-mâché A French word that describes a material consisting of paper pulp mixed with glue or paste. It can be molded into various shapes when wet and becomes hard when dry.

paraffin Blocks of wax used in candle making, cooking, and other craft projects.

Passover A sacred holiday that commemorates the liberation of the Jewish people from enslavement.

perennial flowers Flowers that can be planted once and usually come up year after year (such as bleeding hearts, daisies, hostas, woodruff, and herbs).

Pesach The Hebrew word for Passover.

pinking shears Scissors that make a notched edge when cutting paper, material, cardboard, and other materials.

pompoms Cottony balls of various colors and sizes that are used in craft projects.

poster paints Vivid, water-based, nonpermanent paints that are easy for children to handle.

potpourri A blend of sweet-smelling flowers, herbs, spices, and oils that is sometimes mixed with decorative objects such as pinecones or shells.

quilted panel A prequilted material panel that contains a mural or special design.

raffia   A fibrous ribbon that is used in craft projects and is made from a plant.

raffia filler   Small bits of straw-like fibers that are natural or dyed and can be used in craft projects.

rub-on transfers   Designs that can be transferred onto a project by rubbing them with a wooden tool.

sachet   Interesting blends of herbs and flowers that are dried and packaged in bags or envelopes.

salt dough   A sculpting dough made out of flour, water, and salt that hardens when baked.

scrapbook pack   Tablets or packs of paper used in scrapbook making that contain print designs, backgrounds, cutouts, and patterns for enhancing a scrapbook or photo album.

scrunchies   Hair holders.

sculpting clay   A pliable material that can be molded into sculptures and baked to harden.

Seder dinner   A traditional dinner gathering held in the home at Passover.

Seder plate   A centerpiece dish containing symbolic foods; it is placed on the Seder table during the Seder dinner.

Shaker peg shelf   A decorative shelf with pegs for hanging objects.

shamash   The raised helper candle in the middle of a Menorah that is used to light the other candles.

shrink-wrap   Plastic wrap that can be applied to a basket; it will shrink to fit tightly when heated with a hair dryer.

snow paint   A white, textured paint that comes in a jar and can be painted onto a project to resemble snow.

soap chips   Bags of colored soap pieces that are added to soap molds for a decorative touch.

soap molds   The forms that hold the melted glycerin until it hardens into soap.

Spanish moss   A natural plant used in flower arrangements and other craft projects.

sponge painting   Painting a project using sponge shapes dipped in paint.

sponge stamps   Shapes made out of sponges that can be used to form designs with paint.

spouncer   A stencil paintbrush that resembles a piece of wood with a sponge molded onto the end.

stained glass paint   A transparent, colored paint that resembles stained glass.

statice   A dried branch of tiny white flowers, similar to baby's breath, that is used in arrangements or other craft projects.

stencil paint   A special powdery paint used with stencils.

stencil paintbrushes   Special paintbrushes used for stenciling that are shorter and blunter than regular brushes.

stencils   Designs cut out of plastic that can be filled in with stencil paint to create pictures on projects.

Sterno   Canned cooking fuel used to heat fondue pots or chafing dishes.

stone finish paint   Spray paint that creates a stone or cement-like finish on projects.

tacky glue   Clear glue used in craft projects; it is thicker than white glue and stays in place when applied.

terrarium   A glass container holding layers of soil, sand, and/or gravel; it is used for growing plants, housing small animals, or displaying nature artifacts.

textile medium   A liquid helper that transforms acrylic paints into washable fabric paint.

textured paper   Fancy papers used for making cards, origami, or scrapbook packs.

trivet   A decorative object used to protect a surface from heat or spills.

tulle   A fine, silk, open mesh material used for making wedding veils, scarves, and so on.

ujamaa   An African-American term for taking pride in the cultural expressions of African-Americans (such as music, art forms, or dance).

ujima   An African-American term for working together as a team to support the goals of the family and/or community.

umoja   An African-American term for sticking together as a family.

unity cup   A ceremonial communal cup that is filled with a drink and used in a Kwanzaa celebration.

white glue   Traditional school glue used in craft projects.

wired ribbon   Wire-edged ribbon that keeps its form when shaped into a bow.

zawadi   An African-American term for the gifts given at Kwanzaa.

zeroa   The Hebrew word for a shank bone. Zeroa is placed on the Seder plate during the Seder dinner to symbolize the sacrificial lamb offering the Jews made to Hashem.

Holiday Calendar

Here's a handy list of traditional (and some not-so-traditional) holidays celebrated in the United States:

January 1	New Year's Day
Third Monday in January	Martin Luther King Day
February 2	Groundhog Day
February 14	Valentine's Day
Third Monday in February February 22	Presidents' Day/ Washington's Birthday
March 17	St. Patrick's Day
April 1	April Fool's Day
April 22	Earth Day
Wednesday of last full week in April	Secretaries' Day
First Sunday after the first full moon after March 21	Easter (in 2001: April 15; in 2002: March 31)
Dates vary according to the Jewish calendar	Passover (in 2001: April 8; in 2002: March 28)
May 6	Nurse's Day
First Thursday in May	National Day of Prayer
Second Sunday in May	Mother's Day
Third Saturday in May	Armed Forces Day
Last Monday in May	Memorial Day
Third Sunday in June	Father's Day
June 19	Juneteenth (liberation of slaves)
July 4	Independence Day
Fourth Sunday in July	Parent's Day

First Sunday in August	Friendship Day
First Monday in September	Labor Day
Sunday after Labor Day	Grandparent's Day
September 17	Citizenship Day or Constitution Day
Second Sunday in October	National Children's Day
October 16	Bosses' Day
Second Monday in October	Columbus Day
Third Sunday in October	Sweetest Day
October 26	Mother-in-Law's Day
October 31	Halloween
November 11	Veterans Day
Fourth Thursday in November	Thanksgiving
December 7	Pearl Harbor Remembrance Day
December 25	Christmas
Dates vary	Hanukkah (in 2001 December 10 to 17; in 2002 November 30 to December 7)
December 26 to 31	Kwanzaa

You can use this handy reference sheet to fill in family and friends' birthdays and anniversaries, and any other special occasions you'd like to celebrate.

Personal Holidays and Dates to Remember

Date   Occasion

_____   _____

_____   _____

_____   _____

_____   _____

_____   _____

_____   _____

Index

H

I-J

K

L

M